CONTENTS

The Soviet Politburo 1984-85   vii

PROLOGUE   ix

PART ONE   *IMPASSE*   11

PART TWO   *REFORM*   37

PART THREE   *RESISTANCE*   61

PART FOUR   *REACTION*   89

PART FIVE   *REVOLUTION*   111

PART SIX   *AFTERMATH*   225

RUSSIAN REVOLUTION 1985
A Contemporary Fable

'It begins with unrest among Soviet miners; a
smouldering dissatisfaction which flares into
head-on clashes with bosses, and finally to open
revolution. It leaves you feeling that it could all
happen ... and possibly will.'
Manchester Evening News

'A remarkable account of the bloody path to
democratic socialism and its impact on domestic
and international affairs. The author combines
imagination with a deep knowledge and
understanding of the Communist world.'
Sunderland Echo

'Intricately researched and convincingly written'
Northern Echo

'Compulsive reading'

Sunday Telegraph

By David Downing and published by New English Library:

THE MOSCOW OPTION: An Alternative
Second World War
THE DEVIL'S VIRTUOSOS: German Generals
at War 1940–45
AN ATLAS OF TERRITORIAL AND
BORDER DISPUTES

By David Downing and Gary Herman:

WAR WITHOUT END, PEACE WITHOUT
HOPE:
Thirty Years of the Arab-Israeli Conflict

RUSSIAN REVOLUTION 1985

A Contemporary Fable

David Downing

NEW ENGLISH LIBRARY

First published in Great Britain in 1983 by New English
Library

Copyright © 1983 by David Downing

First NEL Paperback Edition April 1984
Reprinted April 1984
Reprinted May 1984

NEL Books are published by
New English Library,
Mill Road, Dunton Green,
Sevenoaks, Kent.
Editorial office: 47 Bedford Square, London WC1B 3DP

Printed and bound in Great Britain by
Cox & Wyman Ltd, Reading

British Library C.I.P.

Downing, David
   Russian revolution 1985.
   I. Title
   823'.914[F]   PR6054.0/

ISBN 0-450-05684-8

The Soviet Politburo: February 1984 to October 1985

ANDROPOV, Yuri Vladimirovich	General Secretary
CHERNENKO, Konstantin Ustinovich	Secretariat
DEMICHEV, Pyotr Nilovich	Secretariat (Light Industry)
ALIYEV, Geydar Aliyevich	Azerbaijan First Secretary
GORBACHEV, Mikhail Sergeyevich	Secretariat (Agriculture)
GRISHIN, Viktor Vasilyevich	Moscow First Secretary
GROMYKO, Andrei Andreyevich	President of the Soviet Union
PONOMARIEV, Boris Nikolayevich	Secretariat (Fraternal Relations)
RASHIDOV, Sharaf Rashidovich	Uzbekistan First Secretariat
ROMANOV, Grigori Vasilyevich	Secretariat (Party Organisation)
SHCHERBITSKY, Vladimir Vasilyevich	Ukraine First Secretary
SOLOMENTSEV, Mikhail Sergeyevich	Central Control Commission
TIKHONOV, Nikolai Aleksandrovich	Prime Minister
USTINOV, Dmitri Fyedorovich	Defence Minister

PROLOGUE

IN THE early hours of a January day, in the 68th Year of the Revolution, the lights flicker and dim in the Mausoleum. The Guardians of this Holy Place, suspecting a faulty fuse, go in search of a replacement, preferably one manufactured in the first ten days of a plan month. But when they return the sarcophagus is empty and He is gone.

Later that morning a man is seen walking among the people. The shabby clothes, the large head cocked to one side as He listens, the twinkling eyes, all evoke the countless ikons spread around the city. Not surprisingly, everyone recognises him. He speaks of strange matters, of socialist democracy, of people's rights, of power to the Soviets.

As He addresses the growing crowd in the Beautiful Square, a large polished car draws to a halt and through its smoked-glass bulletproof windows another man, tall and ascetic-looking, stares out. It is the Grand Interrogator, the Chairman of the KGB. His face darkens. He stretches forth his finger and commands the men in raincoats to seize Him. And so great is his power and so accustomed are the people to obey him, so humble and submissive are they to his will, that the crowd immediately makes way for the men in raincoats and, amid the deathlike hush that descends upon the square, they lay hands upon Him and lead Him away. The crowd, like one man, at once bows down to the ground before the old Interrogator, who hands them sheafs of statistics and passes on. The men in raincoats take their prisoner to the Lubyanka.

In the middle of the following night, the steel door of His cell is suddenly thrown open and the Grand Interrogator himself *slowly enters. He stops in the doorway and gazes for a long time, for more than a minute, into His face. At last he approaches Him slowly and says to Him: 'Is it you? You?'*

But receiving no answer, he adds quickly: 'Do not answer, be silent. And, indeed, what can you say? I know too well what you would say. Besides, you have no right to add anything to what you have already said in the days of old. Why, then, did you come to meddle with us?

'Was it not you who said so often in those days, "we shall construct socialism"? But now you have seen our "socialist" system,' the old interrogator adds suddenly with a pensive smile. 'Yes, this business has cost us a great deal,' he goes on, looking sternly at Him, 'but we've completed it at last in Your name. For sixty years we've been troubled by this "socialism", but now it's over and done with for good.'

(Excerpt from Zinaida Kopaneva's short story 'The Grand Interrogator', first published in *Waterfront;* 18 April 1985; Nikolayev, Ukraine SSR)

PART ONE

IMPASSE (1962-82)

They chatter about the future
Keep silence for the past
The present waits in queues
Each one longer than the last
They tell us, come, be patient
Another year, or maybe two
Comrades, a little more effort
And there'll be a car for you
      With their hands on their hearts
      They read lists of lies
      And then they all take a bow
      Ah comrades, it might have worked once
      It isn't working now

(from the popular song 'Not working now' by Sergei Lavin)

ON 1 JUNE 1962 it was announced in *Pravda* that the Soviet people were to pay 30 per cent more for their meat, 25 per cent more for their butter. The popular reaction was not favourable: a riotous assembly in Grozny, impromptu mass meetings in Krasnodar and Donetsk, wildcat strikes in Yaroslavl, widespread 'hooliganism' in Gorky. Even the capital was affected, with the Moskvitch auto workers downing tools for most of the day.

By the following morning most of the Soviet Union had resumed normal service. Only in one small Don Valley town, situated some twenty-five miles northwest of Rostov, did the protest assume a more violent form. Here the bureaucrats had proved more than usually incompetent, allowing the town's major industrial works to announce a cut in the piecerate norms on the very day that prices had risen. At a stroke, or two strokes, the workers at the electric locomotive plant had seen their living standard cut in half. It was too much.

Accounts of what turned anger into action remain confused and contradictory. The late Russian author Alexander Solzhenitsyn claimed, in *The Gulag Archipelago (III),* that a spontaneous mass meeting took place at the plant. When the works manager tried to intervene he was asked, simply, 'What are we going to live on now?' His reply (or Solzhenitsyn's) was a masterpiece of insensitivity: 'You're used to guzzling meat pies — put jam in them instead.' Not surprisingly 'he and his retinue barely escaped being torn to pieces'.

According to John Kolasky, a Canadian communist who spent two years studying in the Ukraine, no such exchange took place. On the contrary, the management simply refused to accept a delegation from the shop floor. This, though less dramatic, sounds more likely. It was certainly just as insulting.

13

The workers took action. Trains were stopped on the line running past the works, slogans scrawled on the walls, loco horns and factory sirens set wailing and blowing. The militia arrived, was forbidden entry and departed. The army arrived and occupied half of the works while the workers held a meeting in the other half. The management stared out of its windows, talked urgently on the telephone. Alarm bells were set ringing up the rungs of the various hierarchies.

More workers arrived for the next shift, but those already there showed no inclination to return home. According to Solzhenitsyn arrests were made during the night, but if so enough workers remained to plan a march on the town. When morning came they set off, many with their families, for the centre of Novocherkassk. Carrying red flags, banners bearing peaceful demands, even portraits of Lenin, they were joined by workers from other factories, who brought news of spreading strikes.

In Lenin Square the marchers found a crowd already gathered in front of the Party offices. Ringed around them were troops, both Army and KGB, looking both nervous and well-armed. Insults were exchanged. When the local Party Secretary attempted to address his flock he was shouted down.

Meanwhile the troops were being replaced. Unknown to the crowd, the order to open fire had already had given and refused. More compliant units, strangers to the district, were brought forward, and when the order was given once more, it was obeyed. Only one officer had both the courage and the conviction to resist. He ostentatiously took out his Party card, tore it to shreds and shot himself.

The rest of the troops fired straight into the crowd, dropping people in tens. Those demonstrators who could still run, did so. Within minutes only the troops and their victims remained.

One of Solzhenitsyn's witnesses describes the scene: 'The puddles of blood have formed in the depressions in the pavement. I am not exaggerating; I never suspected till now that there could be so much blood. The benches in the public gardens are spattered with blood, there are bloodstains on its sanded paths and on the whitewashed tree-trunks in the public garden. The whole square is scored with tank tracks. A red flag which the demonstrators had been carrying is propped against the wall of the Party headquarters and a grey cap splashed with red-brown blood has been slung over the top of the pole. Across the facade of the Party buildings hangs a red banner, there for some time past: THE PEOPLE AND THE PARTY ARE ONE.'

The dead were carried away in town buses. In the days that followed Novocherkassk was cordoned off from the rest of the Soviet Union, as the wheels of justice ground through the survivors. The only people 'allowed' to leave the town were relatives of the dead, and they were bound for the remoter parts of remote Siberia. The 'ringleaders' were tried and executed. Silence was decreed. The traces were comprehensively covered.

In return, the Party delivered ample butter and sausage to the shop shelves, albeit at the new price. The locomotive workers were duly grateful, promising, a bare week after the massacre, to fulfil their current plan ahead of schedule.

Solzhenitsyn thought the events in Novocherkassk marked 'a turning point in the modern history of Russia'. This remains debatable, but 1962 was certainly a watershed year for the Communist Party of the Soviet Union, the first since the war in which living standards had failed to rise.

This was particularly depressing for a Party leadership which had just committed itself, in the 1961 Programme of the CPSU to the achievement of 'full communism within twenty years'. And this was not an isolated piece of boasting. Five years had passed since Soviet technology had sent Sputnik and the first ICBM soaring skywards and Party leader Khrushchev had littered those years with dizzying promises of imminent abundance. By 1964 the Soviet worker would have the world's shortest working week, by 1970 a *per capita* income equal to his or her American counterpart. When 'full communism' dawned in 1980 there would be no one left to emulate.

These predictions were too wild for the purposes of propaganda; Khrushchev, for one, really believed them. He had reorganised industry, agriculture, even the Party itself. He was trying to reorganise Eastern Europe and Soviet-American relations. He had lifted the terror, ploughed the vast 'Virgin

15

Lands' of Kazakhstan, sacrificed the alliance with China to the needs of Soviet growth. He had put his own position on the line.

None of it worked. The reorganisation of industry simply forced the basic problems into expressing themselves differently; one series of bottlenecks became another. Agriculture continued to stagnate; the Party continued to resist any erosion of its economic functions. Eastern Europe refused to accept a fully integrated COMECON; the United States showed no interest in peaceful coexistence. Quite the contrary — in 1961 Kennedy and MacNamara were busy setting in motion the quarter-century arms race. China was violently resentful, the 'Virgin Lands' by 1963 a dust bowl wreathed in black clouds.

The terror stayed lifted, as much for the Party's peace of mind as for the people's. But even this had adverse repercussions throughout the society — dangerously weakening the power of command in what remained, to all intents and purposes, a command system.

Khrushchev was kicked out. 'We can no longer afford you,' Mikhail Suslov told him coldly at the famous Politburo meeting. The following day the Chinese celebrated by exploding their first atomic device.

The Khrushchev-less Politburo was keen to present a collective facade, but the holders of the main offices in Party and Government inevitably stood out above their colleagues. Leonid Brezhnev and Alexei Kosygin exemplified the coalition of 'moderates' who now ruled the Soviet Union, with Brezhnev, the Party apparatchik, slightly to the left, in Soviet parlance, of centre, and Kosygin, the reform-minded state bureaucrat, slightly to the right. To Brezhnev's left the old Stalinist hacks were reduced to nostalgia, to Kosygin's right the reformists were reduced to optimism. At the hub of the Party wheel Mikhail Suslov, guardian of ideological rectitude, tacked the Party sails to make the most of a dying wind.

What were they to do? Khrushchev had not created the problems, merely failed, noisily, to solve them. What exactly were the problems? Why was the Soviet growth rate slowing so dramatically?

Basically, the plant had outgrown its pot. For more than two decades, from the early thirties to the middle fifties, the advantages of a centrally planned society had outweighed the disadvantages. The Soviet leadership had been able to mount the sort of singleminded mobilisation of human and material resources which free enterprise economies find possible only in wartime. This was no accident; the Soviet Union had been perpetually at war, with underdevelopment, the hapless kulaks, the Wehrmacht, the consequences of occupation. For a quarter of a century there had been no respite. What was needed was produced by the state for the state. The people were not consulted, but at least they had the compensation of knowing that no person or class was utilising scarce capital as profit. At least they could see the new factories growing up, firstly in the fields, secondly amidst the ruins left by war. All the enemies of the Soviet state were being defeated; the economy was growing at an astonishing rate.

But centralised planning had always involved disadvantages too, and as the war receded these became increasingly evident, a drag on growth. To move the economy from productive balance to productive balance at a high rate of growth required the fullest possible use of resources. No slack could be left in the system; everyone was working at full tilt for everyone else. The danger was obvious — a hold-up in one mine or factory or marshalling yard was likely to reverberate through entire sectors of the economy. If the lumberjacks failed to meet their quota, then the deskmakers would be idle for weeks on end and the planners might end up doing their calculations on the floor.

Over the years management and workers devised ways of countering this uncertainty of supply. Managers would under-estimate the productive potential of their enterprises when sub-mitting draft plans to the central authorities, because they could be surer of hitting a lower target. At the same time they would overstate their supply requirements so as to be sure of receiving what was really necessary. To compensate for late deliveries and the consequent periods of forced idleness, the habit evolved of cramming all work into the last portion of the month, the so-called 'storming' period, and the quality of the product suffered as a result. All these 'solutions' to uncertain supply involved a large and growing burden of sheer waste for the economy to carry.

The centralised system also tended to stifle initiative. The planners, ensconced in their Moscow turrets, could not do the manager's job for him, could not know all that he knew, and that they needed to know, of the particular circumstances affecting his enterprise. But they did have to hand down a production target which kept that enterprise in tune with the rest of the economy. The manager could only be judged by whether or not he fulfilled his quota, not by the manner of his success or failure in this regard. A manager of a machine tool factory might reason that widening the range and improving the quality of his tools would be bound to benefit both his customers and the economy as a whole. But that was not his decision to take; only the planners, with their supposed ability to view the broader picture, could decide such things. The same manager, moreover, was only too aware that the time spent installing new and better machinery would put the fulfilment of his current quota at risk. And many other enterprises were dependent on his quota-fulfilment to fulfil their own. The manager could apply to the central authorities for permission to introduce the new machinery and adjust his current target downwards, but the planners were unlikely to welcome the volume of work — adjusting targets throughout the sector, adjusting investment programmes, income funds, etc., etc. — which would be involved. They would make such adjustments when it was absolutely necessary, and reluctantly even then. In the Soviet economy, to innovate from the bottom was to rock the boat.

A level of centralisation which produced such waste and such chronic conservatism was bound to also engender a generalised apathy among both managers and workers. Obeying economic orders was one thing, obeying orders which bore no obvious relation to the real situation was something else. Year after year the Soviet work force lived with the consequences of the planners' inevitable ignorance, doing things the way Moscow said they should be done, when common sense often dictated quite another way. Cynicism became the norm. The black economy, largely supplied from goods produced in excess of deliberately low targets, grew and grew.

18

Both the advantages and disadvantages of the system were still visible in the 1960s, but the balance between them had changed. In Stalin's day apathy had been overcome by exhortation, discipline and terror. The innovation required for building the basic industrial infrastructure had been well within the reach of the centralised research and development agencies. Waste had not been a crucial factor so long as the economy had access to spare capital and labour.

Now things were different. The spare capital and labour had been consumed by growth. The workers had grown immune to exhortation and the post-Stalin leadership had been unwilling to impose stricter controls. As the economy had grown more complex, as more products were made and the number of economic interrelationships multiplied, the task of the planners had become ever more difficult. The level of information needed was receding out of reach; the newer products were technologically more complex and less susceptible to quantification by the million ton. More decisions were, by necessity, being devolved to the managerial level, yet the whole logic of the system was preventing the managers from taking them. It was time for change.

This was easier imagined than done. When Khrushchev had taken up the gauntlet — or at least started looking for it — the system had already been twenty-five years old. It had gathered inertia and proved extremely resistant to any form of change. A huge bureaucratic apparatus, jealous of its powers and privileges, was inextricably entwined around the limbs of the economy. The Party had been transformed over the years into an enforcement agency for the planners' law; it was the huge army of local functionaries who kept the whole precarious show on the road.

Nor was it only the Party. The Armed Forces enjoyed their priority status when it came to commandeering talent, capital or materials. Many managers liked a system which paid them well, yet demanded little in the way of creative responsibility. And the workers too, so long as the standard of living continued to edge upwards, had reason to be satisfied. Most of the spoils of 1917 had long been wrenched from their grasp, but security of employment still remained and few were eager to exchange it for the hypothetical wonders of higher productivity. No one was anxious to pay 'real' prices for food, transport and other subsidised products and services.

There were people and sectors in favour of change, but they were few and far between. Many economists and mathematicians stressed the need for reform, some managers hungered for more responsibility. An increasing number of individuals in the Party, some highly placed, recognised the inevitability of radical reform and wanted to implement it before matters got out of hand. The KGB was known to contain such reformists; the more evidence there was of nascent working class opposition, the more they dreaded the massive unrest which a further slowing of the economic growth rate might provoke.

It was a peculiar situation. Change was necessary for the well-being of the economy, but few saw it as being in their interests. The outcome was predictable: a tentative stab at reform, based on the belief that it was better to do too little than too much.

The Brezhnev-Kosygin Politburo acted with due circum-spection. All the options were meticulously considered, as the Politburo minutes for late 1964 attest. Four basic 'solutions' to the one basic problem were discussed; they could loosely be termed the 'managerial', 'administrative', 'market' and 'external' solutions. It was to be the failure of each, one after the other, which would set the scene for revolution.

Before embarking on its programme the Politburo took steps to mitigate the potential blow. A new campaign against the intelligentsia was mounted; its first famous victims were Sinyavsky and Daniel in 1965. The other major source of possible opposition, the industrial working class, was treated quite differently. The gap between blue- and white-collar wages was narrowed back towards the differentials obtaining in Stalin's day. For several years there were to be no major mani-festations of proletarian discontent.

The 'administrative' solution carried the least risk and the least hopes. The system would not be fundamentally altered, but it would be managed rather better. Planning would be improved by increasing computerisation, work discipline by more skilful exhortation techniques and new bonus systems.

The new leadership would make less mistakes than Khrushchev.

The 'managerial' solution involved a limited devolution of power to the managers, a 'loosening' of the plan to accommodate circumstances which the planners could not take into account. The first steps in this direction were taken in 1965 with the economic reforms associated with Kosygin. New indicators were introduced stressing profitability, innovation and quality; bonuses and incentives were juggled. On paper the reign of the purely quantitative target had ended, leaving the managers with more than a modicum of independence. But it was only on paper; opposition from the planners and the local Party functionaries swiftly nullified the reform measures, and the net effect inside the Soviet Union was minimal.

In Eastern Europe, by contrast, things were happening, though hardly in the manner intended. At a Politburo meeting early in 1965 it had been decided, by the narrowest of majorities, that Kadar and his colleagues in Hungary could introduce a truly radical economic reform. There had been no question of restricting the Hungarians to 'managerial' changes; subject to the usual political qualifications they were free to create a full-scale socialist 'market' economy, with the planners playing a guiding rather than an administrative role. And, as the years went by, it all seemed to be going surprisingly well. The economic results were encouraging, the political doubts uncomfirmed.

What made this success story even harder to swallow was the disastrous succession of events in neighbouring Czechoslovakia. Here a much more circumscribed reform programme got totally out of control, confirming all the doubters' worst fears. Clearly, reform was not something to be rushed into. Hungary would be watched with great interest, tanks at the ready.

For the moment, for the Soviet Union itself, there seemed an easier path to follow — the 'external' solution. If Soviet productivity could not be raised without creating widespread internal opposition, then that higher productivity could still, hopefully, be imported from the West.

*　　*　　*

As the men in the Kremlin pondered the price they were prepared to pay for détente and its technological perks, their industrial working class was pondering the price of the failure of Kosygin's reforms:

1967 . . . a major strike at the Kharkov Tractor Plant, the first in the Soviet Union for three years, was settled on the workers' terms after several days.

1967 . . . in Priuluk, a Ukrainian town fifty miles west of Kiev, a local man was unjustly arrested by the militia and subsequently beaten to death at the police station. Next day the procession of mourners was passing by the station when the militia commander inadvertently came out of the door. One woman cried out, 'Down with the Soviet SS!' This was enough to send the crowd surging towards the building. They smashed everything that came to hand, including the faces of the available militiamen.

As the news spread, workers in the town's factories downed tools and took to the streets. Troops were called in and fire engine hoses were used to dampen the popular ardour. Five men were arrested.

The whole town came out on strike; the local authorities fled. A letter was sent to the Central Committee in Moscow demanding the release of those arrested, the handing over of the guilty militiamen and the dismissal of *all* Party and Government employees in the town. If more troops were brought in, the letter warned, the people would blow up the gas pipeline which passed by the town.

One Army general arrived. He publicly trampled the militia captain's insignia, announced the release of the five arrested men, but refused to hand over the guilty militiamen to 'lynch law'. This proved sufficient.

1969 . . . in Sverdlovsk oblast a rubber plant was hit by strikes.

1969 . . . women working at an arms factory in Gorky downed tools and announced that they would only resume work once enough food had been found to feed their families.

1969 . . . a thousand miles to the south, in Krasnodar, an

almost identical protest occurred, with workers refusing to attend their factories until such time as the shops had something to exchange for their wages.

1970 . . . a number of factories in Vladimir were hit by apparently coordinated strikes.

1971 . . . a three day strike halted the huge Kirov Factory in the Chelyabinsk suburb of Kopeyske.

1972 . . . Dnepropetrovsk was hit by a wave of strikes, with thousands demanding better pay and a general rise in their standard of living. Having failed to isolate the strikes, the authorities brought in troops and many workers were killed or wounded. A month later the strikes restarted. This time the pay demands were met.

1972 . . . in Dneprodzerzhinsk, Brezhnev's home town, an 'unfortunate incident' occurred. A drunken group of militiamen arrested some equally drunken members of a wedding party, loaded them into a van and zigzagged off down the street. Seconds later the van crashed. The militiamen managed to save themselves, but the arrested group were still locked in the back when the vehicle caught fire. Relatives, friends and a swiftly gathering crowd marched on the militia station and sacked it. They then marched on the Party headquarters. Ordered to disperse, the crowd charged the building instead. The militia opened fire, killing at least ten.

1973 . . . the largest factories in Vitebsk were strikebound after the attempted introduction of new piecerate norms. Two days later the attempt was abandoned by management, apparently on advice from the local KGB.

1973 . . . several thousand workers walked out of the machine-building factory on Kiev's Brest-Litovsk Chausee, demanding better pay and conditions. The director of the plant phoned the Ukraine Party HQ and within hours a member of the Republican Politburo had met with the workers' delegates and given in to their demands. By mid-afternoon the bulk of the administrative staff had been sacked, the workers' pay increased and work resumed.

All of these widely-spaced examples of industrial action demonstrated, first, a profound dissatisfaction with work conditions and pay and, second, a profound distrust of authority, both inside and outside the place of work. The ease with which the minor incidents at Priuluk and Dneprodzerzhinsk escalated into mass action offered a vivid insight into the shortness of the Soviet proletarian fuse.

In most cases the local authorities responded in like manner. They swiftly acted to remove the causes of particular grievances, conceding demands with a speed which would have astonished unions in the West. Of course, the quicker the settlement, the less chance the news would spread, evoking similar action elsewhere. And afterwards the KGB could do its best to winkle out the 'ringleaders'.

It proved an effective response, at least in the short term. It was also the only response available. With no market economy to enforce economic pressures, with no insecurity of employment to frighten the workers, the state was forced to rely on a judicious mixture of concessions and administrative repression. Hopefully the West would come to the Kremlin's aid before things got any worse.

Importing efficiency and technology from the capitalist realm was not a new idea; in the 1920s and in the latter years of the Khrushchev era there had been a considerable inflow. The difference, now, lay in the scope of the 'technology transfer' envisaged and the central role accorded it in Soviet planning for the future. The Kremlin was thinking in terms of entire plants, of voluminous amounts of Western-patented know-how, of literally hundreds of millions of roubles.

Kosygin, addressing the Twenty-third Congress of the CPSU in 1966, had noted that a higher level of economic exchange between the blocs would have 'a positive effect upon the international situation'. What he really meant was that a lessening of East-West tension was the *sine qua non* of better business. A friend in need would be a friend indeed.

The Americans ignored him. They had heard it all before, distrusted Soviet intentions and were basically uninterested, for reasons of their own, in an international détente. This had been

24

the case ever since 1945. From Washington's point of view the ideal situation was one of low-level hostility, not low-level friendship. There were no overpowering economic reasons for either cutting the American arms bill or expanding Soviet-American trade, but American dominance in the free enterprise world did rely heavily on the existence of a global 'enemy'. This need intensified during the 1960s as new difficulties arose in relations with Western Europe and Japan, and as the involvement in Vietnam deepened.

Fortunately for the Soviet leadership there were others in the West more willing to pick up the rouble-draped olive branch. The Cuban Missile Crisis had left nerves jangling around the world. This apparent brush with global death, choreographed by the superpowers in blissful disregard of their allies' feelings, had been widely resented. Gaullist France, anxious for this and other reasons to erode American predominance in Western Europe, took the first steps towards improving relations with Moscow, but it was the continent's other major power which took up the running in earnest. Kennedy's adoption of the 'flexible response' strategy had grim implications for West Germany. The doctrine implicitly recognised the possibility of a limited nuclear war and the West Germans had a shrewd idea of just where it would be limited to. The leadership in Bonn began to debate the broad outlines of a bargain with the Kremlin.

A mutually beneficial deal was not hard to find. West Germany could offer the Soviet Union a formal recognition of the *de facto* postwar settlement and much-needed technological assistance. The Soviet Union could offer West Germany a reduced risk of obliteration, closer ties with its brother-state across the Elbe and access to Eastern bloc markets for its industry. European détente was born.

Others joined in and soon the men in the Kremlin had reason to slap each other on the back. By 1968 Soviet trade with West Germany, Italy, Great Britain and Japan had dramatically increased. Even the rumpus over Czechoslovakia failed to interrupt the new flow of business.

But no sooner had the vodka glasses hit the hearth than disillusion began to set in. European détente was good, but not good enough. Some of the technology required — most notably computers and oil-extraction equipment — was either only available from the United States or would not be supplied by the Europeans without American approval. And the need for this technology kept growing, as a series of crises rocked the Soviet bloc — Czechoslovakia, armed conflict with China in 1969, serious industrial trouble in Poland. The reaction of the Baltic Coast workers provided an ominous premonition of multiplying Novocherkassks. The Americans had to be dragged into détente.

For once, fortune was favouring the Kremlin: or so it seemed. By 1970 American policy was in a frightful mess and the leadership in Washington was searching round for straws to clutch. The determination to police the free enterprise world had landed the United States knee-deep in the Vietnamese quagmire and, though the possibility of eventual defeat was still unmentionable, the economic consequences of the struggle were already proving disastrous. America was paying for the war by printing money and setting in motion, in the process, the spiral of global inflation which was to haunt the rest of the decade. The West Europeans and Japanese were angry about American economic policy and doubly angry at their own apparent impotence in the face of it. The Third World remained violently resentful; there seemed no end to the need for this bank-breaking American omnipresence.

And yet, Nixon and Kissinger mused, perhaps the Russians could lift them off this row of unpalatable hooks. A superpower condominium might cower the West Europeans and Japanese. Moscow might be able to pressure Hanoi into something which looked vaguely like 'withdrawal with honour'. If the Soviets agreed to stop meddling in the Third World, then there might be scope for reducing the American police role. Increased trade might help to balance the American ledger. And more. Selling large quantities of grain to the Soviets would be doubly profitable; less would be available for sale within the free enterprise world, the market would tighten and prices would soar. The more they mused, the more sense it all seemed to make. Superpower détente was born.

In 1972 Nixon and Brezhnev signed the various documents. The one thought he was being promised world stability, the other a technological bonanza. Both were wrong.

Nixon and Kissinger had made three false assumptions, which together amounted to building a self-destruct button into détente. First, and more crucially, they apparently believed that the United States could escape scotfree from the consequences of hiking world food prices. But the oil-producing countries, facing hugely inflated food bills, were disinclined to let matters rest; they used the coincidence of a tightening oil market and the Yom Kippur War to hike their own prices fourfold. This ushered in a general world recession, which in turn exacerbated the differences between the United States and the rest of the free enterprise world. The second and third assumptions, that Western Europe and Japan would be cowered by the grandeur of détente and that Third World stability was simply conditional on Soviet restraint, were swiftly put to the test and found wanting. From about 1975 onwards successive American administrations had little choice but to resurrect more traditional policies; nothing else but increasing doses of cold war ideology would suffice to hold the West together. The Kremlin was told, with decreasing tact, that it would have to seek its credits and technology elsewhere.

But worse was to come. The Americans had managed the diplomatic somersault, but landing on their feet proved impossible. Vietnam had destroyed the American public's willingness to indulge in global policing, and the return to cold warrior status was not accompanied by a restructuring of the military muscle needed to make the old policies 'work'. Nixon and Kissinger had tried to solve this problem by picking out 'regional powers' and arming them to the teeth; Carter tried to solve it by reenlisting the American public in a global crusade for 'human rights'. Unfortunately for Carter, some of the more odious transgressors of human rights were none other than Kissinger's 'regional powers'. The scene was set for disaster.

It arrived in 1978-79. Two pillars of Kissinger's world, in the strategically important regions of Central America and the Middle East, came crashing down. First Nicaragua, then Iran was lost to the West. The toppling of the Peacock Throne also had formidable economic repercussions, a further enormous hike in the world oil price, another deepening of the general world recession.

Although the Soviet Union had not been fishing, much less catching anything in these particular waters, the American administration's gut response was to bury détente. While a new and cheaper method of world policing — the Rapid Deployment Force — was transferred from the drawingboard to reality, the old Soviet scapegoat was being dusted off and held up once again as the centrepiece of American policy. As fortune would have it, Mao Tse-tung had just died in Peking and his successors proved more than willing, for purely mercenary reasons, to join Washington in a new anti-Soviet crusade. In Europe, too, the recession had brought together governments eager to embrace a more aggressive stance and agreement was reached on modernising the theatre nuclear weapons systems. From the Kremlin's point of view the world had suddenly turned sour.

Things were not much better inside the Soviet bloc. The Soviet and satellite economies, with the important exception of the Hungarians, were still suffering from declining growth rates. Now the defence bills would have to rise once more. Someone was going to suffer a drop in living standards.

But not without a struggle; the Soviet working class was taking the first, faltering steps towards self-organisation. In November 1977 an independent union had been set up; largely thanks to the dynamism of one Ukrainian miner, Vladimir Khlebanov. It soon had members in widely diffuse regions of the Soviet Union and, in February 1978, the leadership of this Association of Free Trade Unions (FTUA) addressed an open letter to the Central Committee, stressing worker discontent with a wide variety of industrial abuses, including management pilfering, dilution of production materials, bribery, an excessive accident rate and other commonplace violations of the Soviet labour code.

The signatories were invited to the *Izvestia* and KGB offices in Moscow, where they were given promises of an investigation into the specific complaints. Whether from overconfidence, or from a desire to advertise the strength of its support, the FTUA leadership then published a list of two hundred members. The investigation of the complaints predictably turned into an investigation of the complainers. Khlebanov himself was confined to a psychiatric hospital after being diagnosed as a paranoiac. It was this abnormality, the official report claimed, which explained why Khlebanov had 'been making complaints since as long ago as 1958, and saying that the management in the mines has been cheating the workers over their pay'.

The swift demise of the FTUA was followed by the swift birth of the Free Inter-Professional Union of Workers (SMOT). This time only the leadership ventured out into the open, with the expected consequences. Some were driven from the country, some exiled internally, some confined in psychiatric hospitals, the infamous *pityushkas*. The unnamed members disappeared underground, the KGB in hot pursuit.

In March 1980 a third union, UNITY, emerged in the West Ukraine, in 1982 a fourth, Workers' Rights, in the Dnieper bend towns. The Polish example fired the creation of Solidarity lookalikes in the Baltic republics. None of these organisations functioned openly and their members were in constant danger of apprehension by the minions of the Second Chief Directorate of the KGB. But the number of those committed to an 'independent' platform steadily grew and the number of potential supporters with them. When the time eventually came for a flexing of industrial muscle, there would be more to flex than at any time since 1917.

The Kremlin's pile of woe was certainly reaching skywards. The régime was now engaged in a war in neighbouring Afghanistan which threatened to become a Soviet version of Vietnam. And across the other side of Empire the Polish economy had taken another spectacular nose dive, this time complete with dangerous political implications.

The Afghan 'adventure' had begun, like the war in Vietnam, with high hopes and a tolerably clear conscience. In 1978 a coup had brought the communists to power in Kabul and the Soviets had started lavishing aid on their new comrades. The latter, with a newcomer's zeal, had begun the task of dragging a reluctant Afghanistan into the twentieth century. So far, so progressive.

Then things started to go wrong. The cadres on the ground proved too impatient, too clumsy, and were soon alienating most of their potential supporters, reinforcing the very traditional structures which they were seeking to replace. The Party leader, Taraki, called for a change of pace, a slowing of the revolutionary process. Moscow agreed.

Unfortunately for all concerned, Taraki's right hand man, Hafizullah Amin, had other ideas. He favoured the more direct approach, one that Stalin would have recognised from his kulak-bashing days. Having disposed of Taraki, Amin put his ideas to the test.

The results were spectacular. In a matter of weeks the corpses were piling up and a full-blooded civil war was under way. The Soviet leadership was left with a most unwelcome choice — to wash their hands of the whole business or to step in and take charge. With détente already rotting in the diplomatic cupboard they chose the latter. It was to prove a costly error.

While the gunships were hovering over the Hindu Kush the Polish workers were winning the unprecedented right to elect their own trade union, Solidarity. For over a year this national union openly struggled for a dilution of the Party's power monopoly, but once it became clear that the hardliners on both sides were indisposed to share power, a military restoration of 'order' became inevitable. Late in 1981 martial law was imposed, and the union's activities 'temporarily' banned. Moscow sighed with relief, but the victory was a hollow one. 'Order' offered no solution to Poland's economic and political crisis. It offered time, but time for what?

By the beginning of the 1980s the future facing the Soviet Union looked bleak. The 'managerial' solution had been virtually abandoned, the 'market' solution had not even been tried. The 'administrative' solution offered only peripheral gains, the 'external' solution had collapsed with détente. Maintaining military parity with an arms-race-inclined Reagan Administration, fighting an endless war in Afghanistan, baling out the Polish economy — all were likely to prove extremely expensive. The same group of men which had been guiding the fortunes of the state fifteen years earlier still occupied the chairs in the Politburo chamber. They were older, maybe wiser, but they had no new ideas.

The Twenty-sixth Congress of the CPSU, held early in 1981, was a gloom-ridden affair. Kosygin's successor as Premier, Nikolai Tikhonov, lamented the low productivity and high wastage typical of the Soviet economy, claiming that it was caused by 'inertia and the habits left over from the period when the quantity of output rather than quality was stressed'. This would change of course, though Tikhonov neglected to explain how.

The trade unions were given the full treatment, lavished with praise and encouraged to reach those parts of the system which no other organisation could. No space was to be left for the growth of a Soviet Solidarity.

The persistent failure of agriculture — the latest harvest had been the third bad one in a row — was underscored by Brezhnev himself. 'The food problem,' he believed, was 'the central problem of the whole five year plan in the economic and political sense.' Like Tikhonov he knew the destination, but not the route.

But the Congress did not confine itself only to pious hopes. Some steps of real significance were taken and would doubtless have received greater publicity had they not touched on such politically sensitive issues. The latest carrots were clearly on display — new pay scales, new bonus systems tied to technical innovation. Some of the population would be given the opportunity to get rich. But an old stick was being brandished in the background; those riches would be gained, in the short term at least, at the expense of other Soviet citizens. And not only in wages terms. The régime was trying, very carefully, to make it easier for enterprises to shed labour, both as a means of improving productivity and as a spur to labour mobility. In short, the Soviet working class was to bear the burden of a Soviet economic recovery. Thatcherism was alive and well in Moscow.

Predictably enough, 1981-2 witnessed a new wave of industrial unrest. Short stoppages and the so-called 'Italian strikes' — a slowing, rather than cessation, of work — became almost commonplace. And there were several incidents of major industrial action.

November 1981 . . . at the huge Kama River Lorry Works general dissatisfaction with pay and conditions was brought to a head by the collapse of a recreational centre, less than five years after its construction. After several stormy meetings, in which the workers demanded an immediate revision of work norms and improved amenities, the entire work force came out on strike. The stoppage lasted several days, before being settled largely on the workers' terms.

February 1982 . . . several men were laid off at the Marine Engineering Combine in Nikolayev and, when they demanded alternative employment, were told that several plants on the Far Eastern coast urgently needed marine engineers. Again, the entire work force downed tools. After two days and a visit from high-level Republican Party officials the men were reinstated and the management fired.

May 1982 . . . a similar situation occurred at the Gorky Automobile Plant, when the installation of new West German machinery cost several hundred men their jobs. They, too, were offered alternative employment in the East and they, too, received strike backing from their fellow-workers. This time, however, the management refused to concede, militia were used to break up workers' meetings, more 'troublemakers' were dismissed and the strike was eventually broken.

September 1982 . . . in the Moscow industrial suburb of Kuncevo an attempt to raise norms, simultaneously, at several factories was resisted by the work forces. 'Italian strikes' proliferated, until several workers were beaten up by unknown assailants, occasioning a general stoppage. In reprisal for the beatings a locally-famous director was 'kidnapped' and thrown into the Moscow River. For several days a series of minor street skirmishes took place between young workers and 'special industrial security forces', ostensibly acting on orders from the local Party committee. Eventually a tacit compromise was formulated and the workers returned to the factories. In the ensuing weeks many of their prominent spokesmen were arrested, and in November the norms were raised once more.

Such activity, though only the tip of a large iceberg, might have been borne with more equanimity if the overall situation of the economy was improving. But, in the industrial sphere at least, it was not. When the Politburo gathered on 4 July 1982 to discuss the 'first-year' reports on the 1981-85 Plan, the news was anything but good.

Candidate member Mikhail Solomentsev remembered this session. 'It was notable for two reasons. First, for the atmosphere around the table, which was the most depressing I had experienced. We had two sets of figures in front of us, the real ones and those for public consumption, and at first I mistook the latter for the former. No one could really believe them. None of the targets was being met, except, irony of ironies, that year's grain harvest. And that target had been scaled down after the shortfalls of the previous years.

'Second, and of more lasting importance, this was the day that the outlines of the debate solidified. When Chernenko slipped in some snide aside about the 1981-82 reforms — "the price of encouraging a capitalist mentality" or some such phrase — he got more then he bargained for. Shcherbitsky, who'd never been noted for his strong backing of the reformist case, suddenly launched into an attack, almost a personal assault, on Chernenko.

'It was this sort of "narrow, obstructionist thinking", spread downwards from the very top, which was "hampering all the Party's efforts at sensible reform". And it was "the lack of any progress in this crucial area" which was directly responsible for our "economic failure". "Yes, failure," he almost shouted, shaking the report in the air, "what else can we call this?"

'Chernenko was somewhat taken aback by this, but he was soon on the counter-attack. Our "unsatisfactory economic performance" followed, "as spring follows winter", from the attempt to by-pass the Party in matters of economic management. It was the "reckless" introduction of "economic levers" — "just an intelligentsia name for managerial irresponsibility" — which was doing all the damage. "Weaken the centre, make the planners' job impossible, and this" — he was shaking his copy now — "is the result."

'The argument continued for several hours. Nothing was said which hadn't been said before, but there was a venomous intensity in the air which was profoundly new. The next day I noticed that one Western correspondent had somehow got news of the session; he claimed that "the bitter squabbles now convulsing the Kremlin" were all tied in to the "succession struggle". Would that it had been so simple! It was the level of our economic difficulties which was intensifying the debate within the chamber, which was producing a sudden polarisation as regards policy options. For years the centrists had managed to play the Stalinists off against the reformists and *vice versa*, persuading each side that doing nothing was infinitely preferable to doing what the other side wanted. But at this meeting the centre seemed to be vanishing, the need for difficult decisions drawing finally nigh. The figures in front of us were the product of "doing nothing". No change of policy, or so some of us were beginning to believe, could prove more risky than total economic stagnation.'

Unlike the members of the Politburo, most Soviet citizens lived with the reality, not the statistics. In the summer of 1982, Jean-Paul Bonnet, a French journalist with much experience of the country, found them more depressed than ever about the economic situation. 'It's all falling to pieces,' was one constant refrain, 'It's a catastrophe,' was another. No one seemed to place any credence in the official figures, and everyone had an anecdote to illustrate the prevailing chaos — warehouses full of rotting food a block away from empty shops; empty trains careering across the steppe in pursuit of mileage quotas while loaded wagons in the oblast next door waited vainly for collection . . . the list was endless. But the chief complaint concerned increasingly frequent shortages of basic foodstuffs, particularly milk and meat so far as Moscow was concerned. And

Bonnet was left in no doubt that conditions outside the capital were much, much worse. 'In Kuybyshev the word for cabbage is now the word for food,' one student told him.

Nor was there any real belief that things were going to improve. On the contrary, most people thought the worst was yet to come. 'In ten years from now,' one cabdriver told the Frenchman, 'we will look back on this as an era of prosperity.'

Few had any doubts as to where the blame lay. The Americans were criticised for the arms race, the East Europeans for 'all taking and no giving', but neither could compete with the country's leadership when it came to a popular *j'accuse*. It was 'the servants of the people', with their special stores and limousines and hunting lodges and pampered children, who were responsible for the mess. 'We would not resent the privileges if we thought, for one moment, that they knew what they were doing,' one teacher told Bonnet. 'But they're all such mediocrities. They have to be the way our system works in practice. They know they don't have any answers; at some point in the last twenty years they realised, consciously or not, that the problems were simply too big for the system to handle. And they decided, again consciously or not, that the only thing left for them to do was to live like kings. None of them believes in it anymore. How could they? They're old, and they just hope it all holds together while they're still here.'

This total erosion of faith in the Soviet system was Bonnet's strongest impression. 'Each time I have visited the Soviet Union there have always been people, intelligent ordinary people, prepared to defend the system, to state a belief in its potential, no matter how serious the current difficulties might be. This time I found no one prepared to do so. One Party official told me: "Nobody argues anymore about politics, they simply give a sad, knowing smirk and change the subject. It's too farcical for serious discussion, and too serious to joke about." Another official, rather the worse for drink, confided in me: "Soviet planning is nonexistent. It's like trying to plan a kindergarten picnic; the children are told what is expected of them, they all nod their heads and then rush off in a hundred different directions." An old friend from Moscow University explained the extent to which barter had replaced buying as the main form of economic exchange, and then sarcastically remarked that the régime "should claim more credit for such a swift transition to pure communism".'

What was replacing the lost faith in a brighter future? There was no single answer. Bonnet's friends among the intelligentsia had 'turned inwards, into family life, career-building, leisure pursuits. What could they do to change the wider world?' A few dissidents thought otherwise, but cut off from the rest of the population, obliged by definition to throw down an open challenge, they were mostly easy prey for the KGB.

The industrial working class was largely passive in political terms, and not much more active when it came to working for the state. The black economy paid better. Within this class a small minority were activity engaged in opposing the state machine and there were signs and rumours that such activities were on the increase. But the 'independents', like the dissidents, were largely isolated from other opposition groups; it would take a serious worsening of the economic situation, and a fair degree of either incompetence or daring from the ruling group, for them to pose a potent threat to the system as a whole.

The same could be said, with even more certainty, of the various religious and nationalist groups. There was no organised opposition, no means of expressing a collective *nyet*.

Only in their vices did the Soviet people demonstrate an overpowering unity of purpose. In every corner of the land the consumption of vodka and its illegal surrogates had been rising and rising, to the point where alcoholism had assumed the status of a national calamity. Sport, nationalism and religion all vied for second place, but the ubiquitous 'Commodity No 1' had no real competitor. Bonnet concluded his article thus: 'One night we were returning from a concert in the Kremlin when the taxi-driver suddenly swerved to avoid a pair of drunks lying in the middle of the road. Looking back, I saw that neither had so much as noticed their close brush with a lasting unconsciousness. Lying there, they seemed to typify the Soviet Union's place on the road of history, massively resigned, waiting to be run over.'

PART TWO

REFORM (November 1982-October 1984)

*The most efficient instigator of a
revolution is the government at which
it will be aimed.*

Vladimir Matushevich

IN THE West Brezhnev's long-awaited demise was greeted with the usual flood of speculative pronouncements. Kremlinologists were dragged from their university studies and mercilessly pumped for predictions. Needless to say, they each managed to interpret the available information differently, a quite remarkable feat when the sum total of that information appeared to be the pecking order visible around the lamented leader's coffin.

In the Soviet Union there was also a great deal of guesswork, much of it even less well-informed. The reaction of the ordinary Soviet citizen, according to those on the spot, was a mixture of vague curiosity and indifference. On the streets, on the shop floor, in the queues, people discussed the leader's death as they might have discussed the weather. 'I wonder what they'll do now,' was the stock attitude. No one seriously believed that things would radically change.

Those who had shared, those who wished to share, the fallen Secretary's podium of power, had rather more to lose. In the West the smart money was on either Kirilenko or Chernenko to take the top job, but the former was soon found to be conspicuous by his absence at Party and State gatherings and the latter was soon being criticised in print. The General Secretaryship went instead to the man who had, until recently, led the KGB, Yuri Vladimirovich Andropov.

The Western press gave due prominence to the KGB angle, and speculation was further intensified by changes in the composition of the Politburo. Long-time Brezhnev aide Kirilenko was dropped, while Geydar Aliyev, the KGB-nurtured Party chief of Azerbaijan, was raised to full membership.

But these proved to be the only immediate changes of any

significance, and the experts concluded, correctly as it turned out, that the power-struggle in the Kremlin was still far from resolved. The forces ranged against the new General Secretary remained considerable.

The basic division afflicting the old Brezhnev Politburo — and, by implication, the larger body of the Central Committee — lay not between the hardliners and the softliners as such, nor between the young upstarts and the old fossils. It lay between people of talent and people of mediocrity, between those who deserved to be where they were and those whose slavish devotion to career advancement had been sustained at the cost of all integrity and imagination. In this respect it resembled most political leaderships, East and West. If, in the Soviet context, the talented and the reformers were hard to tell apart, that was because it didn't take much talent to realise that reforms were urgently necessary.

The mediocrities were mostly those who had clung to Brezhnev's coattails during his long rise to power. At each stage of his career he had picked up devoted lieutenants: Kirilenko in Zaporoz'hye, Shcherbitsky in Dneprodzerzhinsk, Chernenko in Moldavia, Kunayev in Kazakhstan during the 'Virgin Lands' scheme. All of them now sat in the chamber, resembling, with one exception, Disraeli's famous description of the Gladstone Government in 1874 — 'a row of exhausted volcanoes'. Known collectively, and with no little truth, as the 'Dnieper Mafia', these men had formed the core of the Soviet leadership since the mid-sixties.

These were the men who had failed to avert the crisis now confronting the Soviet Union; they could hardly be expected to aspire to anything more than political survival and the privileges it entailed.

But there were important differences between them. Kunayev, as one KGB official noted, was 'a drunken idler'. Kirilenko was an apparatchik *par excellence,* almost robotic in his lack of imagination. Chernenko was considerably more able, but also more profoundly cynical; he had a powerful ally and friend in Defence Minister Ustinov. Shcherbitsky was the exception, ebullient, intelligent, with something of Khrushchev's populist touch. He had not surrendered to the immensity of the problems facing Party and country and slowly but surely he had come to realise that radical change was a necessity which could no longer be deferred.

It was Shcherbitsky who, in 1981-82, had been the prime mover in forming a putative Politburo alliance against his former Mafia colleagues. As a Ukrainian he knew he had little chance of becoming Party Secretary but his major ally, ex-KGB Chairman Yuri Andropov, was much more likely to prove acceptable to the current Central Committee. Andropov himself, contrary to Western stereotype, was probably the most reform-minded of the Brezhnev Politburo. This was not really surprising; heading the KGB for fifteen years had provided him with more than a vague idea of the popular mood.

Shcherbitsky and Andropov enlisted Romanov into their fold without difficulty, and for several reasons. He was relatively young (a mere 60); he was Russian; he was both open to the idea of reform yet associated with Leningrad, traditional home of hardliners. He was more intelligent than his Moscow counterpart, Viktor Grishin. Perhaps most important of all, he was on good terms with Defence Minister Ustinov.

The Marshal was to be the fourth member of the projected 'Quadrumvirate'. He was not exactly a reformer by temperament, but he had begun his career as a Kosygin protégé and, though loyal to the Armed Forces he headed, was not as averse to change as his uniform suggested. For the moment his concern for the deteriorating situation of the Soviet Union, both internally and externally, was sharp enough to place him in the reformers' camp.

It is generally believed — no records exist — that these four men met at Andropov's apartment on Kutuzovsky Prospekt within three hours of Brezhnev's death. There they put the final touches to their plan of campaign. As long as the Quadrumvirate appeared to represent the best interests of both the reform-minded centrists and the determined reformists, it could count on healthy majorities in the Central Committee and the powerful Secretariat. It was planned to use these, during 1983, to boost the much narrower majority in the Politburo itself. The two Government representatives, Tikhonov and Gromyko, and the two younger men, Aliyev and Gorbachev, could be counted upon, at least for the moment. That left five full members — Kunayev, Chernenko, Pelshe, Ponomariev and Grishin—who would definitely oppose the Quadrumvirate's plans.

It was late summer before the Quadrumvirate felt confident enough to demand the necessary plenum of the Central Committee.It was a bellicose session, with both Pelshe and Kunayev coming under strong attack, not least from Chernenko, who seemed quite prepared to desert his former allies in the cause of self-preservation. He might have secured Suslov's position, but for the moment the ideological tide was running against Chernenko, and he was prepared to bide his time.

The Central Committee plenum came as something of an anticlimax, with most of the Quadrumvirate's 'recommendations' receiving 'unamimous support'. Kunayev lost his seat, and Pelshe would have lost his too, had he not conveniently died of a heart attack the day before. Romanov was given higher responsibilities, Gromyko was raised to the Presidency. Only when it came to filling the vacancies did a degree of opposition show itself. Of the three men promoted to full membership only one, Mikhail Solomentsev, was a committed 'reformer'. The other two were Sharaf Rashidov, the hardline Uzbek Party leader, and Pyotr Demichev, a centrist member of the Secretariat. The Quadrumvirate had its improved majority, but only for a limited, not a radical, reform programme. The Central Committee was still hedging its bets.

During its first twelve months in office the régime offered few clues as to its long-term intentions. To most people it seemed as if business was proceeding much as usual, and those earnestly searching for signs of the far-reaching changes predicted for the post-Brezhnev era had to delve deep as ever.

Nevertheless, November 1983 did throw up two straws for the wind. At the beginning of the month a new Tarkovsky film was premiered in Moscow. Loosely based on one of the Strugatsky brothers' science fiction novels, *Hard to be a God* ostensibly dealt with the tribulations of an Earthborn surveyor on a feudal planet. The book had been published during Khrushchev's last year in office and its attack on clumsy and corrupt bureaucracy was so scantily veiled as to warrant the adjective 'diaphanous'. Tarkovsky's film pulled even less metaphorical punches than the book.

Since the film had been made in 1982, its release at this time could not be taken as a definite statement of cultural intent by the new Politburo. More significantly, *Hard to be a God* was given a fulsome reception by the official critics, one of whom, writing in *Literary Gazette,* went so far as to draw explicit parallels between the Strugatskys' feudal overlords and 'certain reactionary elements existing within our socialist society'. Another article greeted the film as a 'welcome addition to the long line of socialist triumphs in cinematography'. Further official approval was expressed by the decision to enter the film for the following year's Cannes Festival.

All of which, some Kremlin-watchers decided, might well prove to have been an 'accident'. The film had probably 'slipped through', been misunderstood by the censors, might soon be disowned. But this theory soon received something of a setback — the other straw in the wind could not conceivably have been launched by accident.

On 23 November the Komsomol magazine *Kommunist* published an article on Lenin, in itself a far from unusual occurrence. It was one line which sparked the controversy, one line which sent Kremlinologists around the world into furies of speculation — 'Nikolai Bukharin, one of Lenin's leading collaborators . . . '

The importance of this clue could not be exaggerated. For half a century, since his death at Stalin's hands, Bukharin had been virtually a non-person. Khrushchev had once hinted at a possible rehabilitation, before apparently shrinking from the consequences. Bukharin's name was dynamite in the Soviet context, for the simple reason that it implied a real alternative.

In the West the opposition to Stalin had always been associated with the name of Trotsky, but in reality Trotsky's policy programme for the Soviet future had been remarkably similar to that of his persecutor. And though there is little doubt that Trotsky would have attempted to push through his programme in a more humane manner, it was not Stalin's brutality which had shaped the Soviet political economy, it was

43

his policies. In this respect, in the late 1920s and early 1930s, it had been Bukharin who had consistently opposed him, who had stood out against forced collectivisation, the manic obsession with heavy industry, completely integrated planning, the sharpening of the police state. The name of Bukharin, for those who had heard it, stood for balanced growth, greater political tolerance, an economy in which market principles would have a part to play beneath a looser planning umbrella.

To admit to his having been one of Lenin's 'leading collaborators' was akin to associating the fount of all wisdom with such policies and that meant associating the present leadership with them as well. The Kremlinologists held their breath, waiting for more. Perhaps some magazine would reprint Lenin's last articles, in which he explicitly advised such a softly-softly approach. Copies of such esoteric journals as the *Siberian Hydroelectric Review* were scanned with an intensity beyond the wildest dreams of their editors.

Early in November the new Politburo had commissioned a number of major reports and by March 1984 they were available for perusal. There was no good news. Gosplan estimated that real growth in the economy over the next quinquennium would be less than 1 per cent per annum and that from a much lower base than anticipated at the commencement of the current five year plan. A relative disaster seemed to be looming and Gosplan was having increasing trouble with its concoction of official statistics.

Even the more gullible were beginning to question the régime's economic claims, as the first survey conducted by the new Public Opinion Research Organisation demonstrated. Despite the understandable fear of retribution, a full 26 per cent of the ten thousand sampled admitted to placing no credence whatsoever in official statistics. As if to rub salt in the wound, a further 16 per cent thought the figures for economic growth 'slightly inflated'.

This survey produced a number of interesting results. When asked to place selected 'social difficulties' in order of importance, the sample responded thus (the figures for Moscow and Leningrad residents — 20 per cent of the sample — are separated out in brackets):

Housing	36% (26%)
Basic shortages	34% (15%)
Crime	14% (29%)
Wage levels	7% (13%)
Alcoholism	7% (8%)
The threat of war	2% (9%)

Presumably the figures for Moscow and Leningrad were separated out for internal-strategic reasons — problems in the big cities were more visible and traditionally more threatening — but the separation certainly afforded an insight into the gulf separating them from the rest of the country. Only the perennial dissatisfaction with housing seemed universal. Both the wage level and shortage figures reflected the priority given to supplying the big cities, the greater fear of war a greater appreciation of the risks involved. The appearance of crime as the single major problem experienced by Muscovites and Leningraders pointed to the swiftness with which these two cities, long the safest in the world, had succumbed to the global tide of urban lawlessness.

When asked to accord priority to a number of 'positive' policies, the sample responded with rather more unanimity:

Expansion of consumer industries	44% (28%)
Higher wages	18% (29%)
Strengthening of national security	11% (12%)
Security of employment	10% (4%)
Strengthening of law enforcement agencies	9% (13%)
Broadening of socialist democracy	8% (14%)

The people's priorities were clearly economic, even to the extent of ignoring, or perhaps taking for granted, the importance traditionally given to security of employment within the Soviet system. The rising crime rate had not provoked an overpowering call for a strengthening of the police, the Soviet population having apparently realised, better than its counterparts in the West, the extent to which the latter would mitigate the former. What the Soviet people wanted was more money and more goods to spend it on — the good life as defined by Khrushchev.

Or so it seemed. In matter of fact, this part of the poll was rigged; the answers given were truthful enough, but the sample had been heavily weighted to produce the desired response. The ten thousand citizens involved, supposedly a 'wide cross section of Soviet society', were mostly middle-level bureaucrats and enterprise managers. The more thoughtful members of the intelligentsia and most of the industrial working class areas had been deliberately avoided; the former would place more stress on the need for a 'broadening of socialist democracy', the latter would cling to 'security of employment'. This was not what Andropov and Shcherbitsky had in mind at this stage; they had their sights set on a radical economic reform and they knew that risks would have to be run politically. It was important for them to be able to show their enemies — and, to some extent, their allies — that the risks were not too severe, even to the extent of deliberately concealing them. After all, the risks involved in *not* introducing such reforms were becoming all too obvious.

Another report bolstered their case. For nearly two decades the Hungarians had been used, to their own benefit, as the Soviet bloc's testing ground for the 'market' solution. The result of this experiment, though hardly definitive, was encouraging. Hungary's economy was the most buoyant in the bloc and its political leaders slept far easier in their beds than their comrades in Warsaw, Bucharest or Prague.

This could be interpreted in more ways than one, of course. At a more than usually rancorous Politburo session in April Chernenko asked, presumably with a sneer: 'How long do you think Kadar's road to socialism would last without our troops on his border?' He answered his own question: 'About ten minutes.'

Chernenko was far from alone in fearing the consequences of a major break with the past, but at this time, in the Party and State journals the tide seemed overwhelmingly in favour of reform. Another article in *Kommunist*, ostensibly concerned with the 'second Industrial Revolution', mapped out a possible path through the minefield. The anonymous author stressed the need for democratising the economic process, of devolving managerial decisions, of 'countering the pernicious doctrine of political orthodoxy over professional expertise'. The Party would then be released from 'the onerous burden of being everywhere, doing everything', would find itself free to 'guide and inspire the Soviet people on the road to communism'.

In most of the academic journals the main topic of discussion seemed to be the 'creative evolution of Marxist economic theory'. The reformers of the 1960s — those that were still alive — suddenly found their ideas back in fashion; even the work of the Czech economist Oto Sik was once again available for serious consideration. The major problem, around which all these economists danced like Bukharinist moths round a Stalinist flame, was the ideological status of 'market relations'. Were these capitalist phenomena pure and simple, or were they merely a neutral statement of an undeniable reality? Could there be, as Sik argued, socialist market relations? The Hungarian experiment tended to prove that there could, but facts were one thing, ideology quite another.

During this period of intense debate within the ruling circles of Soviet society, the most obvious sign of changing attitudes could be found in the country's relations with the rest of the world. The report on Afghanistan had proved as depressing as that on the economy, reading like a Pentagon review of the situation in Vietnam *circa* 1964. Victory over the rebels was still considered possible, but only if a further quarter-million troops could be committed. The cost of this trebling of the military presence was attached. It was far in excess of what the Soviet economy could afford.

The Red Army was in no danger of losing the war. For three years now a virtual stalemate had reigned, with the Soviet units in comfortable control of the major cities and highways, and the rebels controlling, or at least denying their enemy control of, the countryside. The level of Soviet casualties was still running at about twenty a day, or six thousand a year, a figure that bore favourable comparison with the road accident statistics in many Western countries.

But if this cost could be born with relative equanimity, the corrupting effect of the war on those conscripted to fight it presented more serious problems. More than half a million

Soviet citizens had now done duty in Afghanistan, had been exposed to a society alien to their own. The effects were hard to judge, but in at least two respects could already be seen as profoundly detrimental. Many Soviet soldiers had sampled the delights of Afghan marijuana and some had graduated to the sterner joys of opium and morphine. Many had brought their habits home and the swift spread of illicit drug networks in Moscow and Leningrad had been partly responsible for the sky-rocketing crime rates.

A further and more threatening indication of the war's capacity to upset the *status quo* was the spontaneous appearance of unofficial 'soldiers' councils' *(soviets)* in active service units. These were usually concerned only with improving the traditionally poor conditions of Soviet military life and in most cases were disarmed through timely concessions. But disputes involving political issues also occurred and, most serious of all, there were signs that the habits of military democracy were being brought home from the war by regular as well as conscript units.

An end to the war then, was a Politburo priority for both political and economic reasons. But how to end it? The military wanted the creation, by diplomatic means, of a breathing space. If, they argued, the flow of Western and Chinese aid to the rebels could be halted, if the sanctuaries in Pakistan could be isolated from the war, then it might prove possible, by widening the basis of the régime in Kabul, to secure a satisfactory compromise. If the moderate wing of the Islamic opposition could be seduced into a partnership, then the wilder rebels could be reduced to the 'banditry' role which the propaganda machine had long ascribed to them.

All of which depended on a change of heart in Washington. Admittedly there seemed little hope of this in the spring of 1984. The Reagan Administration, driven through alternating bouts of hysteria and catatonia by successive disasters in Central America, was extremely loth to lose its one cast iron proof of Soviet perfidy and aggression. A resuscitation of détente just didn't suit the mood on Capitol Hill.

But, the Soviet experts at the Institute of the USA and Canada pointed out, a Presidential election was due that autumn. The polls showed the Democrat candidate some points ahead of the incumbent President Reagan, and he was known to favour a lessening of Cold War tension. Alternatively, Reagan himself, in a last-ditch attempt to retain his White House stage, might welcome the opportunity to steal his opponent's thunder. As long as the Americans believed that Moscow and /or Havana were behind every guerrilla on the Central Asian mainland then Moscow had a card to play. Guatemala for Afghanistan might sound to the Americans like a feasible trade-off.

There was also the possibility that such an understanding could be extended to the moribund arms talks in Geneva. The cost of running an arms race might be crippling the Soviet economy, but it was also wreaking havoc in the Western world. If anything was to cost Reagan his reelection it would be the calamitous level of American unemployment, itself the product of starving the civilian economy of capital in favour of the arms industry. Surely, the Soviet experts insisted, the mutuality of interests would lead to a deal. And if it did, then the Soviet planners would be left with a sizable fund of spare capital and labour, all of which could be used to cushion the blow of a radical economic reform.

Accordingly, on 26 April Foreign Minister Sidorov met Secretary of State Shultz in Reykjavik for talks. No details were announced in the press, merely a bland statement, but Sidorov was able to report back that the Americans had shown interest. When the Quadrumvirate took their places on the Mausoleum reviewing stand for the May Day parade they cannot have been too dissatisfied with their first four months of power.

Some of this satisfaction wore off in the latter half of May. In a ten day period four events of major significance took place and each gave strength to the old adage that no news was better news.

The first took place in Tashkent, the capital of Uzbekistan. For several years the Republic had been displaying increasing signs of social and racial tension and over recent months the level of minor incidents had risen to such a peak that the KGB had considered it necessary to formally convey its concern to the Politburo. This was 12 May; ten days later another minor incident sparked off a major convulsion.

On the evening of 21 May a Russian bus driver refused to take on board a party of women wearing yashmaks. The driver was acting according to regulations, but for once the local militia refused to support her. The argument turned into a fistfight, in which several Russians and several 'natives' were quite badly hurt. Eventually a KGB squad turned up and arrested only the 'natives'. The news spread, fuelling prejudices on both sides of the racial divide.

This incident, like many others before it, would probably have fuelled resentment and nothing more had it not been for an unfortunate coincidence. The following evening Dynamo Kiev were to play the local team, Tashkent Pakhtakor, in an important cup game and the local KGB chief, sensing trouble, sensibly tried to have the match postponed. But the local Party boss was from Kiev and he wanted to see his team play. He decided that the KGB was overreacting.

That evening twice the usual number of spectators turned up and troops were put on standby. Some observers put the subsequent riots down to a bad refereeing decision, some to the fact that the referee was a Russian, but most agreed that the disputed penalty was merely a pretext. In any event, the fighting inside the ground claimed eight lives, the riot in the city centre three times that number. In the ensuing week no less than twelve Russians were assaulted on the streets. It was an awesome reminder of the Soviet nationality problem.

The second important event occurred in the east Ukrainian city of Donetsk. Rumours had been flying around for several months, but it was only on 23 May that the corruption scandal thrust itself into the forefront of all local conversation. The housing shortage in the area was chronic and it was well known that the Russian director of the local construction trust had been using state materials and labour to construct Azov Coast dachas for his family and friends. That week it also became known that he was selling both materials and dachas on the black market.

Such a disregard for 'socialist norms of behaviour' was not

exactly unprecedented, and most people, though greatly resenting such abuses of power, were prepared to confine their opposition to persistent grumbling. But on 22 May one of the few houses actually erected by the trust collapsed on its newly-installed owners, killing one child and severely injuring another. The reason for the disaster was not long forthcoming: the workers involved had used inferior materials, on orders, they insisted, from the trust management.

The whole trust work force, partly from conviction and partly in response to pressure from wives, friends and others, came out on strike. They were addressed by an oblast Party official at a mass meeting the next day, but all he had to offer was 'threats and lies'. Two other enterprises were abandoned by their work forces. Each had its own grievances, but all agreed that the trust director, his cronies in management and on the local Party committee, had to go. There seemed every possibility that the strikes would continue to spread until some action was taken.

An alarmed Ukrainian Politburo dispatched some high-ranking Republican officials to Donetsk with instructions to concede whatever seemed necessary. The director was sacked, along with his management team, and a shakeup in the Party organisation was promised for the near future. The men went back to work, the director to his dacha and the local KGB started asking questions. It was the answers they got, or failed to get, which gave the affair much of its significance. All the facts pointed to a level of organisation among the strikers, both within enterprises and between them, but no trace of that organisation could be found.

The strike at the Likhachev Auto Plant in Moscow on 26 May was, by comparison, a minor affair. It only lasted two hours, ending when the management conceded the workers' demand for a revision of the piecerate norms. This time the KGB investigation team did discover the source of the trouble, and it proved a more ominous finding than the Politburo could have wished for.

What had happened was simplicity itself. A worker had dropped a spanner, completely by accident, and the entire assembly line had taken this as the signal for a walkout. That a strike could begin in such a manner spoke volumes for the reservoir of discontent on the Soviet shop floor, and the fact that it had happened in pampered Moscow only served to heighten the Politburo's sense of skating on thinning ice. Vladimir Shcherbitsky was later to quote this incident as a turning point in his own political consciousness: 'Before the Likhachev strike I was intellectually in favour of reform, considered it as a necessary step forward for our country. After it had occurred I felt the need in my guts, considered reform as our only hope of avoiding an eventual uprising by the workers.'

But the Americans were not to be helpful. In the weeks that followed the Reykjavik meeting a cloud of silence covered Washington; it was as if the Reagan Administration was huddled in a perpetual conference. And then, on 29 May, the bombshell arrived, an exceedingly aggressive statement by the President himself, heaping new accusations on the Kremlin and its alleged allies in Central America.

Two events had precipitated this hardening of the American line. In Guatemala the guerrillas had launched one of their most audacious raids, kidnapping the American Ambassador. On the other side of the world a battalion-strength unit of the Baluchistan People's Liberation Front had captured the Dasht valley town of Turban, a mere ninety miles from the Indian Ocean. The Pakistan Army detachment sent to evict them had been routed.

Both events had taken place in the first week of May, but neither had been divulged to the press for obvious reasons. Then, on 28 May, secrecy was lost — the Ambassador's body was 'mailed' to the French Embassy in Guatemala City. The Reagan Administration opted for the easy way out; as one State Department spokeman noted, off the record: 'When in doubt blame the Soviets, especially when they're fifty miles from the Indian Ocean.' There would be no early resumption of talks, no second wind for détente.

Significantly, *Pravda* carried a full running commentary on the Donetsk scandal, yet failed to provide even a cursory mention of the Likhachev stoppage. Certain facts of Soviet life were now being discussed with increasing candour, but others remained very much *sub rosa*.

Since March *Pravda* had been edited by a Quadrumvirate appointee, and in June he was instructed to both widen the area and increase the intensity of public discussion. Suddenly the letters page seemed full of criticisms both pertinent and wide-ranging; the editorial replies adopted a sharper tone, a willingness to go beyond the stock 'abuses of a good system' answers. A series of articles on the East European states painted a dismal picture of Polish planning and a glowing portrait of the Hungarian system. Another series on Soviet history offered subtle variations on the Leninist theme, digging up quotes from the revered founder which five years earlier had been rotting in the ideological cellars. Almost every other day wide publicity was given to the hydra of corruption and, more traditionally, to the need for continuous Party vigilance in the struggle for purity. More persuasively, so far as the Party in the country was concerned, much play was given to a string of corruption trials and the imposition of maximum sentences on many of those found guilty of misusing state power and property.

This campaign reflected the Quadrumvirate's slowly growing confidence. The events of May, though depressing, had increased its majorities in the Politburo and Central Committee, with only Chernenko, Grishin, Rashidov and Ponomariev now prone to vote against its plans in the smaller forum. The Secretariat and the Ministries were busy working out the details of the reform programme and, as these leaked upwards, there was a visible strengthening of leadership resolve. Reform was such a large, uncertain concept; the reform *programme,* when seen written out in black and white, looked far less threatening, far less of a leap into the unknown.

In July a plenary session of the Central Committee announced the first batch of measures. None seemed particularly radical when viewed in isolation, but when considered as parts of an entirely new strategy they offered grounds for considerable hope. If this was the foundation of the Quadrumvirate's new Soviet house, then the finished structure might look rather more imposing than the old.

The measures themselves were a curious — or perhaps understandable — mixture of the liberal and the puritanical and many observers deduced from this that the Armed Forces and the KGB had been prominent among their sponsors. The legal reforms in particular exemplified this trend; while the laws were tightened their judicial enforcement was rendered less liable to arbitrary interference. Judges were given greater security of tenure, the press given the right of access to all trials. The notorious 'public gathering' tribunals were drastically curtailed. On the other hand, the primacy of Party policy over the law was not challenged and the laws involving dissident activity were recodified with less concern for the niceties of the Constitution.

These changes were welcomed, nevertheless, by the more thoughtful section of the Soviet intelligentsia; they did mark progress on the road to the Rule of Law, even if the laws themselves still seemed frequently unacceptable. Also welcome was the spate of measures dealing with education, most of which were introduced as a spur to better teaching. The quota system — so many having to pass their exams each year — was to be abolished in 1985. More funds were to be made available for managerial and technical training, more autonomy, on an experimental basis, was to be allowed teachers in the higher grades.

The most surprising decision announced by the plenum involved permission for six thousand Meskhetians to return home from their place of Siberian exile. This figure only represented 3 per cent of the total and the Meskhetians were few in number when compared to other sufferers of Stalin's wartime deportations, but the decision was still a bold one. If the transplant proved troublefree, if the Meskhetians reciprocated the Kremlin's trust and the Georgians made no problems about having them back, then more would follow. Or so it was hinted.

The 'nationality' problem was obviously one of those uppermost in the Politburo's collective mind. Though no actual reforms were promulgated, the non-Russian Republican Party organisations were encouraged to display, wherever possible, 'positive discrimination' in favour of the local peoples. At the same time the various journals were mounting a campaign against roughshod Russification and secularisation in Central Asia. The Uzbek paper *Pravda Vostoka,* which two years earlier had been trumpeting the 'reactionary role of Islam', was now stressing the need for 'co-existence in the ideological sphere', and finding as much joy in Islamic weddings and funerals as it had previously found in the local folk-dancing. More privately, Party officials in the region were being commanded to step up the struggle against 'racial insensitivity', and further fortified with large doses of Lenin's writings on the nationality problem.

The fourth main target of the reformers was the all-pervasiveness of corruption, and here again the puritanical leaning of certain figures high in the Army and KGB apparati were thought to be behind the new assault. Stringent new penalties for concealed stockpiling of materials, sale of state materials, misuse of state funds and abuse of state power were announced. And should anyone doubt the régime's intentions in this matter, it was also reported that the KGB's Second Chief Directorate, which dealt with such activities, was to be greatly expanded. In stark contradiction to the spirit of the legal reforms already noted, it was further announced that special tribunals were being set up to deal with the expected flood of cases.

More informally, notice was given that the flow of scientific and technical information within the Soviet Union would henceforth be subject to less restriction. No details were made public, but the intent was clear. Right through the first week of August *Pravda* carried a series of articles pointedly exposing the economic consequences of 'the cult of secrecy for secrecy's sake'.

This plethora of reforms received a predictably mixed reception. The non-Party intelligentsia was understandably enthusiastic, welcoming change both as an end in itself and as a harbinger of improved economic performance. The dissident reaction varied; while some claimed that the measures represented no more than the usual cosmetic exercise, others insisted that the thin end of a wedge was infinitely preferable to no wedge at all. This analysis was shared by many middle- and lower-level Party functionaries, though with diametrically opposed sentiments. Many trembled at the prospect of a sustained anti-corruption campaign and Chernenko's theory that the KGB was becoming a danger to the Party received more than a few new recruits.

For the mass of the population, excluding two thousand happy Meskhetians, the reforms seemed at first an interesting irrelevance. The anti-corruption drive was certainly popular and became more so through August as a number of prominent heads were actually seen to roll. But for most people the economy remained the major cause for concern and so far nothing had been done to alleviate the recurring shortages. Measures had been promised for the autumn. Measures had been promised before.

Still, visitors to Moscow that summer found more than the usual quota of optimists. This could partly be attributed to the Soviet triumphs in the Los Angeles Olympics, partly to the undoubted smugness with which Soviet citizens eyed the burning ghettos of another Reaganesque summer, but Westerners with friends in the Soviet capital remarked, almost to a man, on the visible growth in confidence with regard to the Soviet future. There was a sense of movement, almost a sense of awe in face of the authorities' obvious determination to lift the country out of its deepening rut.

The economic debate continued. The opponents of reform, though now a definite minority in the Party's higher reaches, doggedly stated and re-stated their unbounded faith in the Marxian labour theory of value. Economic efficiency, they insisted, was not everything; the primary task, as ever, was the strengthening of socialism.

The reformist economists poured scorn upon these 'dogmatists'. They insisted that the labour theory of value and a controlled use of market relations were far from incompatible. And economic efficiency could not be simply ignored. 'One cannot discount the concept of opportunity-cost just because Marx failed to explicitly condone it in *Das Kapital*,' wrote Sergei Kirillin, one of the newly fashionable gurus at the Leningrad University economics department. In the same article he quoted the 1920s economist Yurovsky — 'only the memory of the fact that interest on capital forms a class income in capitalist society can serve as a psychological basis for a refusal to make calculations of this type. No rational basis for such a refusal exists.'

The debate went on, but the Politburo's mind was made up. In the third week of September another plenum of the Central Committee was convened to approve the economic reform programme. The measures were much as expected by informed opinion, but the mode of presentation came as a surprise to all but the initiated. In subsequent weeks a (probably apocryphal) story went the rounds in Moscow; it recounted how Chernenko, when first confronted with the detailed proposals, had suggested sarcastically that they call the programme NEP 2. Another more likely explanation of the chosen designation was given by Solomentsev, who claimed that it had been adopted to express both the significance of the change and the essential continuity with Party history which it supposedly represented. Either way, the name struck some hardliners as close to blasphemy, and several long-standing Central Committee members were rumoured to have torn up their Party cards in a comradely burst of drunken angst.

NEP 2, to quote Secretary Andropov, was 'a further giant stride on the road to full communism', 'a further example, if such example were needed, of the Party's untiring devotion to the creative development of Marxism-Leninism'. It was also, as many realised with either a leap of the heart or a shiver down the spine, the beginning of the end for the half-century-old economic system fashioned by Stalin and his minions.

The essential aim, as the fulsome commentaries carried by the media made clear, was a relaxation of the centre's grip on the micro-economic market, and the consequent encouragement of initiative, innovation and creative responsibility at the productive level of the economy. These business attributes were necessary not merely for their own undoubted sake, but also because further growth in the Soviet situation of labour and capital shortage had to be 'intensive', based on raising productivity in existing enterprises rather than the proliferation of new ones. As if to emphasise this point, strict new guidelines for the establishment of any new enterprise west of the Urals were announced.

All this, of course, represented a considerable shift in the role of the planners. Whether it amounted to a diminishing role was another matter and one which the press did its best to ignore. To judge from *Pravda*'s commentaries the planners were still gods, only gods of a new type, not the old obsessives fretting over every nut and bolt in the economy, more like Olympian philosophers, computing their long-range plans and offering general guidance to the masses toiling on the plains below. The levers of power they possessed were more indirect, more strictly 'economic'; the days of the exhaustive blueprint were over, now it was time for manipulation rather than administration, of working through the banks, the tax system, the capital funds, the long-range plans.

The planners' forced withdrawal from the sphere of day-to-day activity left space for new hands on the economic tiller and for several months now the enterprise managers and directors had been given progressively more rein. Eventually they would be taking decisions concerning production levels, investment levels, wage distribution, the source of their inputs and even — the reforms were studiously vague on this point — the level of employment. Of course, they would not be taking such decisions in a vacuum; the freedom to draft their own one year operational plans was still circumscribed by the obligations inherent in the centrally-drafted five year plans. And, as if this old god was not powerful enough, a strange new god was lurking in the wings — the concept of profitability. It would take time to master the new business arts involved, and NEP 2 was explicitly stated to be a 'programme extending over several years'. There were few illusions as to how difficult this transition period would be.

The main human problem confronting the reform, however, was neither the planners, sulking at their desks, nor the managers, ambivalently eyeing a future full of increased freedom and increased responsibilities. The main human problem concerned the vast bulk of the population, the work forces spread across the length and breadth of the Union. For the new plan-market balance to succeed there had to be a radical reform of the price structure, and in this context, as any Westerner knows, reform means up. The market sector could not operate 'rationally' unless prices reflected, far more accurately than hitherto, the reality of the supply-demand situation. Free prices, it was recognised, were politically impossible for many items, and they were consequently applied only to luxury goods. Most staples were to remain subsidised, fixed at an artificially low level, but between these two extremes a large range of items were to be priced on a sliding maximum-minimum scale.

Herein lay the rub. In a situation of excess demand, which this indubitably was, the natural tendency of the sliding prices would be upward. If profitability was taken seriously by the managers, they would naturally favour producing those goods with the higher prices. Since the essential items were still subject to price restraint, they would soon become scarce, creating incredible bottlenecks and widespread shortages throughout the system. The answer, though hard to accept, was easy to see — the excess demand had to be lopped off before the price reform got into its stride. This could be done by deflating wage levels, raising norms and generally dropping the working population's standard of living.

The reformers tried hard to cushion the inevitable blow. Apart from maintaining huge subsidies on the absolute basics of life, they introduced new bonus systems tying higher wages to higher productivity and decreed substantial rises in pension payments. A deliberate effort was made to lower expectations, to present the inevitable hardship as a necessary sacrifice. In a TV interview Shcherbitsky noted that it was 'unrealistic' to expect a rise in living standards year after year. 'Sometimes,' he said, 'it is necessary to pause to take breath, to put the emphasis on consolidating what has already been achieved.' A pointed, if humourless cartoon in *Pravda* showed a newly-arrived country boy conversing with a prosperous-looking city worker. 'I was better off where I was before,' he says. 'Ah, it's always like that,' replies the city-dweller, 'any change seems hard at first. You'll soon find out that it was worth it.'

Side by side with this undoubtedly genuine effort to secure public acquiescence in the reform programme, the authorities mounted a campaign against 'anti-socialist elements who decry all progress, whose ideology is nothing but a cloak for their devotion to yesterday's truths'. The KGB Industrial Security Service was also highly active that autumn, sustaining a surveillance operation of heroic proportions. In one Moscow factory it was rumoured that 'only the *shpiks** remain, endlessly reporting on each other's indiscretions'.

* Paid informers.

PART THREE

RESISTANCE (October 1984-1985)

*It begins to seem as if miners are running
the world. First they bring down Mr Botha,
then Mrs Thatcher, and now the Kremlin's
new rulers are under threat.*

(from a *Guardian* editorial,
'Underground Opposition', 5 April 1985)

NEP 2 was rather like a British incomes policy — the situation demanded it, most people thought it a good idea, but precious few people wanted it applied to themselves. The letters to *Pravda,* faked and genuine, were unanimous in their approval, but in offices and factories across the country conversations centred on the problems posed by the new policies. The Soviet population had been too long inured in its Stalinist trench for an 'over the top' order to look anything less than a disturbing and dangerous gamble.

As the weeks went by, the different Soviet interest groups became increasingly aware of exactly how the reforms were affecting them and in most cases the reaction was profoundly negative. It was hoped that the Armed Forces, which had prudently been allowed to retain all the perks of priority status, would remain disinterested spectators, but like its counterparts around the world the Soviet military was not short on men who turned white at the mere thought of change. Significantly, *Red Star,* the Armed Forces journal, continued to provide one of the few platforms still available for the propagation of Stalinist economics.

The long-frustrated 'thinking half' of the Soviet intelligentsia was the only group to give the reforms its unstinted support. The intellectuals, scientists, technicians, economists — all saw the new policies as both 'rational' and as a chance to enhance their own futures in a more 'progressive' Soviet Union. The other, administrative half of the intelligentsia saw things very differently; the reforms, if successful, would lessen the need for purely bureaucratic skills, would demand from it a flexibility of response which was fundamentally foreign to its experience.

The higher reaches of the Party reflected the division of

opinion within the intelligentsia. Majority opinion backed the reforming Politburo, with varying degrees of approval and trepidation, but a sizable minority continued to protest against the new line on both pragmatic and ideological grounds. These conservatives had a powerful leader in Konstantin Chernenko, who still felt secure enough to voice his continued opposition to the reform programme. When disaster came, as Chernenko thought (and presumably hoped) it would, he would be well-placed to 'rescue' the Party.

He had abundant support among one group — the planners. Despite all the publicity given to its new, 'higher' role, the planning establishment was awash with resentment. One high-level official later remembered the many instances of deliberate sabotage which had occurred in the latter months of 1984. 'Everyone was talking of how "they" had scuttled Kosygin's reform in the sixties, even though few of them had been out of short trousers at the time.' The Quadrumvirate, realising its mistake, purged the top leadership in November, but the new appointees made little impression. Work on the new five year plan, scheduled to begin the following year, proceeded at a criminally slow pace.

In the middle reaches of the Party, in the regional, Republican and oblast headquarters, the majority for reform was either wafer thin or nonexistent. These men and women were used to taking Moscow's orders, but they were also used to having their own orders obeyed, and some formally obedient economic bosses were now behaving as if the local Party had ceased to exist. There was a hint of redundance in the air.

And if this was true of the middle reaches, it was far truer at the lowest levels of the Party organisation. The ordinary functionary had always been the planners' watchdog on the spot, the person who got things through with or without the assistance of the nominally superior manager. The latter's new responsibilities had been won at the former's expense and now the roles were reversed. Arbitrary interference by non-specialist hacks bearing a Party card was no longer assured of a welcome.

This was the general picture. Naturally enough there were many functionaries at all levels who welcomed the reforms, who had been secretly hoping for such changes for years. These people knew the system was not working as well as it could, they had spent their working lives trying to make up for its idiocies and they were more than prepared to give the changes a try. Like the managers, they had suffered from the arbitrary whims of the far-off planners and where relations between the two were already good the reforms tended to benefit both.

So much for the Party. The managers, it might be imagined, would show a far greater interest in the positive aspects of the reform. But, alas for the Quadrumvirate, this proved only sometimes to be the case. In the first place they were given next to no help by the recalcitrant planners. After years of being deluged with instructions, the managers suddenly found themselves bereft of even the most perfunctory guidance. For men and women inexperienced in 'business' this was a cruel blow, and it was one particularly outlandish example of such 'non-cooperation' on the planners' part which had occasioned the Gosplan purge in November.

But the problem went still deeper. The managers were not simply inexperienced, they were also, in many cases, uninterested. Conditioned by the habits of a working lifetime to dislike risk, responsibility and uncertainty, they proved a group of people singularly ill-suited to the discipline of an imperfect market. In a way they were offered the worst of both worlds; though still crucially dependent on their workers' diligence, their suppliers' punctuality, the planners' skill, they were now also expected to work miracles. The rewards for success were certainly greater, but many wondered whether it was worth it. The relationship with the local Party man, which had hitherto been both straightforward and annoying, was now ambiguous and difficult.

Most serious of all, the relationship between the managers and their workers was slowly changing to the formers' detriment. The lack of worker power in the Soviet Union had always been easy to understand and maintain — it was based on the workers' distance from decision-making. The granting of power to the managers changed all that; now, if the workers wanted to change the *modus operandi* in their factory, they merely had to convince the manager, by whatever means were available. This was one half of the reforms' most devastating legacy. The other lay in its creation of the workers' need for such pressures to be applied.

The reforms offered the industrial working class nothing more positive than visions of future prosperity. The new bonus systems were seen, quite realistically, as a means of extracting more work for the same real wages. But even this verged on optimism in the long run, for the bonuses of the workers, like those of the managers, were frequently dependent on forces beyond their control. Both were reliant on planners, suppliers and each other; in the new situation created by the reforms the workers were especially vulnerable to the level of managerial competence. And since this, in the last months of 1984, proved in many cases dismally inadequate, the majority of the industrial working class suffered a real decline in living standards.

The reform programme offered other disbenefits. The bonus systems, by profiting a few at the expense of the many, produced a widening of differentials which was much resented. But for most workers the major problem was the clear threat to traditional work practices. More and more workers were suffering enforced 'job mobility' as managers sought to stretch the rules governing security of employment. Discipline at the work place was being tightened, with the same threat of 'redeployment' being used to enforce compliance. All of which, many thought, was 'not the way things were done'. Most of the Soviet Union had been spared the ravages of the Protestant work ethic and the underlying resistance to any rise in the tempo of work — 'We're not Germans,' as one steelworker told a touring Central Committee member — was profound and virtually universal.

The deterioration in living standards and the new sources of resentment on the shop floor might not have received political expression had it not been for two other consequences of the wider reform programme. Poverty was bad enough in itself; it seemed close to cruelty when set against the portrait of official high life painted by a string of sensational corruption trials. Through November and December the media was full of the reformists' clean-up campaign, and since many of the accused were enterprise managers, the workers' faith in their own managements was hardly likely to be enhanced. Of course it was good to see justice done, and the régime could be given credit for doing it, but the overall effect was to increase the hunger for a more general settling of accounts.

The second development, already noted, was the gradual realisation by many work forces of their own increasing power. Some of those who had drafted the reforms had pointed out that increased worker participation was the natural corollary of managerial autonomy, but the Politburo had considered such a development politically premature, not to say dangerous, and had shelved the idea pending a favourable debut by the managers. But shelving workers' participation could not prevent the emergence of new, implicit power structures within enterprises. The managers were more dependent on their workers — profitability demanded quality, and quality could not be 'ordered' as easily as quantity — and the workers knew it. At the lowest rung of the economic ladder the reforms were beginning to break down the old, rigid hierarchy of Soviet society. Increasing the level of KGB surveillance could not compensate for such a fundamental shift in the constellation of forces; no number of *shpiks,* as any Marxist-Leninist should have known, could alter the facts of productive life.

The winter of 1984-85 was long and hard. For Western correspondents, marooned in Moscow, the progress of the reforms was as difficult to perceive clearly as the cupolas of the Kremlin through near-persistent snow. Their contacts among the intelligentsia seemed unable to decide between wild optimism and the more familiar cynical pessimism. The newspapers still trumpeted the 'Leninist renewal', but on rare trips beyond their cloistered world the correspondents found the surface of Soviet life as placid, as leaden as ever.

This calm was deceptive, as those in possession of hard information knew only too well. In the KGB building on Dzerzhinsky Square, in the offices of the Party Secretariat spread around the capital, the reports poured in for the computers to digest. Something was changing, something fundamental. But what?

The computers took several months to construct a coherent picture. At first there appeared to be no pattern, no uniformity of response to the reformers' efforts. At some enterprises the rise in productivity, even in so short a period, exceeded the wildest hopes, yet at other plants there was an actual fall in the rate. Gradually, however, patterns did begin to emerge. The computers discovered a strong correlation between the vigour of the anti-corruption campaign and economic performance in particular areas. This was most marked in the industrial south Ukraine, where the old Dnieper Mafia retained the power to protect many highly-placed officials, and where industrial performance remained extremely sluggish.

A more obvious correlation was detected between economic progress and the age of the industry concerned. In old-established sectors, notably coal, steel, textiles and railway engineering, progress was virtually nonexistent; in the newer consumer industries it was generally rapid, if somewhat uneven. Again Ukraine scored badly.

Not surprisingly the incidence of industrial unrest, usually expressed in the form of 'Italian' strikes or chronic absenteeism, was highest in those areas still muddied with corruption and cursed with declining industries. Equally predictably, the reformists tended to stress the former factor; they had always claimed that working class opposition could only be averted by a truly thoroughgoing reform. Unfortunately the reformists were mistaken in this belief, at least in so far as the short term was concerned. In these areas corruption was clearly a secondary issue; the opposition to the reform was based on its immediate economic effects, in the shops, on the factory floor, in the workers' pockets. And in certain key areas, like the Donbass and the Dnieper bend towns, that opposition was rendered more effective by the high level of illicit working class organisation.

It was here that the real trouble would begin. Here, in the old industrial areas, the needed productivity gains could not be provided by the magical wave of managerial wands. Indeed, there were only two possible sources of such growth. One was a huge injection of capital investment, and this was not to be forthcoming, the planners having decided, quite rightly from a purely economic point of view, that their limited resources could be better utilised elsewhere. The other was a sustained disregard of such negative factors as guaranteed working weeks, safety procedures and realistic piecerate norms. This was the course adopted; it was the only one available. The corrupt administrations and management teams which afflicted these areas were certainly viewed with a venomous eye, but their removal would only scratch the surface of the real problem.

A few well-meaning officials in the Ukraine industrial belt tried to bring the brewing storm to Moscow's attention, but without success. The leadership was more interested in finding the good news needed to confound its critics and a 50 per cent productivity leap in some Siberian salmon cannery was infinitely more heartening than vague rumbles of discontent emanating from Ukraine. 'Teething troubles', it was thought, were inevitable. Even Lenin had needed to take one step back for each two steps forward.

Agriculture had been left out of the 1984 reform programme, partly because the Secretariat was already overburdened with work, partly because it was felt that this problem of problems needed to be approached with particular care. Over the last half-century many solutions had been sought for the ills afflicting the rural sector, ranging from Stalin's requisition by terror, through Khrushchev's maize obsession, to Brezhnev's attempt to turn agriculture into an industry. None had worked, or even looked like working, so far as a large and sustained increase in productivity was concerned.

And yet, despite this apparent catalogue of failure, the level of grain production had steadily risen to the point where the Soviet Union was self-sufficient in cereal for human consumption. It was the growing livestock population which consumed, in the bad years, the huge volume of imported grain.

Fortunately for the Quadrumvirate, the 1983 and 1984 harvests had shown a substantial improvement on previous years and the level of imports had fallen to some 15 per cent of the overall requirement. The signs for 1985, as the winter passed, were also good. It was felt that agricultural reform could be delayed without fear of serious consequences.

This, in retrospect, might have been an error, though hardly one for which the Quadrumvirate could be blamed. The 1985 harvest would be worse than expected, but not that much worse, and the import requirement would still be lower than it had been in 1980-82. The real disaster took place in Washington, when the new administration at the Department of Agriculture announced, with what seemed precipitate haste, the withdrawal of twelve million American acres from crop production in the ensuing year.

This was not aimed at Moscow, nor at Africa where it was to create one of the century's most appalling famines. The decision was taken in response to the serious danger of rampant soil erosion in several Mid-Western states. For years the topsoil had been disappearing at a rate faster than nature could match, and the Agriculture Department, fearing another 'dustbowl crisis', had stepped in to place the nation's long-term interest above that of the (richly compensated) farmers. It was a far-sighted move, one of the few in the six year history of the Reagan Presidency, but its external consequences were to be unfortunately severe. As far as Moscow was concerned, the grain available for import would be both insufficient in quantity and much more expensive.

And it still had to be secured, against stiff competition from other potential buyers more amenable to the White House. As the spring of 1985 approached it became increasingly clear that the Soviet Union was being relegated to the back of the queue.

The unexpected reelection of the octogenarian Reagan the previous November had thrown Washington into turmoil. The Democrats now had an overwhelming majority in Congress and many considered that the President's reelection by virtual default — his opponent's closet had been found full of gruesome skeletons only days before the vote — had deprived him of a moral mandate. Unfortunately the US Constitution had not been drawn up with such contingencies in mind, and in matters foreign Reagan and his executive team showed no inclination to submit to Congressional direction. The embers of Cold War, which had been allowed to cool somewhat during the campaign, were now being fanned again. The Soviet Union was

70

as useful a scapegoat as ever; the Soviet reforms, which had been cautiously welcomed by the Democrat candidate, were scorned as snares and delusions, mere stratagems in the Kremlin's unremitting campaign for world dominion.

This ludicrous scenario was used to 'explain' the new series of reverses to the American global position. The further weakening of the Pakistani hold on Baluchistan, which could legitimately be ascribed to a measure of Soviet interference, was now equated with the accelerating collapse of the military régime in Islamabad, which could not. The fundamentalist coup in Iraq and the spreading urban strife in Brazil and Argentina, all as anathematic to Moscow as they were to Washington, were seen in the same simplistic light. Some of Reagan's more lunatic colleagues were even heard to suggest that the 'long, hot summers' of 1983 and 1984 had been inspired by Soviet agents.

All of which boded ill for the Kremlin. With the US and Canada either unable or unwilling to sell grain to the Soviet Union and with the beleaguered government in Argentina attempting to win back its North American ally, the possibility of a large shortfall was already becoming apparent. And with the Reagan Administration still apparently set on pursuing an unlimited arms race, there could be no large-scale shift of capital and manpower resources into the Soviet civilian economy. The reforms might, *might* be proceeding well, but the international climate was taking another turn for the worse.

Within the Soviet Union the new-look economy was displaying increasing signs of strain. Opinion differed as to whether it was the reforms themselves, or a deliberate campaign of obstruction, which was creating the difficulties, but no one disputed that they were potentially serious.

The chief cause for concern lay not in the matter of production levels — these continued to fluctuate wildly from enterprise to enterprise — but in the distributive system. The flow of goods between enterprises and between the enterprises and the retailers seemed to be bedevilled by even more bottle-necks than usual and the level of shortages in the shops was assuming Polish proportions. In some areas the spring brought

71

extreme harship, with even previously abundant commodities conspicuously absent from the shelves.

Enthusiasm for the reforms, never exactly high, began to ebb. And as if this wasn't bad enough from the régime's point of view, the growing discontent of the ordinary Soviet worker was increasingly finding 'expression' in the growth of illegal workers' organisations. The 'independents', as these parallel unions were usually called, neither supported the reform programme nor the system it was intended to reform. If in some ways they reflected the simple desire for greater egalitarianism — often expressed in Stalin nostalgia — in others they represented a radical break with all Soviet history, a conscious search for a 'real' socialism, one which would involve far more radical reforms than any yet envisaged by the Quadrumvirate.

The influence of these 'independents' was, at this time, as much a matter of rumour as of action. It was a 'rumour', moreover, largely restricted to certain areas, most notably the southern Ukraine, industrial Central Asia and the Ural cities. It was not that the 'independents' operated underground, it was more a matter of the informality of the ties involved; they represented solidarity rather than a specific programme, shared feelings rather than conspiratorial attitudes. The KGB, avidly searching for committed cells of committed enemies of the state, discovered little. In a sense the strength of worker opposition to the régime was growing so great and so diffuse as to be almost invisible.

In the Politburo chamber this particular threat, though taken seriously, was seen very much as a symptom of the wider problem. The reformers saw the successful implementation of their programme as the only way of rendering the 'independents' impotent, the anti-reformers considered them eminently squashable should the will be found. The main topic of debate remained the reforms themselves — were they working, albeit slowly, or were they undoing the very fabric of the Soviet state? Chernenko had no doubts on this score. 'The current policies are threatening to lay waste sixty years of building socialism in this country,' he stated angrily at the session on 14 April. He demanded a reversal of many decentralising measures, a tightening of 'ideological vigilance', a return to a 'socialist interpretation' of the law. To Andropov's mild assertion that 'miracles could not be expected in a matter of months', he replied that a 'miracle' was very possible if the Party did not realise the error of its current ways.

And he was gathering support. For some weeks two of the new Politburo members, Demichev and Aliyev, had been wavering in their support for the reform programme. When Chernenko pushed through a virtual note of no confidence in Quadrumvirate policy on 23 April both switched camps, leaving only an eight to six majority in the reformists' favour. The latter needed some good news, and quickly. They didn't get it.

In the Donbass coalfield the impact of the reforms had been almost totally negative. The miners were now working longer hours for less pay. The quantity of goods in the shops had declined markedly since Christmas. The anti-corruption campaign had mysteriously passed the region by, though it was common knowledge that the oblast Party and KGB were up to their necks in large-scale black market activity.

There had been strong support in the area for the 'independents' since the late 1960s and, despite the arrest of succeeding individual leaders, this support had not noticeably waned. Indeed, as resentment increased during the winter of 1984-85, the ranks of those committed to parallel unionism began to swell. By late April, to those working there, the Donbass bore all the hallmarks of the proverbial powder keg.

The fuse was ignited at a *vstrechny** plan meeting of the Makeyevka 3 pit on Thursday 25 April. The following account of this meeting comes from Boris Gilyarovsky, one of the miners' unofficial leaders.

'The *vstrechny* meeting was unlike any I had ever attended. The scene was the same, the canteen decked out with pretty graphs charting our march into the brilliant future, the miners filing in

* Literally a counterplan, supposedly put forward by the work force as an improved version of the official plan.

73

looking exhausted (such meetings were almost always held at the end of the day shift), the bosses sat behind the table at the far end, looking as well fed as ever.

'The atmosphere, though, was very different. The bosses couldn't help looking prosperous, but the usual smug expressions had been transformed for the occasion into an artful mixture of businesslike determination and fatherly concern. They knew there was trouble in the air.

'A few *shpiks* tried to set the usual tone, feet up on the tables, sports magazines well in evidence; some even tried feigning sleep, surreptitiously opening one eye to see if their example was being followed. It wasn't.

'The director began his address with a long panegyric of the new industrial policies, dropping quotes from Lenin like so much litter, every now and then glancing to his left at the raion secretary. The latter didn't seem to be listening, and he wasn't the only one. Perhaps the intention was to bore us to death, perhaps the director was worried about his career prospects. But we were patient. No one had brought any booze and the magazines stayed wedged in our pockets. Sooner or later they would have to get down to business.

'Eventually, with an air of extreme reluctance and a bonhomie so false that even his companions on the high table winced, the director introduced the new work schedules "proposed by our most conscientious comrades from Work Brigade 4". This brigade was currently on the dawn shift, but the presumed hope that all the men were safely home in bed was soon shattered. "We proposed no such fucking thing!" a voice shouted from the back.

'The director managed to ignore this interruption, but another swiftly followed. Without saying a word, one of the younger miners — who I later learned was Vasili Suvorov — strode purposefully across to the noticeboard and pinned a new graph alongside the one detailing our latest ascent into industrial glory. Suvorov's graph also showed a bright red line working its way skyward, and for a moment the bosses scented unexpected support. "What growth rate does this diagram purport to show, comrade?" the raion secretary asked. "Serious injuries!" Suvorov shouted over his shoulder.

'For a few seconds there was absolute silence. Then both the director and the secretary began to speak, only to be drowned out by a huge burst of applause from their obedient work force.

'Eventually the secretary managed to make himself heard. "This is disgraceful behaviour. You should be ashamed of yourselves. I am ashamed at this moment ['So you should be!' someone shouted] . . . I do not apologise. Our nation ['Yours!'] is going through a difficult period. Everyone has to make sacrifices ['What about you lot then?'] . . . these new schedules have been worked out with all due attention to safety procedures. We do not need that" — he pointed angrily at Suvorov's graph — "to remind us of the tragic accidents which have occurred in the last few months. Everyone is conscious of the need to protect lives. Your union representatives ['They've got sod all to do with us!'] have conscientiously studied these proposals, and made amendments to them in your interests. You are behaving like spoilt children, expecting the good life without accepting the need to work for it. I . . . "

'At this point Suvorov stood up and began to shout angrily over the secretary's peroration. "If you call the good life living five to a room with no running water and not even enough coal, the coal *we* dig, to keep a stove alight through the winter, then I am ashamed of you, of us for listening to you, and all the other *chinovniks** like you. Try doing a day's work, and then maybe you'll have the right to speak."

'More thunderous applause, and the men on the high table were beginning to look distinctly uneasy. Scared even. The director and the secretary exchanged whispers, and it was the former who now got up to speak.

'This time the tone was conciliatory. "I see that there are some who harbour doubts about the new schedules [*loud laughter*], and that a natural sympathy for the victims of last week's accident has made some of you angry . . . justifiably so, perhaps . . . but also perhaps unreasonably so. I would remind you that the bonuses connected to these schedules are considerable, please think about that. I recognise that a decision cannot

---

* Literally bureaucrats, but with an old and decidedly unfavourable connotation.

be made today ['We've already made it!'] . . . we will think over what has been said and come back to you. This meeting is closed.''

'We were left in possession of the canteen, and a general sense of euphoria. The tiredness seemed to have worn off. Now the bottles could be brought out for a celebration . . . '

The elation of Gilyarovsky and his comrades proved shortlived. When they clocked in next morning the office yard was swarming with raincoated gebists, and the new schedules were posted up on the noticeboard. Inside the office Vasili Suvorov was being questioned by two men in uniform.

The arriving miners made no move to prepare for work, simply gathering in an ever-growing crowd across the yard. The situation became increasingly tense, with the miners whispering among themselves and jeering at the gebists and bosses. Then, to the latter's surprise, the men trooped into the changing rooms and, a few minutes later, took the lifts below ground.

If the authorities thought they had won a victory they were mistaken. Someone had suggested a meeting underground, beyond the reach of unwelcome ears, and this was now being convened half a mile down. According to Gilyarovsky there was hardly any debate, simply a reaffirmation of shared resolve. Half an hour after disappearing, the miners arrived back at the surface. A delegation of three informed the director that no more work would be done until the schedules were revoked and Suvorov released. He shrugged his shoulders and glanced at the uniformed officers through the door, as if to indicate that the matter had been taken out of his hands.

There was nothing extraordinary about the events which took place at the Makeyevka 3 pit on 25–26 April. Strikes in the Soviet Union were not rare and neither was the arrest of individuals known to have instigated them. If the authorities had acted quickly, had made concessions or merely promised them, there is little reason to believe that the strike would not have ended as swiftly as it had begun.

But the authorities did not respond in such a manner and the resultant spread of the strike was extraordinary by Soviet standards. By nightfall on the Friday twelve other pits in the vicinity had come out in support of the Makeyevka 3 miners' rejection of the new schedules and by Monday morning miners as far afield as Slavyansk and Novoshakhtinsk, at opposite ends of the Donbass, were refusing to go underground. Forty thousand men were defying their directors and, by implication, the rulers in the Kremlin.

The Donbass strike was presumably uppermost in the minds of the Politburo members as they reviewed the traditional May Day parade, for the moment the festivities were over an emergency session began in the chamber overlooking Alexandrov Gardens.

Chernenko's mind was made up: 'If we concede special privileges to the Donbass miners the whole country will cease work until they have them too. We cannot shirk this challenge.' He thought there were two possible courses of action. 'We can wait them out. My information is that a strike cannot be sustained for more than a fortnight at most. But there is a risk that the example could spread during that time, so I recommend the second course — send in the troops, however many are necessary. A soldier behind every miner if that is what it takes.'

Nor was Chernenko reluctant to place the strike in a wider context. He was 'bound to say that the necessity for such action would not have arisen but for the reckless abandonment of sound policies over the last few months.' It would not be enough to defeat the miners, who were only, he added sarcastically, 'pulling on the economic levers which this bureau has mistakenly placed within their reach'.

Gorbachev was unimpressed, asking drily whether Chernenko thought that the miners were 'striking against our betrayal of socialism'. Chernenko didn't find that amusing, merely naive. Perhaps Gorbachev's long absorption in agricultural matters had affected him adversely. Had he 'any notion of what is at stake here?'

Andropov came to Gorbachev's defence. He found it 'incredible' that Chernenko could envisage sending 40,000 troops down the mines. 'This is not 1937.'

Shcherbitsky tried reason. 'Let me spell something out for you, Konstantin Ustinovich. We have agreed, most of us, that our problems can no longer be solved by the old, purely administrative methods. If we revert to them at the first hint of trouble, nothing will be solved. Nothing. Of course we could get the miners back to work by holding guns in their backs — I could get you to agree with me if I held a gun in your back. But you would not agree with me enthusiastically, or work willingly for my ideas once the gun was removed. On the contrary, you would see the gun as proof that the ideas are wrong.'

'They are wrong,' Chernenko replied.

Demichev put the centrists' point of view. He had no wish to use the Army in such a situation, but a long strike would be profoundly unsettling. What was Shcherbitsky suggesting as a solution?

'Talk,' Shcherbitsky said.

Chernenko laughed. 'And what do you intend to say? "The Politburo would be most grateful if you would go back to work"?'

'Something like that. As I understand it this whole business began with one worker objecting to new schedules on safety grounds; and then some local Party idiot overreacted. It doesn't sound like an insuperable problem, so long as we act quickly. And it certainly doesn't bring the whole renewal programme into question; in my view it emphasises the need for it.'

Andropov agreed. 'What purpose will ten Novocherkassks serve? This is not an uprising. There have been no attacks on Party offices, no bloodshed. Comrade Chernenko is exaggerating the situation for reasons that are perfectly clear to us all. I propose that a member of this bureau be appointed to head a delegation to Donetsk — I suggest Vladimir Vasilyevich. If the miners prove unreasonable, then we can consider Comrade Chernenko's "solution" to the problem.'

Shcherbitsky was due to arrive at Makeyevka 3 at 2 pm on

Saturday 4 May. Boris Gilyarovsky was one of the waiting miners' delegates:

'The hours before the first negotiating session seemed endless. Most of us were very nervous, drinking tea and smoking so heavily that you could hardly see across the room. I found it hard to shake the feeling that we'd placed ourselves out on a very rickety limb and that the big boss was about to arrive with a sharp saw in his hand. And I wasn't the only one thinking such thoughts.

'Suvorov, though, seemed eager for the fray. He'd been released the day before, and he now did his best to encourage the rest of us. ''It's them that should be nervous, not us. We've got eighty thousand miners out there ready to back us up; the bosses can't dig the coal themselves. Believe me, they wouldn't be sending a member of the Politburo if they weren't prepared to do a deal.''

'The telephone rang. It was the boys at the gate telling us they'd arrived. We watched from the window, until the line of Chaikas edged their way round the sorting sheds and drew to a halt below. A chauffeur leapt out, opened the rear door and out stepped Shcherbitsky, a dark blue suit capped with silver hair. The rest of his party followed him into the building.

'The canteen where the trouble had started was being used for the meeting, but the furniture arrangements had been changed. There was no raised table now, just one long line of tables laid end to end, and rows of chairs for all who could squeeze in. Suvorov's graph was still on the wall.

'The ten members of our team took seats along the side left vacant by the Party delegation. The oblast secretary introduced the latter — I don't remember all the names, but there were people from the Ukraine Central Committee, Gosplan, the Ministry of Energy, the Trade Union. Konstantin Gunchenko, the Makeyevka 2 delegate who'd been chosen as our chief spokesman, did the same for our side, naming each of us and saying which pit we represented. Shcherbitsky looked relaxed. He smiled at us.

'The oblast secretary then suggested that we outline what we expected from the meeting, since it was our action which had made it ''necessary''. Gunchenko, in his slow drawling voice, then began to read out our statement, which basically consisted of the eight demands. At the same time copies of the statement were passed along the table to the officials. None of them bothered to read it.

'When Gunchenko had finished, Suvorov suggested that the best way to proceed would be to take the demands one by one. The oblast secretary looked at Shcherbitsky, who looked at the ceiling.

' "I would like first to say a few general words, to make my position as clear as possible. I am here because the Party views this situation with the utmost seriousness and because I would like to help clear up the misunderstandings which created this situation. No, do not misunderstand *me*. I realise you have grievances, genuine grievances. It is quite clear that serious mistakes have been made in this area and in this industry in particular. There are things to be put right, that is obvious. Soviet workers do not take the action you have taken without reason. I am not convinced — but perhaps you can convince me — that you have pursued the wisest course open to you. And I must tell you, in all frankness, that the government cannot grant, just like that, all your demands. There has to be give and take. I have not come to dispense gifts, to promise the earth, to solve all your problems and the problems of our country with a few beautifully chosen words. I am here to find the common ground that exists, that must exist, between us. Confrontation is a sterile business. I am open to your suggestions, you must be open to ours. Right, let us begin.

' "I see no problems with points one and two. We have no desire to victimise anyone who attempts criticism in a genuinely constructive spirit. The directors of four mines have already been replaced; those of the remainder will have their records investigated. Point Three. Here I see problems. I'm sure that you accept the need for higher productivity, despite your refusal to accept the plans drawn up by the Ministry of Energy. Do you have a counterplan of your own which manages to combine higher yields and acceptable safety levels?"

'It was a smooth performance. Someone had once told me that only a blockhead could rise to the top in our country, but Shcherbitsky was certainly no blockhead. He sounded tough, he sounded concerned, he sounded reasonable. "Give and take", of course. This was not our wretched raion secretary. If he'd suggested "give and take" we'd have asked him when he'd last given anything. This was a member of the Politburo, the "collective Tsar" as some called it, and he exuded a consciousness of his own power, even when surrounded by several hundred miners who had every reason to string him up.

'Still, the question had been anticipated. Suvorov said that yes, the "strike committee" — he emphasised the words — did have a plan for increasing productivity that involved an actual lessening of accident risk. More pieces of paper were passed down the table and this time they got read. The KGB had slipped up for once.

'Ten minutes passed, with only the rustle of papers and the sound of matches being struck to break the silence. Shcherbitsky was obviously out of his depth when it came to technical matters, but he had grasped one aspect of our plan — the cost. Just to be sure, he asked for the Ministry man to reply.

' "The author of these proposals has made an understandable error. The machinery mentioned here is not suitable for use in this area. The decision was reached several . . . "

'Suvorov interrupted: "Are you trying to tell a miner who has used these machines in Vorkuta that he doesn't know whether they are suitable for the mine he works in now. You know as well as I do that their use would be more expensive here, not impossible. That is why the East has priority."

'Now it was Shcherbitsky's turn to interrupt. "Comrade, let us not get carried away by emotion. Let us say you are right. We are still left with too few machines to go around. Someone has to have priority. You are surely not suggesting that the miners in the East should work in more dangerous conditions so that your safety can be enhanced. The planners have to safeguard the overall interests of the state, and the newer mines in the East are much more productive. It makes more sense to invest in new machinery for them, surely?"

' "The point," Suvorov retorted, "is the shortage itself. No miners, anywhere in the Soviet Union, should still, in 1985, have to face the sort of danger we face every day. We are willing — the proposals you have just read show how willing — to increase our productivity, but we demand that such an increase should not be paid for in miners' blood. It cannot be beyond the planners' expertise to produce enough of these machines to go around.''

'Shcherbitsky was writing something down on the back of our proposals. Everyone waited. He smiled. "I cannot answer for the planners, but I will look into the matter. Let us move on . . ."

'Five hours later the meeting broke up, with another scheduled for Monday. By this time the ashtrays had overflowed and Shcherbitsky's piece of paper was overflowing with things he was "going to look into". Once the officials had left we all sat around the table feeling half-dazed. The worst had not happened, at least not yet.'

A week later the Donbass miners were back at work. The so-called 'Makeyevka Agreement', signed with a total lack of official publicity on Friday 10 May, promised them better housing, more money, more goods to buy with it, new safety machinery — all the purely economic demands — as soon as it was humanely possible. Or, to put it another way, as soon as the Soviet economy could be coaxed into producing them. It was not a brilliant victory for the miners, but it was certainly victory enough, and the vast majority could neither afford nor wished to risk the consequences of further prolonging the strike. From the Politburo's point of view it appeared as if a dangerous situation had been, albeit expensively, averted.

This proved rather optimistic. In the ensuing weeks the Quadrumvirate and its supporters were to stress, over and over again, that Shcherbitsky had conceded nothing of vital importance to the miners. Promises had been made, and would of course be kept if it proved at all possible, but the nature of the relationship between ruled and rulers had not been brought into question. New houses, new machines, better-stocked shops — these were the sort of demands which the Kremlin could accommodate, albeit at someone else's expense.

82

Chernenko disagreed, and for once the instincts of the old Stalinist were not playing him false. The provisions of the 'Makeyevka Agreement' might not contain any dangerous precedent, but the very fact of the deal did. The Government had bargained, had been seen to bargain, with a group of workers; that was the crucial point, not the success or failure of the bargaining.

It was point not lost on the workers of the southern Ukraine. While the meetings were still underway in the Makeyevka 3 canteen, a series of strikes had erupted in the wide area bounded by Rostov in the east and Odessa in the west. Many had been inspired by the miners' example, but not all — in several instances it was discovered that the strikers had been unaware of the Donbass confrontation. In most cases the basic issues involved were the same — poor conditions, shortages, the raising of norms — and the managements concerned, mindful of the Donbass example, proved willing to make concessions. Most of the strikes lasted less than six hours.

But some did prove harder to break. In the Dnieper bend towns of Dnepropetrovsk, Dneprodzerzhinsk, Zaporoz'hye and Marganec the second week of May bore witness to a prolonged struggle between workers (often supported by their managements) and a determined group of city Party machines. In the last-named town several people died in a pitch battle between workers and militia, when the latter were instructed to end the former's occupation of their clothing factory.

The Quadrumvirate's attitude towards this rash of the Makeyevka 'disease' was both patient and pragmatic. The instructions handed down to the local Party machines — the instructions so blatantly ignored in the Dnieper bend towns — emphasised the need for accommodation, for defusing the situation through negotiation and, where necessary, concessions. Force was only to be used, or threatened, in two circumstances: in disputes involving plants manufacturing strategic materials or in the event of violent demonstrations beyond the limits of the work place.

In most cases this approach proved successful, at least temporarily. But in two areas it was to fail, and in the long term these failures would prove more significant than the more numerous successes. By 13 May some hundred thousand workers in the Dnieper bend towns had been out on strike for more than a week and the atmosphere had grown increasingly tense as rumours of direct action by the workers vied with rumours of punitive action by the authorities. In Moscow it was decided that Shcherbitsky, who had begun his Party career in Dneprodzerzhinsk, should be sent south once more.

His mission was to prove successful, but in the process it was also to cast a cloak over more significant developments elsewhere. In Nikolayev, a city of a million inhabitants on the Bug estuary, some extraordinary things were happening.

In the week of the Makeyevka 3 meetings two scandals had, almost unnoticed by the rest of the country, rocked the Black Sea city. The first concerned revelations of the privileges enjoyed by local Party children at their special kindergarten. Each day apparently, fresh fruit and vegetables were being flown all the way from Georgia — five hundred miles distant — for this group of sixteen children. The list of amenities at the kindergarten was simply astonishing; it boasted three video-recorders (virtually unknown in the Soviet Union), language laboratory facilities which the city's university would have envied, enough toys to stock a floor of Moscow's Detsky Mir and a ratio of one teacher to every two children.

On the day that these oft-rumoured facts received verification at a local Party meeting, a dockworker interrupted a political meeting at the Lenin Marine Engineering Works to charge the management with selling new safety machinery to a similar works in Odessa. This worker had been involved in unloading and readdressing the imported machinery; he thought his 'comrades at the Lenin Works would be interested to know why it has never arrived.'

One of the links connecting these two scandals was their exposure by Party members out of sympathy with the local Party machine. This latter, staffed by careerist Mafia appointees, known to be both corrupt and virtually immune to the anti-corruption campaign, had next to no support in the city. Another, related factor of importance was the strength of the local 'independents', a strength evident as far back as 1976 in the disproportionately high number of Nikolayev workers involved in Vladimir Khlebanov's FTUA. Caught between a corrupt administration and widespread support for an 'independent' line, many Party members gravitated towards the latter, creating a potentially explosive situation on the shop floors.

The workers' response to the twin scandals was consequently more considered than similar actions taken elsewhere. They did not simply pour out on strike. The Marine Engineering workers forcefully repossessed their safety machinery from the railway yard, and in all the major plants — the Lenin Works, the Sverdlov Flour Milling Combine, the shipyards and docks — the management was either ejected or, most insulting of all, simply ignored. In Nikolayev, as the mid-point of May approached, workers' management was becoming a reality.

Far away in Moscow, however, this situation appeared less serious than the violent strife convulsing the Dnieper bend towns and for two fateful weeks Nikolayev was left largely to its own, increasingly daring, devices. In the large enterprises which had dispensed with the luxury of management, committees were convened and charged with investigating ways of improving both economic performance and the conditions of the work forces. Hundreds of workers, from the newest recruits to the oldest of hands, were questioned, asked for suggestions concerning their own departments. Experiments were begun to test such suggestions. This was industrial democracy in action.

And, in many cases, the experiments proved remarkably successful, even in the short period allowed them. In the flour-milling combine an increase in productivity of quite staggering proportions was realised, all within the existing framework of the operational plan and without recourse to labour shedding or longer hours. These results, later submitted to the Politburo in a top secret memorandum, were to play a significant role in the events of autumn.

Party members were particularly prominent in these experiments and also in the more visible political upsurge taking place in the city. Many of the top officials had fled and were busy sending elaborate tissues of falsehood to their superiors in Moscow, but most of the middle and lower rank functionaries had embraced the new developments with emotions that wavered between intense trepidation and immense excitement. For many of them the ideology which had shaped their intellectual lives seemed, for the first time, to be reflecting the reality of their working lives.

Nowhere was this more evident than in the three issues of the newsheet *Waterfront* published on 14, 16 and 18 May. The speed with which events were reshaping local political consciousness was reflected in its cyclostyled columns, as criticism of symptoms was swiftly honed into a far-reaching diagnosis of the disease. The first issue was largely devoted to detailing the two scandals which had crystallised opposition to the local Party machine; the second went further, launching a bitter attack on the men responsible. Nor did it shrink from general observations. 'Lies are not lies for them,' the editorial stated, 'justice is not justice, equality is not equality, man is not man. They preach socialism and mean nothing more than a system which keeps them going. They preach unity and mean themselves and any others who are up to the same game. They preach democracy and mean doing what they tell you to do. They would have prospered under the Tsars.'

The third issue, brought out when the Politburo was already swivelling its beady gaze towards the errant city, went further still. The reform programme, 'this renewal of the unrenewable', was sharply criticised on two specific grounds. First, because it involved the working class in bearing the brunt of the burden whilst denying that same class any responsibility for its success or failure, second, because it provided for 'no broadening of socialist democracy whatsoever', only 'a further cloak for the endless machinations of an incompetent and corrupt minority'. 'This leadership' — whether of the city or the state was not made clear — 'though emotionally suited to the running of a huge capitalist corporation, unfortunately lacks the basic competence needed for performing even this distasteful task.' It was high time, the writer concluded, that 'the workers' state be run by the workers, not by a clique which falsely claims to represent their interests.'

In the middle of the same page, in cartoon form, a famous Soviet joke received its first airing in print. In the opening box Felix Dzerzhinsky, the first head of the Cheka, is being resurrected by Soviet scientists; in the second they tell him that all the old Bolsheviks are being resurrected in order of seniority. Thirdly, Dzerzhinsky is seen rushing through the door of Lenin's Mausoleum, only to find, in the fourth box, a note pinned to the empty sarcophagus which reads: 'Have taken a look round. Obviously we have to begin all over again. See you in Zurich. Yours, *Vladimir Ilych*.'

PART FOUR

REACTION (May–October 1985)

Inside the Izvestia *building*
electricians are writing the news
the journalists are out on the roof
replacing the slogan's fuse
and deep in the mausoleum
where the body twitches in dreams
the praetorians swap copies of Playboy
for the tightest American jeans

another night at the circus
they say it's the best in the world
the magicians can fool you completely
and the animals do what they're told

(from the Vlasov/Sidorova song 'Circus')

NIKOLAYEV MIGHT be isolated from the rest of the country, but the news reaching Moscow in the third week of May suggested that the social aspirations finding expression in the port city were far from unrepresentative. Although the troubles in southern Ukraine seemed to be abating, new sources of unrest were appearing, mostly in areas previously noted for industrial stability.

On 17 May a series of strikes hit the Kazakh capital of Alma Ata, another stronghold of the 'independents'. Though the spark was industrial — a large group of workers had been fired on trumped-up charges by a manager eager for productivity bonuses — the strikes soon took on national and racial undertones and a number of Russians and Ukrainians were attacked on the streets.

On the same day, a large demonstration of striking workers took to the streets of Kaunus, the Lithuanian capital, bearing portraits of the Pope and placards proclaiming the lethal word 'Solidarity'. The demonstration was dispersed by militia using tear gas, leaving several workers injured and many arrested.

On the following day the burning fuse reached the outskirts of Moscow itself, as workers downed tools at the 75th Anniversary Engineering Works in the suburb of Chovrino. The issue here was the state of the toilets.

For the Politburo, sitting in almost continuous session some ten miles to the southeast, this apparently petty dispute seems to have been the proverbial last straw. Over the preceding fortnight the chamber had born witness to expressions of growing concern, and high on the list of worriers were two members of the Quadrumvirate, Secretary Romanov and Defence Minister Ustinov. Even Andropov's perennial sanguineness seems to have been shaken by the events in Nikolayev. Reforms were one thing, sedition quite another.

The time for stern action was fast approaching. It is not known for certain when the crucial decision was taken, but according to one unconfirmed report the deed was done at a private meeting of the Quadrumvirate early in the morning of 19 May. Ustinov apparently demanded a crackdown as his price for accepting a continuance of the reform programme, pointing out that such a policy was infinitely preferable to the purely reactionary course championed by Chernenko and his growing band of allies. Romanov agreed enthusiastically, Andropov and Shcherbitsky with ill-concealed reluctance, and only on condition that parallel action was taken against those obstructing the reforms.

At the full Politburo session which took place that afternoon, and which was notable for Chernenko's insistence on reading lengthy quotations from the third issue of *Waterfront,* the Quadrumvirate's compromise was accepted. Only Solomentsev and Gorbachev voted against a crackdown.

But the hawks had scored only a partial victory. Another motion, put by Chernenko and seconded by Grishin, which demanded a replacement of the current, Andropov-appointed, head of the KGB, was defeated by nine votes to five. The Politburo was still evenly balanced, still constrained between the necessity and the danger of its reform programme.

On Monday 20 May *Pravda*'s front page sounded the appropriate tocsin. 'During the process of Leninist renewal,' the leader-writer intoned, 'it is especially important that every communist, every Soviet citizen, exercises ideological militancy, prepares himself to oppose the fictions of hostile propaganda with the eternal truths of Marxist-Leninist teaching.'

'Using the renewal process as a convenient pretext,' the article went on, 'a huge variety of anti-Soviet organisations and services, founded by the imperialists, are searching out morally unsteady, weak, politically immature people. Sometimes people fall into their net who have sunk to indulging in egotism and self-advertisement — people eager to make themselves heard as loudly as possible, not through honest labour for the sake of the motherland, but by any suspicious means whatsoever, not even excluding praise for our ideological enemies. Renegades and turncoats cannot count on going unpunished.'

The editor received predictably massive support from the public, which for the past few days had been using the letters page to conduct a vigorous debate on the rights and wrongs of long-haired athletes representing the Soviet Union. On 20 May this controversy, which many observers considered unresolved, abruptly vanished. In its stead appeared criticism of the 'growing anarchy' in Soviet society, of the new 'Nepmen' crawling out of the economic woodwork, of 'people who seek to take advantage of renewal', and the perils such people posed to the 'purity of Soviet life'. 'We do not wish a Western style of life in the Soviet Union,' one correspondent noted loyally, before launching himself into a blistering assault on the profit motive. 'My comrades and I wish to express our increasing concern,' wrote a chemical worker from Solikamsk, 'at the steady growth of a profiteering mentality in our district.'

For a people accustomed to reading between the lines of its premier newspaper, the message could not have been clearer, and indeed, for many of those most affected the opportunities for reading *Pravda* that morning were severely limited. Throughout the preceding night the Soviet Union had resounded to the noise of doors being kicked in, as thousands of suspected 'independents' were rounded up for interrogation and probable trial. If the streets of Moscow that morning seemed much the same as ever, in the towns of the Dnieper bend, the Donbass, the Baltic Republics and Central Asia troops were much in evidence. Only Nikolayev was left ominously alone.

That evening President Gromyko addressed the nation on TV:

'Citizens of the Soviet Union, I address you as President of our country. I address you on matters of the utmost importance.

'During these last few weeks certain events have taken place which go beyond, far beyond, the necessary limitations laid down for the process of socialist renewal. Those who have toiled to raise our country's standard of living, to develop its riches, to defend its borders and its social system against our class enemies, have found their achievements belittled and their mistakes magnified out of all proportion. The work of generations has been derided by those who have most benefitted from it.

'In recent days many public institutions have been occupied and acts of violence committed against public officials. There have been frequent examples of terror, threats, moral mob trials and direct coercion. Crimes, robberies and break-ins have spread like a wave through the country. Fortunes measured in milliards of roubles are even now being made by the sharks of the economic underground.

'Citizens, this is not what the people expected from the economic programme we embarked upon last autumn. The people expect energy, determination and, above all, a sense of responsibility from all those involved — and that is every last one of us — in the implementation of the programme.

'It cannot be said that the government lacked goodwill, moderation, patience — perhaps we even erred on the side of tolerance. We saw in the programme an opportunity to deepen the system of socialist democracy, to begin the solution of our economic difficulties in a spirit of goodwill and determination. To some extent our hopes have been fulfilled. In many branches of our industry both the quantity and the quality of goods produced have increased and the wages of those directly involved have also risen.

'But in some areas, in some industries, this has not happened. Certain individuals have used the economic programme as an excuse for presenting their own political programmes, programmes which do not lie within the bounds of socialist legality. In ordinary times their arguments would have been ignored by the Soviet worker, but in such times of hardship as those we have recently endured, it is understandable that some of these arguments have found a ready, if reluctant, audience. We understood this and we took no precipitate action, believing that common sense would in the end prevail.

'Our faith in this matter, however, has not been fully justified. The extremists have taken our tolerance for weakness and have grown bolder. Some have appealed to the West for "justice"; a strange choice of champion indeed. Justice from states who now have no work for a quarter of their workers!

'We could not allow this state of affairs to continue indefinitely. The programme of economic renewal is necessary for our country, for the people's well-being, for security against the threat of war which is posed by the desperation of the imperialists. Those who have sought to disrupt the programme, to use the opportunities it presented for their own selfish ends, have reached the end of the people's patience. As I speak the more serious offenders are being taken into police custody.

'Citizens, just as there is no turning back from the road laid down by Lenin, so there is no turning back from the reforms introduced, in his name and spirit, last autumn. The steps taken today only serve to preserve the fundamental premises of Leninist renewal. All the reforms will be continued in an atmosphere of order, businesslike discussion and discipline.

'A difficult period is ahead of us. To make tomorrow better, we must recognise the hard realities which confront us today. We must understand the need to make sacrifices, if the future we wish for our children is to become the reality.'

Western commentators remarked on the similarity between this address and that delivered in similar circumstances several years earlier by Poland's General Jaruzelski. But though the sentiments and, in some cases, the actual words were the same — both addresses were drafted by the CPSU Secretariat — the Gromyko speech contained precious little in the matter of specific measures. There was no declaration of martial law, no ban on strikes (they were implicitly outlawed in any case) and, most significantly, no change in the ranks of the Party leadership. Most observers correctly concluded from all this that the reform programme was still a going concern.

Tuesday's *Pravda* provided confirmation and a decided softening of Monday's tone. Under a by-line well-known to reflect top-level thinking, the paper called for 'a unity which triumphs over the undoubted errors of recent months', and warned against 'a fleeing from reality, into either a mythical past or unfounded pessimism for the future'. The renewal programme should be approached in 'a radical and disciplined manner', in an 'atmosphere of vigilant responsibility'.

This article was presumably read with both interest and trepidation in Nikolayev, where the much-publicised crackdown was still awaited. The Party bosses had still not returned from 'exile', the major work places were still being run by their workers. Nikolayev, on the morning of Tuesday 21 May, remained an 'independent' enclave on the shore of the Soviet Union.

In the preceding fortnight two 'leaders' had emerged from among the ranks of the industrial workers. One was Vladimir Travkin, the 24-year-old son of a Russian Party functionary and his Ukrainian wife. He had been an exemplary Pioneer and an exemplary Konsomol member, but his sense of mission had been soured by service in Afghanistan. Stationed in Herat for six months in 1983, Travkin had taken a lead in organising one of the first soldiers' soviets, whose avowed purpose was a substantial improvement in the lot of the ordinary Soviet conscript. For such temerity he had been transferred to an active service unit in the Panshir Valley.

He survived this, but the authorities did not forget him. His term completed, Travkin found a job befitting his educational qualifications impossible to come by. For a year he worked as a clerk at the chemical combine in his home town of Chernigov, and here he came into contact with some surviving veterans of Khlebanov's FTUA. When the NEP 2 was introduced he moved south to the union-conscious city of Nikolayev with several letters of introduction. He got work at the flour-milling combine and was one of those most involved in organising the widespread opposition to new work schedules. An enormous capacity for hard work, an ability to get on with almost anyone and a tremendous oratorical flair had since raised him to a position of some eminence among the port city's workers.

Nadezhda Yaschenko had a longer record of opposition to the authorities. Six of her forty-four years had been spent in prisons and psychiatric hospitals for her part in organising 'independent' branches in the Nikolayev shipyards. She had been released the previous summer and by some gross oversight on the part of the city machine had managed to regain her previous job and recommence her union activities. Better-educated than Travkin and equally determined, Yaschenko had been the foremost strategist of the city's 'peaceful revolution'.

Both were present at a meeting of the various works committee representatives on the evening of 20 May. All knew that action by the authorities must be imminent, but what form it would take remained a mystery until late that evening. Then a railway worker arrived with the news that the Army had commandeered the track east to Fedorovka for the next twenty-four hours. The implication was obvious.

Meeting force with force was out of the question: but then so was a meek surrender. Surely something could be done; the solidarity of the workers, of the whole city, was unquestionable, and so much had been achieved. The sending of a delegation to Moscow was discussed, but no decision was taken. A mass meeting would be held on the following morning. Let them shrug aside twenty thousand 'hooligans'.

That same evening 'they' were also meeting, fifty miles to the southwest in the Kherson Party offices. The leaders of the oblast central committee had been flown down to greet Politburo members Chernenko and Ponomariev. Also present were the commanders of the Nikolayev naval base, the Odessa Military District and the oblast KGB.

No records were kept of their discussion, but one of the Nikolayev officials later recounted the gist of it in court. Chernenko had come determined to make an example of the Black Sea city. One phrase — 'we cannot put them all in *pityushkas*' — particularly stuck in the official's mind. He also noted the relish with which Chernenko supervised the planning of the military operation, talking about 'the city as if it were occupied by the Germans'. Ponomariev, by contrast, 'seemed nervous about the whole business, and spent much of the meeting on the phone to Moscow'.

* * *

Both meetings ended around midnight and by this time the convoy of trains carrying the Uzbek and Kazakh troop battalions was already past Snigirevka Junction, heading west. It reached the outskirts of Nikolayev around five in the morning and here the troops were disembarked. They had been used in Dnepropetrovsk the previous week and were expecting more of the same. 'We kept waiting for the tear gas canisters and masks to be issued,' one soldier later testified, 'but they never were.'

Tuesday morning was fine, a sunny sky with only the gentlest of breezes wafting up the estuary. The mass meeting was held inside the grounds of the flour-milling combine, in the shadow of the gigantic silos originally built to hold grain destined for export. One young worker, Tatiana Tolyshkina, wrote a vivid account of the event:

'Members of the works committees addressed us, putting the pros and cons of continuing the occupations. There must have been twenty-five thousand people packed into the yard and those at the rear could hear little of what was being said. Still, they cheered and applauded whenever those at the front did so — everyone knew that there was basic agreement. A few *shpiks* muttered cynical asides, but no one took any notice of them and they soon disappeared. We knew our demands were fair, were right, were realistic; a decent life, that's all they added to.

'Travkin got a great cheer when he took the microphone and he even managed to carry his voice to the farthest corners of the yard. "If we submit," he shouted, "if we just crawl back on our knees and ask forgiveness from that scum, then it will all have been for nothing. They will bring greater force to bear and we will have no choice but to bow before that. But they cannot bring greater justice to bear, they cannot wipe out the memory of these last two weeks, cannot make us forget what we, *we*, have achieved in that time. So, they will chain us to our machines and our desks in the name of socialism. It will bring them a respite, perhaps, a few more years of privilege at our expense, but they cannot solve anything without us and deep down they must know that too. They are frightened now, frightened of us, and who knows where that fear will drive them. But, I tell you, sooner or later they will have to unchain us and give us a better reason to work. Not just more money, though heaven knows we could use it. Not just more things and better things to buy, though we want that too. But dignity, a sense of worth, a share in decisions, an end to corruption and all that goes with it. I beg you, do not be fooled by promises of more bread.

' "The other day someone told me of a phrase used by Trotsky back in 1905. Now I know Trotsky is like a word for evil in our country now and I don't profess to know whether he was as black as they say. Perhaps he was a knight in shining armour. But he said this about some promises made by the Tsar; he called them 'a whip wrapped up in a constitution'. I think we should remember that phrase."

'This is not a verbatim report of Travkin's speech, it is what I remember, how accurately I don't know. But the general tone of defiance was quite unmistakable and unforgettable, and he got a tremendously enthusiastic response from almost everyone present. It was hard to believe in those moments that our situation was so desperate. When a helicopter flew so low across the crowd that it only narrowly missed one of the grain elevators you could see a thousand fists shaking against the sky — it was like an Eisenstein film. The sense of solidarity, the feelings of power and elation which a huge crowd united in spirit emanates, was very strong that morning. No one knew that two gunboats had dropped anchor in mid-river behind the elevators, let alone that fighting had broken out aboard them when some sailors refused to man the guns.

'Another helicopter appeared overhead, this time hovering at around fifty metres and an amplified voice ordered the crowd to disperse. No one moved, but the voice droned on, competing with the racket made by the machine. Perhaps this was a genuine attempt to avoid bloodshed, more likely it was a deliberate ploy to distract the crowd's attention. If so it was successful, for everyone seemed hypnotised by this monstrous metal bird hanging above us, intoning its hopeless message.

'Things moved quickly after that. Something was happening at the back of the yard and what sounded like gunfire could be heard above the noise of the helicopter. We later learned that the guards on the gates had been shot down by plainclothes men and that the gate itself had been bulldozed by a tank, letting in the Asian soldiers.

'A voice from the platform was screaming at everyone to sit down, not to resist, but at the back they were learning that these soldiers had orders which hadn't taken surrender into account. They were shooting wildly, some straight into the crowd, some, from compassion or excitement, into the air, some even at each other. The crowd was pressing forward, trying to escape, but there weren't enough exits and another danger had appeared. "Oh shit, twenty-fours," as I heard someone groan. Three helicopter gunships were now circling above the yard, firing down into the mass of humanity. One passed in front of the sun, and the next thing I knew I was waking up in a hospital ward full of moaning patients and armed guards.''

On Wednesday 22 May, halfway down page two, *Pravda* devoted four lines to the 'resolution of certain problems' in the city of Nikolayev. 'Hooligan elements' had incited workers into anti-Soviet acts of violence and a number of arrests had been made. The situation was now back to normal and a photograph —taken in 1981 — showed a smiling group of workers exchanging the time of day with Ukrainian Party Secretary Vladimir Shcherbitsky.

In fact four hundred and seventeen workers were killed that morning. More than five thousand were arrested, including Nadezhda Yaschenko and the crews of the two naval gunboats. But of Vladimir Travkin the authorities could find no trace. For three days he had hidden in the works, less than fifty metres from the bloodstrewn yard, listening to the chatter of the convicts brought in to clear up the mess. When the combine reopened for business his co-workers smuggled him out, and fellow FTUA members on the railway arranged for him to reach Moscow. There he secured a false passport, grew a moustache and secured a job at one of the huge factories on Enthusiasts' Highway. The Politburo had not heard the last of him.

*　　*　　*

In sanctioning a crackdown the Politburo had surrendered to the most Soviet of gut reactions — if control is being wrenched away from the centre, then the centre has to wrench it back. On 19 May few of its members had looked far beyond that. The hardliners doubtless hoped that it would be the thin end of their wedge, would be followed by a gradual reimposition of all the old and trusted methods of administrative direction.

The text of Gromyko's address, however, showed quite clearly that the hardliners still lacked the power to force through a 'great leap backwards'. The Party's commitment to the 'Leninist renewal' had been reaffirmed; there was still a clear Politburo majority in favour of some level of reform. So where would the crackdown end? What were the new limits? How would the new balance of forces be reflected in policy terms?

Some sort of decision was taken at the session on Friday 24 May. As usual, Chernenko led off for the hardliners. The Party's first task, he claimed, was to 'reestablish the basis of socialist order'. The managers were crying out for more guidance, they no longer knew what was expected of them. 'The conscientious ones have no time for the actual business of producing goods, the lazy ones are simply using their new "freedom" as an excuse for failure.' The workers, bereft of 'the most elementary discipline', were reacting just as he had predicted they would, on the one hand 'shirking all responsibility', on the other making life impossible for their superiors. 'In the last few weeks we have seen where such a situation inevitably leads, into an assault on the very foundations of socialist thinking.'

But it was no longer enough, Chernenko thought, to merely reestablish control over the economy. The anti-corruption campaign, 'though legitimate in its own terms', had become a destabilising factor in the life of the country. The people had been given the false impression that the majority of officials was corrupt and some 'unscrupulous opponents of socialism' had used such popular misgivings to 'launch attacks on any form of authority'. The fight against corruption should continue, but more discreetly.

As for the legal reforms, these had also proved 'counterproductive'. In some cases 'an excessive devotion to

101

legal forms' had been instrumental 'in obstructing the pursuit of socialist justice'. These reforms should be rescinded at once, and a more careful investigation mounted into any changes that might prove necessary.

Chernenko concluded by demanding the 'restoration of adequate control to the planning organs' and new laws aimed at restoring labour discipline. 'We have been drifting this way and that, comrades. Now we must demonstrate resolution. Nothing else will suffice.'

Shcherbitsky replied for the reformists. He argued that the failures, such as they were, could be traced to quite different sources, to 'those people who have deliberately sought to misrepresent the reform programme and to obstruct its implementation', and to the excessive use of 'resolution' in past years. 'But,' he continued, 'let us examine these "failures". We have seen disturbances in the past few weeks, some of them quite serious. It is interesting that the most serious of all have occurred in precisely those areas where resistance to the reform programme by our own people has been most marked. Be that as it may, we have never, at any time, been in the slightest danger of losing control of the situation. The success of the measures taken this week is ample proof of that. And I would remind you all that the programme was introduced in the full knowledge that some measure of active dissent was inevitable.

'But if these disturbances are to be used as evidence of failure, as the only evidence apparently, then let us examine the successes.' Shcherbitsky had a sheaf of them, the records of enterprise after enterprise whose performance had been substantially boosted by the reform. 'I cannot understand,' he went on, 'how Comrade Chernenko can ignore this evidence. Or is he determined to defend "socialism" all the way to penury? That way lies nothing but disturbance, enough to destroy us all. Or does "Comrade" Chernenko intend to deal with the rest of the Soviet Union the way he dealt with Nikolayev?'

At this point in the proceedings, according to Solomentsev, 'a brawl seemed almost possible. Even in my time Politburo sessions had not been noted for comradely good cheer, but I had never witnessed such an open display of mutual contempt.

It was hard to believe that Chernenko and Shcherbitsky had worked together so closely in the Brezhnev years.'

The tension eased as other members spoke in defence of the protagonists, but everyone knew that the issue would be ultimately decided by the three men sitting at the top of the table: Andropov, Romanov and Ustinov. It was known to Solomentsev, and perhaps others, that Andropov and Ustinov had conferred at length the previous day. Had they reached agreement?

It was Romanov, with approving nods from Ustinov and no dissent from Andropov, who put forward the compromise. 'It seems to me, comrades,' he began, 'that personal differences are threatening to obscure a strong measure of agreement. We cannot afford to ignore either the successes related by Vladimir Vasilyevich or the fear expressed by Konstantin Ustinovich. That much seems clear. We must proceed with the reform programme, but with more caution than hitherto. We need to reestablish, beyond any doubt, the authority of the party and to that end it may prove necessary to suspend, temporarily, some of the devolutionary measures. The Secretariat should be instructed to determine the various options.'

Since neither left nor right wished to alienate the centre, Romanov's proposal was carried unanimously. It seemed to Solomentsev as if a 'new centrist coalition might be emerging, more radical than that existing under Brezhnev, less adventurous than that originally envisaged by the Quadrumvirate'. He did not welcome the prospect. Perhaps flattering himself with hindsight's aid, Solomentsev 'wondered that day whether the Politburo had chosen the worst possible course. Shcherbitsky's way offered hope, Chernenko's way power; a compromise between them seemed likely to plunge the Soviet Union between two stools.'

From the policeman's perspective the crackdown was eminently successful. There was no outcry, either from within the Party or without, and no fresh wave of strikes in support of those arrested. For the moment the Soviet Union seemed shocked into silence, not so much by the authorities' action as by the weeks of unrest which had provoked it. A few dissidents mounted a brief protest in Red Square, a few odd strikes erupted and swiftly petered out. Repression still worked.

But repression in the service of whom and what? There was no longer a coherent answer; the Soviet leadership was approaching the condition which had characterised Hitler's régime in its final years, one of empires within empire, each pursuing conflicting interests beneath a single umbrella of autocratic power. There was no real policy agreement. Deprived of its solid grip on the past, its hold on the future fearfully loosened, the Soviet leadership was simply freewheeling towards catastrophe.

It still spoke with one voice, but that voice seemed to speak for several minds. Only in matters foreign could a consensus be found, and this only for a preservation of the *status quo*. In Afghanistan the war went on, with neither victory nor defeat in sight. The East European régimes, though untouched as yet by the internal Soviet unrest, continued to act as a drain on the Soviet exchequer; this year it was Romania's turn to cash the biggest fraternal cheques. The remnants of European détente were clung to with desperation, as the Kremlin bent over backwards in its attempts not to antagonise Strauss' Christian Democrat government. The United States remained unreachable, with the Reagan Administration demanding the restoration of the pre-crackdown situation within the Soviet Union, oblivious to the fact that it had previously condemned that very situation as a confidence trick.

In domestic affairs it proved more difficult to preserve the *status quo*, partly because no one could agree what it was. The Press still waxed lyrical about the potential for economic renewal, but the designation NEP 2 was now rarely mentioned and much new emphasis was being given to the dangers of over-optimism in general and 'reckless innovation' in particular. The story was similar as regards the anti-corruption campaign. Though still official Party policy, the campaign's prosecution was now hedged with so many restrictions as to deter all but the most conscientious of citizens.

The new catch-all, predictably enough, was 'discipline'. Party discipline, work discipline, student discipline, family discipline. Almost everything from bad economic results to street crime could be laid at the door of discipline's arch foe, the dreaded 'anarchy'. Appropriate dictums from Lenin adorned every available facade. Causing problems was 'an infantile disorder', and so was solving them 'recklessly'.

This distaste for disorder was shared by neo-Stalinists and reformists alike and as an ideological stopgap it proved fairly serviceable. But it fell far short of the coherent policy which was so desperately needed. Romanov's flippant faith in the Secretariat's ability to devise such a policy was soon shown to be groundless; the Secretariat was as riven by disagreement as the Politburo and the Central Committee and the provision of a clear-cut compromise between planner power and managerial power would have taxed the most united of men. In lieu of such a policy a series of makeshift instructions intended to 'correct the balance' were issued, and in most cases these were open to a wide variety of interpretations.

The job of interpreting them, and thus in effect of deciding what was to remain of the reforms, fell to the mass of Party functionaries up and down the country. Not surprisingly their decisions reflected the existing lack of unity at all levels, and from region to region, city to city, the implementation of the Secretariat's instructions took many different forms. This in turn spread further confusion and indecision throughout the economic life-support system. Planners and functionaries sought to regain their lost prerogatives in the name of reaction as managers sought to retain them in the name of reform. Behind the political reality of order, as expressed in the lack of open dissent, the system as a whole was displaying all the signs of growing anarchy.

The purely economic consequences grew increasingly severe. As summer wore on the distribution system, already dislocated by the reforms, was thrown further out of gear by attempts to reverse them. Food shortages grew more acute in the less sensitive areas as the planners, still effectively in control of the agricultural sector, sought to build stocks against the looming grain crises. In Buenos Aires Soviet diplomats pleaded with the new Argentinian régime.

The industrial working class bore its usual substantial share of the growing hardship, but there were no significant eruptions of organised anger. Most of the major disputes of April and May had been resolved through the granting of notable concessions and the making of fulsome promises and, though the crackdown had involved the arrest of many known 'trouble-makers', the concessions had not been revoked, and promises not rescinded. In the intervening months a vigorous attempt had been made to close differentials. For the moment the workers had some incentive, other than repression, to keep quiet.

This situation, of course, was hardly conducive to economic growth; in many areas the clock had simply been turned back to pre-reform days. The workers were once again ignoring the management and ignoring the régime. The hardliners should have been happy.

But the situation was also profoundly different. For one thing, the economy was performing worse than ever and in the coming months this failure would create a level of hardship not seen in the Soviet Union for several decades. For another, the workers had learnt a great deal from the spring strikes. They knew now that taking over the work place was a better bet than taking to the streets, that simultaneous action was more effective than sporadic stoppages. They had a better idea of who their friends were, knew which managers and functionaries could be trusted and which could not. And, most important of all, they had learnt, in certain key places like Nikolayev, that a real alternative did exist, one moreover which seemed to offer a better deal both for them and their country. The argument that the one had to be sacrificed for the other had lost its power.

From a Western journalist's perspective, the Soviet Union was not the place to be in the summer of 1985. The media had done its usual overkill job during the weeks of unrest and, after deploring the crackdown, had disappeared in search of fresher stories for the delight of its public. In the West itself there was no shortage of political drama.

The Western economy had, as they say, bottomed out once more, but there were no signs of it ever regaining the surface. Unemployment remained the major issue, with the OECD total now approaching forty million. Once again the streets of the developed West were awash with nihilistic violence, as the god materialism failed to deliver material. The different nations seemed to be playing musical riots; this time around Switzerland and West Germany were leading the game, with the United States coming in a close second. Ominously for the White House, the American disturbances were now penetrating its power base in the West, with San Diego hosting the goriest show of the summer.

The Western economies were not being helped by the Middle East's latest plunge into crisis, with Syria riven by virtual civil war and Iran trying to cope, bloodily, with the power vacuum left by Khomeini's assassination. The oil glut of recent years was fast receding into a subject for nostalgic reminiscence and the producers had received a further boost with Mexico's decision to join OPEC. The only good news on the Third World 'front' was the ending of civil war in El Salvador, and in the United States there were many who considered the compromise solution a comprehensive sellout.

All of which made the Soviet bloc seem like an oasis of calm — to everyone but its inhabitants. They watched the tribulations of the West on TV, accompanied by the jubilant voices intoning capitalism's death-rattle, but few really believed it. When had they ever seen or heard any other vision of the West's future? The citizens of the Soviet Union were more concerned about the troubles brewing just beneath the surface of their own society.

Marion Lennox, who had found Moscow so unusually buoyant the previous summer, found the Soviet capital full of apprehension. The few dissidents still at liberty were earnestly analysing the events of May, lamenting their own lack of contacts with the Soviet workers and eagerly awaiting a second chance to establish some. But they were extremely unrepresentative of the Muscovite 'middle class' with whom Lennox came into contact. 'Most better-off Muscovites,' she reported, 'talk about the Soviet workers much as I imagine the old aristocrats spoke of the Bolsheviks, as an almost alien species, full of dark and fathomless instincts, bent only on destroying the little that was tolerable in Soviet society.'

Lennox was shocked by the wave of Brezhnev nostalgia, which seemed to her 'little more than a discreet form of Stalin nostalgia', and by the sudden 'flowering' of a rampant xenophobia. 'The strikers are doing the work of Russia's enemies,' was a constant refrain. 'Some apparently intelligent Muscovites,' she wrote, 'slip with ease into the sort of anti-semitic and anti-asiatic sentiments which only a year ago would have made them blush with shame.' Side by side with such prejudices went a consumption of alcohol 'which even the Russians themselves find breathtaking'.

Some perceived the situation with greater clarity. 'One old friend, whom I'd always relied upon to provide a positive counterpoint to the cynics, seemed doubly depressed. "We are, as the English say it, up shit creek without an oar," he told me. "The reforms are twenty years too late — now it's them or the Party and those gentlemen would rather go down with the ship than save it by jumping overboard." '

Lennox found no shortage of radical solutions to the country's problems. Many of the xenophobes blamed everything on the cost of supporting the 'fraternal millstones', and even among the less nationalistic, the conduct of Soviet foreign policy came in for some heavy criticism. 'They are living in the past, like you in the West,' one university lecturer told her. 'We took over eastern Europe to give us another five hundred miles, the sort of distance Hitler's tanks could cover in a month. Now the American missiles can fly over it in seconds. What good are these countries to us? The régimes are far more unpopular than ours, they cost us a fortune and they give socialism a bad name everywhere. It would be better to let them go.'

The same lecturer was rather less pessimistic about the reforms. 'We have to move towards workers' management, towards industrial democracy as the first step towards political democracy. It won't be as you have it in the West — a centrally planned economy necessarily creates authoritarian pressures — but it will be much more productive, more forward-thinking, than what we have now. We are potentially the world's greatest economic power — and look at us.'

But this lecturer, like most of the few prepared to look

beyond despair, found little cause for optimism in the immediate future. 'The men at the top have convinced themselves that real change is too risky, but they don't have any other ideas. That's why everyone is so depressed. There's a feeling that it has to be either economic disaster or a political explosion, or even both. Most people are afraid of either. And, though you in the West would find this hard to understand, the Russian people would be ashamed of either.'

Certainly the Western commentators who drew parallels between the 'Russian Spring' and similar episodes of Hungarian, Czechoslovak and Polish history were profoundly mistaken. In the summer of 1985 there was no widespread sense of resentment against the Government crackdown, no widespread desire to see the system brought crashing down. The Government was resented because 'order' was the only thing it could impose, and then only 'order' of the more superficial variety. 'The Government no longer rules, it merely reacts,' as one observer complained. There was no democratic ideal nestling close to the Soviet heart, only an earnest longing for someone to 'clear things up', 'get things straight', before it was too late. No one knew what would happen if the Government failed to do this, only that it would be worse than it was now. Like the Party, a large majority of the Soviet population had grown accustomed to the sixty-eight-year-old system. It was hard to imagine any other way of managing the place.

PART FIVE

REVOLUTION

*When a government begs for realism,
reality cannot be far away.*

(Graffito in Moscow)

'IT SOUNDED like a peal of thunder, and the ground trembled underneath our feet.' That was how one shaken clerk at Kramatorsk's Yuri Gargarin pit described the moment of disaster. His words would later assume the status of political metaphor.

It was the early hours of Friday 11 October. The night shift was drawing to a close and the miners, desperately intent on securing overfulfilment bonuses, may well have ignored warning signals. No one ever found out. At around 5.15 am a methane explosion ripped through the third level, killing eighty men outright and dooming more than twice that number in the lower tunnels.

In the hours that followed, two groups of people converged on the pithead. First to arrive, in a steady, aching stream, were the wives, sweethearts, parents and children of the men and corpses trapped underground. Soon afterwards, with rather less emotional involvement but little less anxiety, KGB and Party officials began parking their cars in the colliery yard. While the rescue operation swung into action, the director's office phones were humming with information, suggestions, instructions. In Donetsk and Moscow officials were being tumbled out of their beds, in Kramatorsk itself the local KGB and militia units were being readied for active duty.

The authorities' first instinct was predictable. As the sun crept across the slag heaps, lorryloads of men were blocking the roads and interdicting the railways. All telephone communications between the town and the outside world were cut off as soon as the authorities had rigged up their own exclusive lines.

Predictable and mistaken. At this stage there was every chance that the situation, politically speaking, could have been

113

saved. Had the authorities chosen to treat the explosion as a tragic accident and nothing more, then the resultant furor might well have been subsumed in the natural sharing of grief. As it was, each move taken by the men grouped in the director's office only served to worsen the situation. When the first bodies were brought to the surface, the widows were scarcely allowed time for identification before the waiting ambulances whisked them away. Grief became confused with anger; the authorities' assumption of responsibility began to seem like an admission of guilt.

That day no one reported for work at the other pits in the immediate vicinity; the miners just gathered in an ever-growing crowd around the scene of disaster, until the slag heaps were covered in a mass of silent humanity, watching the ambulances come and go. Officials asked the crowd to disperse, claiming that the rescue effort was being impeded, but the appeal was ignored and no attempt was made to enforce it.

The authorities had no more success in containing the news. That afternoon, almost simultaneously, miners in Slavyansk and Artemovsk abandoned the tunnels to hold open-air meetings. By evening the whole Donbass was talking about the disaster, about how the authorities had tried to keep it quiet, about the bodies being driven away in ambulances to who knew where. Members of the 'independent' unions contacted each other and arranged a meeting for the following day, Sunday, in Makeyevka.

Meanwhile, in Kramatorsk itself, the vast crowd arrayed around the pithead had mutated into a procession, winding its way downhill towards the town centre and the House of Miners. They found the building empty, the pavements lined with militia. Some youths threw stones through the institute's windows, but no attempt was made to restrain them; the local militia commander was under strict instructions to start nothing he couldn't finish. Eventually the crowd dispersed, some back to their homes, some back to the vigil on the slag heaps. For the moment sorrow was more powerful than anger.

The 'independents' who gathered in a storeroom of the

Ordjonikidze footwear factory on Sunday 13 October were mostly young, mostly inexperienced and all thoroughly committed. Knowing the fate of their predecessors, those who had led the strike in the spring, they could hardly be anything else. Of the ten miners who had sat down with Shcherbitsky in the Makeyevka 3 canteen not one was still working in the Donbass. Four had been 'voluntarily' retired, two moved to other regions, one bought off, one falsely discredited, and two committed to psychiatric institutions for 'remedial treatment'.

But these young men could count upon widespread support. The promises of May, though never officially revoked, had certainly not been kept. The safety machinery was still expected 'soon', the new housing was conspicuous by its absence, the new directors were no better than the old ones. Wages were still pitiful and prices continued to edge upwards. The miners were 'sick of being treated like beasts of burden'.

Expecting massive support, some of those present at the 'independent' meeting demanded immediate backing for a regionwide strike. Others were more cautious. The groundwork laid over the previous winter, the careful creation of an informal cellular structure covering the whole of the Donbass, should not be risked lightly. It was agreed to send a delegation of two to Moscow, where they could petition the Central Committee for an immediate honouring of the 'Makeyevka Agreement'. The rest of those present would spread the news of the delegation's journey.

In Kramatorsk the authorities had realised their mistake and several bodies were 'returned' for the first in a series of 'heroes' funerals'. A large wreath from the Central Committee, and the accompanying letter of condolence from Secretary Romanov, were much in evidence. Promises of investigations, improvements, more bonuses, filled the air. A shipment of meat suddenly filled out the town's butchers' shelves. Kramatorsk's mourning was not to be without its compensations.

No meat, however, reached Slavyansk, Artemovsk, or any of the other mining communities. In several of these towns 'Italian strikes' were now under way, punctuated by scuffles between miners and the local militia and 'illustrated' by a resurgence of May's graffiti. During Sunday night one local poet had painted, in huge letters, THE DEEPER YOU DIG, THE STRONGER THE SMELL, on the side of the Artemovsk 6 sorting shed. Next morning, management attempts to erase the offensive message were successfully resisted by the miners.

The tension in Artemovsk and elsewhere was somewhat defused that afternoon when news of the 'independent' delegation to Moscow became widespread. Now perhaps something would be done.

It was 'done' that evening. Without apparently consulting their superiors in Moscow, the local Party and KGB had decided on cowering the miners into submission. Working on the principle 'remove the troublemakers and you remove the trouble', they ordered the arrest of over four hundred miners throughout the region.

The principle proved as false as ever. On Tuesday morning, as news of the arrests filtered through the various shifts, the Donbass coalfield ground to a halt. In pit after pit, the miners disappeared underground with their magazines and packs of cards, until the only digging being done in the region was for the dead of Kramatorsk.

On Tuesday afternoon the two delegates presented themselves at the offices of the Central Committee in Moscow. They received a polite audience, were allocated hotel rooms and asked to wait while the matter was taken up with the relevant authorities. They were not contacted again.

The reaction to the miners' strike varied from place to place, level to level. Some directors and union officials made it clear that they sympathised with the men's action, others tried to ignore it, while others again berated their work forces and tried to persuade the higher authorities of the need for stern countermeasures. But the higher authorities were no less divided. The oblast machine wanted another chance to test its 'principle', the Donetsk-Makeyevka city machine favoured procrastination. Both appealed to the Republican Politburo, which found itself forced to seek guidance from Moscow. In the Kremlin, as the records show, there was one group insisting on a showdown, one warning against a showdown, and one unable to decide. At all levels of the hierarchy the deadlock seemed total. Like a TV set unable to decide on its picture, the Soviet machine needed a sharp, sudden blow to the head.

This 'analysis' seems to have been shared by the oblast KGB, which on Wednesday 16 October proceeded to apply its second, and more realistic, principle — 'a crackdown, once started, is hard to reverse'.

Trudovaja, a suburb of Gorlovka, itself some ten miles north of Makeyevka, had been one of the last mining communities to join the strike in April. The director was reasonably popular and, like most of his managerial team, a local man. The union officials had been more conscientious than most. The miners were certainly unhappy about their pay and conditions, but there was none of the locally-generated bitterness which characterised so many Donbass communities.

The Kramatorsk tragedy was initially seen as that and only that. Those with 'independent' sympathies were told not to try to make political capital out of others' misfortunes. On Monday, Tuesday and Wednesday the Trudovaja pits continued to cough up coal.

By Wednesday, however, sympathies were beginning to shift. There had been no arrests in Trudovaja, but there had been a great number in Gorlovka and the omnipresence of the uniformed militia and their plainclothed brethren was beginning to fray the nerves. At the end of the second shift an impromptu meeting took place in the yard with the arriving third shift and the issues were hotly debated. Opinion was now more evenly divided, some arguing for work as usual, others reminding their co-workers that the 'Makeyevka Agreement' had not been honoured.

This meeting would probably have passed off peaefully enough had not the militia commander decided to break it up. When the miners refused to disperse he ordered the use of tear gas, without first ensuring that the wind was blowing in the required direction. The effect was merely to enrage the miners, who disarmed the outnumbered militia and took their commander 'into custody'. The meeting then continued and it was decided to deliver the commander, in person, to the Hall of Justice in Trudovaja town.

Spirits high, the miners marched into the town, accompanied, quite happily, by many of the disarmed militia. But someone had been busy arranging a reception committee. As they entered the small town square, the miners found themselves confronting a large detachment of KGB troops. For several seconds the two sides stared at each other and then, without any warning, or indeed words of any sort, the troops opened fire. Fifteen miners and six militiamen were killed. Those that could still walk were arrested.

The Politburo which gathered in emergency session on the morning of Thursday 17 October was a dispirited and disunited body of men. The majority for reform had never been large, the majority for crackdown only marginally more substantial. Now there seemed a majority for nothing save inaction. The resurgence of industrial strife as winter grew near, the catastrophic agricultural situation, the deepening hostility of the international environment — all posed questions for which there were no apparent answers.

Of the twelve members who had noted for the crackdown in June, only four — Chernenko, Grishin, Rashidov and Demichev — considered that an intensification of repression would help matters. Of the ten who had voted through the original package of reforms, only four — Andropov, Shcher-bitsky, Solomentsev and Gorbachev — favoured stepping up the pace of change. Romanov and Ustinov were now distancing themselves from both camps, desperately searching for the safety of a middle ground which only existed in their imaginations. Gromyko was showing his age, drawing parallels between past and present which were as irritating as they were inaccurate. The three other members — Aliyev, Tikhonov and Ponomariev — didn't seem to know which way to turn. In this they faithfully reflected the Central Committee as a whole.

Andropov began the session by reading extensive excerpts from a KGB appreciation of the Donbass situation. The local Party and KGB organs were heavily criticised for provoking the trouble. It had 'not yet been ascertained who authorised the action at Trudovaja'. However, it had 'definitely not been authorised by the Collegium in Moscow'.

Whoever had authorised it, the 'action' had provoked 'a serious lack of confidence in the Donbass authorities among the miners'. A situation had been created which was 'potentially more critical than that existing in the spring'. The influence of 'the so-called independent unions' was spreading, despite the 'intensified political and administrative campaign against them'. Only a substantial upturn in the country's economic performance was likely to 'reverse this dangerous trend'. The unknown author concluded his appreciation on a chilling note: 'the capacity of the local organs to deal with the present situation is questionable. If the *status quo ante* is to be restored without recourse to politico-economic methods, preparations should be made for the deployment of regular Army units.'

Andropov invited comments. Grishin considered the report 'prone to understatement'; Chernenko noted, rather unhelpfully, that understatement had become 'a KGB fetish in recent years'.

Demichev, while agreeing with his fellow hardliners, wanted the Donbass situation placed in its 'proper perspective'. Though serious, it was also unrepresentative. Moscow was 'calm', so was Leningrad, Siberia, the Caucasian republics, the Asian republics. If the miners wanted 'conflict', then the miners should have it. 'Whatever measures are necessary for the restoration of order should be taken immediately, regardless of the local consequences.'

Ustinov was not so sanguine. Neither was Romanov, who doubted whether the consequences would be purely local. He favoured a positive approach, a considered approach. 'Almost every act of this ridiculous sequence of events reeks of hysteria.' The accident was mishandled, the strikes were mishandled, Trudovaja was a catastrophe. To send in troops would simply increase the problem.

'Why not send Vladimir Vasilyevich back with another wreath?' Chernenko asked sarcastically.

Shcherbitsky ignored him. 'We cannot sign another "Makeyevka Agreement" when the first one is yet to be implemented.' He had been looking into the matter. 'The safety machinery is provisionally, *provisionally,* allocated for production in the 1986-90 plan. The housing construction funds disappeared somewhere between the oblast and raion levels. The miners are not idiots. They'll want more than promises this time.'

Aliyev thought that Shcherbitsky was proving Demichev's case. If there was nothing to give the miners, then a compromise was impossible. 'We are brought back to the simple choice — order or anarchy? We cannot shirk that choice, no matter how unpleasant it may be. The miners are not the only workers making sacrifices this year. We cannot ensure good weather for the crops, we cannot make the West behave peacefully. It is a bad time for everybody, but we have been through such times before. Even if we had the means to make the miners' lives easier, that would not be fair to other groups. They would demand the same privileges and rightly so. I fail to see what we are arguing about.'

This made Andropov angry. 'Then you must have been asleep for the last year. Let me tell you what will happen if we deploy the Army in the Donbass. The miners will continue their strike, regardless of how many are arrested. The chances of a republicwide, even a countrywide, response are high. The effect on the Party functionaries — I think Mikhail Sergeyevich will confirm this — will be profoundly demoralising. The effect on those used to enforce this version of 'order' should not be underestimated. Study the spring debriefings, Vladimir Ivanovich. We are walking a tightrope.'

'And you have led us onto it, Yuri Vladimirovich,' Chernenko said. 'I suppose now you would advise us to jump off.'

Before Andropov could reply, Gorbachev seized hold of the argument. 'I have been listening to this petty bickering for two hours and time, as we all know, is not limitless. Comrade Andropov wants positive suggestions — very well, I have one. It seems obvious to me that there is much truth in all the arguments put forward; and equally obvious that none of them offers a workable policy. So we should combine them. We agree that concessions to the miners, whether desirable or not, are not practicable. I agree with Comrade Andropov that a massive display of force would be counterproductive. An apparent stalemate. But we must act. If we have nothing to give, then we must 'not give' with the maximum possible effect. We must create a grand gesture, a symbol as powerful as it is, for the moment, empty. I propose a conference, to be held here in Moscow, of workers' delegates from throughout the country. These must be chosen by the workers themselves, without overt interference from the local organs.

'The calling of such a conference would be beneficial for several reasons. It would provide a focus for the workers' discontent. It would give us time. It would pinpoint troublemakers and agitators. Most important, and this is the positive aspect, it would give us the opportunity to regain the workers' confidence. It must not be seen by us, or by the people, as the usual exercise. We should tell them the facts, the real facts. We should explain, patiently, why the economy is performing so abysmally. If the workers' chosen delegates can be brought to believe that there is no escape from a period of hardship, then the sensible ones at least will accept matters. We keep telling the people there is no crisis, when any fool can see that there is. We must admit to it. We must make it clear that the Party is not to blame for it. As Geydar Aliyevich noted, the harvests have been decimated by the weather, not our policies. The West spurns our offers of peace. As it is now, we are blamed for everything, because it is we who admit nothing.

'If this conference fails, as it may well do, if the unrest persists, then we will have to take coercive action. But at least by then we shall be better prepared and there will be many who will have come to see the need for such action. The enforcement agencies will have a clearer sense of purpose. Above all, we shall have regained the initiative.'

There was a lengthy silence around the table as the implications sank in. Where were the hidden snares?

Chernenko didn't like Gorbachev's delegate-selection process; it would 'do untold damage to Party morale'. But even he sounded interested by the idea. Some were later to argue that the hardliners accepted the Conference because its failure would immeasurably strengthen their hand, but Solomentsev saw the situation differently: 'Gorbachev's idea was taken up for one reason and one reason only. It was the only idea we had.'

That evening the Central Committee's 'bold new initiative' was given top billing on the 9 pm (Moscow time) news. The ball of revolution, set in motion by the disaster at Kramatorsk, had been inadvertently speeded on its way.

FRIDAY 18 OCTOBER

Moscow seemed unusually animated that morning. Work attendance, the records show, was the highest for six months. On the trains and buses, in the offices and canteens and queues, people discussed the 'bold new initiative'. What did it all mean? Could it be the break with precedent which they claimed it to be? Or was it just one more Party circus? For the first time since the spring politics seemed a matter worth debating.

Such an unsettling of the normal routine was expected and care had been taken to minimise any unforeseen consequences. The various agencies of order had been instructed to maintain a low profile; it was no good introducing a safety valve if some peasant in a militia uniform took it into his head to stop the steam escaping.

But the trouble, when it came, could hardly have been averted by the most conscientious of policemen. Around eleven that evening a group of teenage boys, rather the worse for drink, started to pester two young girls waiting for a bus in Iljica Square. The girls seemed (to others present) to be coping with the situation, when a vodka troika — three men and a bottle — emerged from the nearby Metro station and decided that the scene was set for knight errantry. A fistfight ensued, during which the girls caught their bus.

The militiamen on duty at the station tried to prise the contestants apart, but one member of the troika proved unwilling to be subdued. When the next crowd of passengers emerged from the Metro doors the first thing that caught their eyes was a young worker lying on the ground, with two militiamen apparently kicking him in the head. One couple, on their way home from the cinema, tried to pull the militiamen off. The latter, now enraged by the difficulties of their calling, turned on the newcomers and the woman, one Natalya Kutakhina, was smashed across the side of the head with a loaded truncheon.

More of the crowd joined in and at this moment, a fresh contingent of militia arrived from the station in Nizhegorodskaya Street. They too released themselves from the tensions of the day by hurling themselves into the fray. The fighting spread up Enthusiasts' Highway, under the Kursk line bridge, fists and staves flying.

Traffic on the Highway was now hopelessly jammed and the long tailback building up on Ulyanovskaya retarded the arrival of militia reinforcements. By this time — a bare twenty minutes had passed since the striking of the first blow — few of those involved had any idea of what had set the whole business in motion. The pent-up frustrations of militia and populace alike were supplying all the momentum that was needed.

At around 11.30 three fire engines from the station on Nizkhegorodskaya managed to reach the Square and hoses were turned on the brawling mass. A more disciplined contingent of militia had now arrived from the Petrovka Street barracks, and this was formed up in lines on the western side of the Square, riot shields and gas masks in readiness. The KGB presence was also becoming noticeable.

The hoses certainly dampened the ardour of the battlers, who slowly coalesced into two groups sullenly watching each other over an area of tarmac studded with prone and groaning bodies. But the crowd showed no inclination to disperse and the tension rose once more when an attempt was made to remove the wounded. The crowd moved forward as if tied together and the order was given to launch the tear gas canisters. This did the trick. As the gas rolled down the Highway the militia advanced, dispersing the crowd with riot staves. By midnight only the forces of order and the ambulances remained.

Three people had died, one of them Natalya Kutakhina, and many required treatment in the hospital on nearby Volgagradski. Forty people had been arrested; they spent the night in the drunks' compound at Petrovka Street. All were released the following morning.

And that, as far as the militia was concerned, was that. Drunken brawls came in many shapes and sizes and, though this had been a large one by Moscow standards, there seemed no reason to believe that it carried any special significance. Three people had lost their lives and doubtless there would have to be some sort of investigation. Friday was always a difficult night.

Police chiefs are not generally noted for their political acumen. Among the high-rise industrial estates of Perovo the 'drunken brawl' was being described as the 'Battle of Iljica Square'. Anger and resentment abounded. Was this what the bosses called a 'bold new initiative'? An olive branch in one hand, a riot stave in the other?

The two dead workers were heroes, Natalya Kutakhina the innocent victim of police brutality. And she was not just any girl. She was well known in the area as a conscientious kindergarten administrator, but her name was better known for the popularity of her father Ivan, a foreman at the Hammer and Sickle Engineering Works on Enthusiasts' Highway. He was something of a local folk hero. Foremen were not usually noted for siding with those working under them, but Kutakhin, a 'Hero of Socialist Labour' from the Khrushchev era, had consistently fought for shop floor rights. Through the negotiations of the previous winter he had proved a thorn in the management's side. Now, it seemed, the authorities had had their revenge; the daughter had paid for the father's temerity.

This battle was far from over.

Iljica Square is some two miles due east of the Kremlin. From the Square, Enthusiasts' Highway runs due east, pointing the way towards Siberia. Once the first stage of journeys undertaken by convicts, pioneers and armies, the Highway now boasts mile upon mile of industrial premises. And behind these, on the southern side, stretches a bewildering jungle of high-rise residential blocks.

October 19 was a designated work day, a 'Red Saturday', and soon the news of the night before was filtering across the shop floors. In the Hammer and Sickle Engineering Works a stoppage was called in mid-morning to discuss the situation. Foremen and union men tried to intervene, but found the men in no mood to listen. The management tried threats, which made matters worse. All figures of 'authority' were ejected from the main machine hall, together with a few known *shpiks,* and the doors locked. The closed-circuit cameras, recently installed as a spur to more glorious victories on the productivity front, were covered over with tarpaulins.

The meeting was long and heated, but by lunchtime the decision had been taken to down tools for the rest of the day. Delegates were dispatched through the maze of back yards to other factories; in many cases they found meetings already under way. Some were discussing the 'battle', others the new piecerates, still others any grievances which had been thrown to the fore by the prevailing atmosphere. By mid-afternoon four miles of factory were overflowing with industrial discontent. There was also a notable buildup of law enforcement vehicles on the highway itself.

At around 4 pm, as the sky began to darken, the Hammer and Sickle workers, some four thousand of them, left their factory and began marching towards the city centre. Other groups joined them, despite the fact that no one seemed to know where the crowd was going. In the end a destination was chosen for it. By the Highway metro station armoured cars had been used to block the way west, and someone, or many someones, shouted out, 'Let's hold a meeting in the Park!'

By 5.30 there must have been over twenty thousand workers gathered around the semicircular lake at the western end of Izmailovski Park. On the Narodnyi Prospekt side of the water an articulated lorry had been brought into use and someone had conjured a megaphone out of thin air. Up and down the road a solid mass of workers prevented the militia from reaching the improvised platform.

But what was to be said? A group of workers, mostly from the Hammer and Sickle, could be seen arguing by the lorry. After a considerable stretch of time and much heckling from the crowd, they all climbed onto the back of the lorry and one took up the megaphone:

'I know that many of the comrades at the back won't be able to hear me, so I ask you that can to pass back whatever seems necessary to know. Unfortunately this meeting lacks official sponsorship [*loud cheers*] and the bosses have neglected to anticipate our need for a good sound system. Like so many other needs they fail to take into account [*more cheers*]. I'm not going to talk for long. We know why we're here. We know what we need. For a start we want our lads released [*they already had been, but for some reason the Hammer and Sickle leaders were still unaware of this*] and we want the buggers who murdered Natalya Mikhailova Kutakhina to be brought to justice. For another thing, we want the norms lowered. But it's no good just wanting things if no one hears a damn thing you say. So first of all, we want to be heard.

'There's a lot of us here, but there's more that isn't. We've decided, if you agree, to hold a real meeting in Pushkin Square tomorrow. What we want is for everyone here to spread the word, tomorrow afternoon at two in Pushkin Square . . . Someone here thinks there should be a show of hands . . . Right, that's what I call a 99.9 per cent majority. So contact everyone you can . . . One more thing — there's a lot of militia about and some of them are probably looking for trouble. Don't give them the excuse. Ah, one last thing — we think the meeting tomorrow should be dry. We're not looking for trouble; we don't want another Nikolayev . . . '

The meeting over, the mood dispersed, the crowd anxiously set off for home. But there was no violence, thanks, it later

126

transpired, to the KGB. Petrovka Street had wanted to make arrests, but Dzerzhinsky Square had vetoed the idea. The militia did, however, take the megaphone into custody.

SUNDAY 20 OCTOBER

The next morning *Pravda* carried a brief and misleading report on the park meeting. 'Workers from several factories on Enthusiasts' Highway,' the paper claimed, had 'gathered spontaneously in Izmailovski Park to discuss the new productivity plans and to suggest ways of improving industrial performance.'

No mention was made of the meeting scheduled for Pushkin Square, but two other pieces had been inserted — at the last minute and in the Moscow edition only — with the coming afternoon in mind. One writer concluded an esoteric article on 'isolated incidences of industrial hooliganism in Magadan' with a plea for responsible behaviour in 'the Soviet work place'. It was of the utmost importance, he claimed, that the forthcoming conference should be approached in a 'positive, Leninist spirit'.

On the practical side, another small notice informed the citizens of the capital that the Novogirejevo-Marksistskaya and Scolkovskaya-Molodoznaya metro lines would be closed 'for essential maintenance work' that day.

The decision to shut down the two metro lines had been taken at an extended Politburo meeting the previous evening. It was a consolation goal for the hardliners, who had demanded nothing less than the prohibition of the projected Pushkin Square rally. To allow it, Aliyev had claimed extravagantly, 'will be to shout our weakness to the sky, to give fresh hope to every enemy of socialism'.

But the majority, albeit with some agonising, had proved able

127

to resist such rhetoric. Some feared the possible consequences of a prohibition: a further deepening of industrial strife, a prejudicing of the conference which now held many of their hopes. Others stressed the need to separate the 'mass of responsible citizens' from the 'small minority of anti-socialist agitators'; banning the meeting, they argued, would produce the opposite effect.

At one point in this rambling, often bitter discussion, Andropov placed the issues in their historical context. In a few crucial sentences he summed up, coherently if inadvertently, the Politburo's dilemma and the inevitability of much that was to follow. 'We have to move forward,' he said. 'We have to widen the area of democracy in the work place — efficient economic administration demands nothing less. At the same time, we have to control that movement politically, to keep it firmly within the bounds of creative Marxism-Leninism. Some individuals will try to exploit this situation for their own political ends. They must be allowed to do so, because they will only isolate themselves. Then they can be dealt with.

'But we cannot, any longer, control matters simply by saying "no" in a loud voice. This is the essence of the matter, and this is what Konstantin Ustinovich will not bring himself to accept. We could maintain such a level of social discipline, of course we could. We could fill Pushkin Square in ten minutes and we could empty it in ten minutes. It is precisely this level of political effectiveness which accounts for our economic difficulties, which hampers our forward movement. I admit to doubts about permitting this meeting; it is a formidable break with precedent, a gamble. But the alternative, Konstantin Ustinovich's way, that is also a gamble, and one that offers no hope for the future at all.'

Despite the closure of the two metro lines, by 2 pm Pushkin Square was overflowing with people. There were hardly any children present — it seemed safer to leave them at home. More surprisingly to many, the militia was also conspicuous by its absence and the famous 'Half Rouble' police station at the bottom of the Square seemed deserted. The only visible sign of

128

authority was a group of men with filming equipment perched high on the roof of the Izvestia building.

The atmosphere, according to one participant, was 'reminiscent of the hour before kick-off at a Dynamo-Spartak derby'. A vast buzz of conversation, the occasional raucous laughter, the shouted greetings, all underlaid by a pervasive tension. No one knew what to expect. Who would speak. What would they say? How far would they go? Were the militia forming up out of sight? No one had seen a single uniform. Or would the bright blue sky suddenly fill with helicopter gunships?

Eventually someone started to speak from the makeshift rostrum atop the Rossiya Cinema steps. The sound equipment let out an agonised series of high frequency moans. Another delay. Then the distant figure began again and suddenly was audible . . .

' . . . this meeting yesterday at the one in Izmailovsky Park. I say we, and I mean that in its real sense. There were no individuals there saying that a meeting had to be held. Everyone voted for it, and I mean everyone. You can see that for yourselves.

'You may be saying to yourselves: "Why's he talking to us? Who is he?" Well, my name's Tolyshkin and I'm talking because somebody has to go first. Anyone who has something to say is welcome to say it; you just have to come up here.

'For those of you who don't know what this is all about, a word of explanation. There's two reasons. First, one of our sister-workers was murdered by the militia on Friday night and we've come to demand some justice. Second, we're at the end of our patience. I know that's easy to say, but there can't be a man here who doesn't know what it's been like these last few months. It just seems to get worse and worse with nobody doing anything about it.

'We're not here to blame people, say it's his fault or theirs. We want to start putting right. No one wants to work harder and harder for less and less, to find that when the bonuses are given out the prices have risen even faster and the queues are longer and then there's nothing worth buying anyway. All of us can see how improvements could be made, but somehow there's always someone with a reason why things should stay as they are.

'There's one important thing to say. To you and those cameras up there, just so as there's no misunderstanding. I'm not, and none of the people I know here are, anti-socialist agitators. We're not dreaming of overthrowing socialism or restoring capitalism or any of that rubbish. I know people who've been to the West and, yes, they're richer than us with their cars and their five rooms for a family. And we'd all like to be richer. But from what I've heard — and I don't mean from our newspapers — the West is not a good place to live. They love their riches so much that they've forgotten to love life. Well, we're Russians and we don't have such distractions. We still love life here, even if the way things work drives us mad. I say this because I see the Western TV cameras here and I know how they'll use their film to insult our country.

'I think we've won a great victory with this meeting. But it's a victory for us, not a defeat for the bosses. They've won a victory too by calling the conference and letting us speak . . . '

Many others did speak and most received tumultuous ovations for saying what the crowd already knew but wanted to hear anyway. Most talked about the situation at their places of work, about corruption and inefficiency and shortages and low wages and how rude the shopgirls were. Some were bluntly critical of the authorities, others more subtle, some naively wondered how such mistakes could be made year after year. Again and again the call went up for the arrest of the militiamen who had killed Natalya Kutakhina.

The anger was real enough, but the occasion itself seemed to blunt the edge of rage. Everyone was too stunned by the fact of the meeting, overwhelmed by their audacity in shouting criticism to the rooftops. People continually glanced up at the cameramen on the Izvestia building, as if to make sure that the authorities still existed, that it wasn't all just a dream. One thoughtful observer later wrote: 'It seemed almost as if the occasion had been arranged as a bizarre tribute to the men who had guided the Soviet Union for so long, who could now afford to sit back and watch their children, the Soviet people, take the first faltering steps towards self-responsibility.'

But at times the sharp edge of rage showed through. One of the last speakers that afternoon, a thin young man with a Ukrainian accent, announced himself as Vladimir Travkin. And if few of the crowd recognised his name, all the men gathered on the Izvestia roof did. They had been looking for him for months. His speech showed why:

'Comrades. Yes, comrades . . . it is good to say the word and mean it. We are all comrades here, except for those up there and those who sit at the other end of the camera cables.

'Comrades, we have heard much about work conditions, about the forthcoming circus organised by the *nachalstvo**, about the tragic death of Natalya Mikhailova. But I do not, in my heart, believe we have approached these matters correctly.

'Natalya Mikhailova's death was no accident. We all know that. But nor should the militiamen who struck the blow take all the blame. We all know where these boys come from. They leave the Army and they're offered this job in Moscow with all its bright lights and they can't resist. Who would go back to the kolkhoz, where there is no future, only Party bigheads ordering you around and doing no work themselves? These boys come here and they know no one except each other and they're fed full of prejudices and given orders which seem to make sense. Who would argue with the preservation of law and order, especially when the alternative is to be sent back to the kolkhoz?

'No, it is not the one who struck the blow who should be strung up, it is the ones who create the situation where such things are bound to happen. I was in Nikolayev in May, at the meeting that morning at the flour-milling combine. Most of you know something of what happened that morning. It was a meeting like this one, even bigger perhaps, and the gunships came, and the troops, and a piece of ground as large as this was drenched in blood. I lost many friends that day, but I don't blame the men in the gunships or the Asian soldiers. They didn't suddenly decide to go out and kill four hundred workers. They were given the choice, the workers or themselves. It's the ones who gave them that choice who deserve our attention.

'This conference of workers' delegates they're calling. We

* The 'bosses'.

should attend it, there's no doubt of that. And we should make sure that it's our people and not theirs who represent us. But don't let's fool ourselves. They don't want to know what we feel or need or want. They know all that — the *shpiks* and gebists haven't been doing nothing all this time. I don't know what it is they want out of this conference, but it sure as hell isn't going to be the same as what we want. And we should remember that.

'One of the comrades said that the authorities had won a victory by letting us meet here. I think he's mistaken. I think they're scared. And they're right to be scared. They know that if they tried to break this up there wouldn't be a single worker at his machine tomorrow.

'Like that comrade, I'm a socialist. And that's what I want, socialism. I've listened to all the demands put this afternoon and I agree with them all, but let's be a little bolder, let's want even more. Let's have all the special shops closed. Why should Soviet goods, made by Soviet workers with Soviet materials, be sold only to those who have non-Soviet currency? Why should some people have access to foreign goods when the rest of us can't even buy Soviet goods? Special shops, special holiday resorts, special hospitals, special schools — what's so damn special about them? Their skill at running the economy?

'I'm not saying that everyone in authority, everyone in the Party, is either corrupt or incompetent. But there's too many who are. And the rest are stuck in the machine. Even when they see what's going wrong they do nothing, because it's easier and safer not to step out of line, and the shops get more special the higher you go. Why bother, that's what they ask themselves. If I don't make this mistake, then someone else will be able to. Nothing's going to change; I'll only be hurting myself. It's a disease, you can see it everywhere, in the factories, the schools, the housing committees. This is not socialism — it's consti-pation. And all the leadership can manage is the odd fart in our direction.

'And what do we do? We must look at ourselves too. We drown the smell in dreams and drink. We dream about the car and the new flat and whether our little girl will be the next Nelli Kim. And we drink. Well, a bottle or two every now and then never hurt anyone, but when I see ten-year-olds drunk on the street when they should be in school then it's different.'

'My time's up. I tell you again, they're scared. They've been running things their way so long that they don't know any other way to do it. And now the country's in real trouble they need *our* help. We mustn't give it to them without getting something in return.'

The speeches came to an end soon after six, but the crowd seemed loth to take the last speaker's advice and disperse. Perhaps it was a reluctance to end such a fine party, perhaps also there was an unwillingness to forsake the safety of numbers. Either way few departed, and spontaneous 'mini-meetings' erupted in various parts of the square. One of these was to prove of more than immediate significance and to end in bloodshed.

A few hundred metres south of the Rossiya Cinema, across Gorky Street, where the southeastern corner of the square gives way to the tree-lined paths which run down the centre of the Tverskoj Boulevard, several hundred people were harangued by a young man standing on one of the drinking fountains. His identity was not vouchsafed, nor ever discovered — fuelling suspicions that he was an *agent provocateur* — but his message was crystal clear. Direct action, and now.

One earlier speaker who had congratulated his audience on their sobriety had obviously not been able to see as far as this corner of the square, or he wouldn't have been quite so pleased. Many of those gathered here had brought a celebratory bottle or three and many were young. By the time the unknown agitator had mounted his marble soapbox, many had been ready for the sort of action he recommended.

Travkin had already, unwittingly, given them a ready target — the special shops. One such was more special than most and famous — if such a word could be applied to something so unmentionable — as any landmark in Moscow. The anonymously named 'Bureau of Passes' on Granovsky Street catered for the biggest of the bigwigs; any day of the week a long line of plush limousines, complete with snoozing chauffeur, could be seen parked outside. 'Let's close this one shop down ourselves,' the man on the fountain suggested, 'and get ourselves some decent food while we're doing it.'

His audience was willing. About four hundred strong, they trekked down Tverskoj and then Gertsena Street, shouting slogans and singing drunken arias. The city seemed denuded of police.

Granovsky Street seemed deserted, the shop apparently unattended. This should have struck someone as strange, but if it did, it wasn't one of those who kicked down the door. The mob poured in behind them, saliva glands working overtime at the thought of French wine, British marmalade and German bockwurst.

Minutes later militia began arriving at both ends of the narrow street.

Several months later, one of the militiamen involved was interviewed by a British journalist:

'We had been on standby at the Petrovka Street barracks all afternoon. Everyone knew that there was a big demonstration in Pushkin Square and we were all dreading being ordered out to disperse it. But as the hours went by we began to breathe a little easier and, I must admit, we broke open a few bottles which the bosses had left us.

'Then, around 6.30, we were ordered to the lorries. We were driven straight down Petrovka, which meant it couldn't be the Square, along Marks Prospekt and into Kalinina. Then we were ordered out. Our officer told us that a crowd of hooligans were smashing up buildings on Granovsky Street — we could guess which one! — and that we were to seal off one end of the street. There wouldn't be any problems, he said, it was just a matter of closing the trap and letting the looters give themselves up.

'Well, this seemed an easy business compared with what we'd been half expecting all afternoon, so spirits were good. We got to the end of the street, formed up and started moving forward slowly. The shop was about two hundred metres down and we could see people pushing through the door like it was time-out at a hockey match and only two minutes to get a piss. Some had seen us and were trying to warn the others. Some ran for it, climbing walls on the other side of the street, hoping, I suppose, to find a way out through the gardens at the back. We weren't expecting a fight.

'Then, out of the blue, things started to rain down on us. At first it was only stones and bottles, but then one of the bottles came lit at one end and we all knew what that was. It wasn't the only one either. A couple of the lads got bad burns and some of us just lost our heads. Maybe it was the booze we'd had, but I think we'd of reacted that way anyway. One guy fired his rifle and the rest of us joined in. Bodies were dropping, and others were sticking their hands in the air. Some of these were shot too.

'Still the Molotovs kept coming — the people throwing them were in one of the yards, out of sight — and then flames started coming out of the building they'd broken into. One of our officers was screaming at us to stop firing; apparently we'd hit one of the men sealing off the other end of the street. A couple of lads were sent forward to lob gas grenades into the yard and soon after that the Molotovs stopped coming. The fight was over.

'The first arrests were being made and from then on there was a long procession of people being loaded into the lorries. Some of them were carrying the most amazing things — stereo equipment and shower units and western computer toys — as if they'd be allowed to keep them! We took note of those who'd been in the yard and a few scores were settled once we had them down at the barracks.'

MONDAY 21 OCTOBER

Confusion was the rule that morning, a confusion which spread outwards from Moscow in the days and hours which followed. The meeting in Pushkin Square might have left a vague sense of euphoria floating in the air, but the violent fracas in Granovsky Street, much exaggerated by rumour, had engendered mixed feelings, simultaneously heightening tension and sobering expectations. And the task facing the industrial workers that morning — electing their delegates, on the usual Trade Union franchise, to the forthcoming conference — was hardly conducive to fostering a renewed sense of normality. In factory after factory chaotic, emotional and, above all, endless meetings were taking place.

The line dividing strikes and occupations from legitimate preparations for the conference was blurred from the outset. At the end of the previous working week more than a few plants, especially in Moscow, had been either strikebound or occupied, with the managements locked out. In only a few instances was work resumed and management readmitted, and in many formerly trouble-free plants the electoral process actually brought work to a halt. Beyond Moscow both workers and authorities seemed uncertain of what was expected of them; in some cases workers seeking to elect delegates were arrested, in others the authorities had to intervene to get the elections held. If the Politburo was expecting its grand gesture to be debated and answered in the workers' tea-breaks it had another think coming.

In this context the intent of Andropov's TV address to the country was presumably two-fold. By firmly stating the Party's position it was hoped to limit the disorder inherent in the delegate-selection process and by stressing the difficulties of the economic situation to limit the expectations inherent in the conference itself. The address was prepared by the Secretariat that afternoon and delivered at 7 pm Moscow time.

'Citizens of the Soviet Union, I address you as General Secretary of the Communist Party, and with the full support of the Soviet Armed Forces.

'Almost five months have passed since the President addressed you in June. At that time a growth of anti-socialist activity within the country created the need for a stricter approach to the maintenance of order and legality. I speak to you now, as much in sorrow as in anger, so that such action may not again prove necessary.

136

'In June the President spoke of a future fit for our children. It was hoped that a more realistic attitude would prevail, that all of us would gain the necessary insight into the effort required to make that future a reality. The majority of Soviet citizens, I am sure, has responded to this challenge in a spirit of selfless determination.

'But, I regret to say, not all. Certain elements in our society, opposed to the socialist policy which guides our development, have refused to accept the necessary limitations laid down by law and have wilfully sought to obstruct the implementation of programmes supported by the vast majority of their fellow citizens. Some of these people are simply trouble-makers, people who delight in obstruction for obstruction's sake, but most, we believe, are victims of misinformation.

'The forthcoming conference of workers' delegates has been called in an attempt to overcome this problem. It is no good to cry for the impossible. Our hopes must be grounded in reality. We must accept the limitations posed by factors which lie beyond our control. The Party cannot command the weather to favour our harvests. It cannot divert much-needed resources away from military programmes so long as the imperialists reject our proposals for world peace and disarmament. The conference of workers' delegates will be invited to discuss the way forward for our economy and will be given all the information it requires for this task. In such a way we can move forward, improving our economic situation and broadening the scope of our socialist democracy.

'Certainly no one is being helped by the wave of industrial stoppages now afflicting a few parts of the country. Every hour spent idle is an hour spent weakening our economy, an hour spent damaging the prospects for our children's future.

'On Sunday last the workers of Moscow held a rally in Pushkin Square and many speeches were given. Confidence was expressed in the forthcoming conference and constructive criticism offered. We welcomed this frank airing of views.

'But, it must be said, a small minority of speakers refused to stay within the bounds of socialist legality. Their speeches contained no positive elements, no criticism of a constructive nature; their aim was purely and simply to incite their fellow workers. As a direct result of this irresponsibility, a mob of hooligans broke into a building and destroyed a large amount of state property.

'The guilty men have, of course, been arrested and will be duly tried. Violence of this nature cannot and will not be condoned. Our streets must remain safe for all who use them and we intend to ensure that they are. Any who think differently will be swiftly dissuaded.

'I lay these facts before you because some confusion seems to have arisen as to the events in question. Some unprincipled elements have attempted to make "heroes" out of the criminals concerned, to draw spurious connections between their detaining and the opinions expressed in Pushkin Square. Nothing could be further from the truth. As I have told you, we welcome positive suggestions for the improvement of economic performance and are holding the conference of workers' delegates with just such a purpose in mind.

'I appeal to those workers who are now refusing to work: elect your delegates, pass on your grievances, your suggestions, and let them take up the matter. Resume your work, while we meet with them. Idleness produces nothing, except, that is, for greater difficulties, more shortages. I appeal to you all, let us move forward together.'

American journalist Bill Olwen watched Andropov's TV speech in the manager's office at the Hammer and Sickle, along with a large contingent of the factory's work force.

'. . . Since this was the factory where the trouble had started, I thought that the men's reaction to the speech might offer some clues as to future developments.

'They listened intently and were obviously genuinely interested in what Andropov had to say. And though the assertion that the authorities had "welcomed" the "frank airing of views" was greeted with a ripple of knowing laughter, the Secretary's evocation of "violence" on "our streets" seemed to strike a real chord.

'The moment the speech ended the respectful silence evaporated, leaving a room full of impassioned arguments.

Vladimir Travkin, who had given the most inflammatory speech in Pushkin Square, was apparently both hero and villain. "He asked for it," one man said in reference to his arrest. "He told the truth," said another. "And twenty people died because of it," the first replied, "because of his egotism."

Others were considering Andropov's appeal for a return to work. Some were adamant about continuing the strike until their "demands" had been met. Others argued that "we can always come out again if the conference is a con". The debates were still going strong when I left at midnight.'

The world was full of meetings that day. Across the Soviet Union industrial work places were at a standstill, the month's plan targets shoved rudely aside. Instead workers argued with workers, with managers, with union officials. Party members disputed with each other. The law enforcement agencies counted their ammunition and, in some cases, began to ponder their loyalties.

At the centres of the storm, in the buildings on Dzerzhinsky Square, Frunze Street and within the Kremlin, officials calculated political odds, drew up and tore up contingency plans. In the universities debates were held, forbidden, allowed, scheduled. The only element of continuity was the rudeness of the shop assistants.

The meeting in Pushkin Square had been widely reported. On Sunday night Western TV screens had shown highlights and through Monday Western experts pontificated on the meaning of it all. Was the monolith wobbling in the wind? Was the mighty Soviet Union, whose existence and purpose had dominated the century for friend and foe alike, on the verge of a cataclysm? And if so, who would pick up the pieces? Or had the Pushkin Square demonstration been nothing more than a KGB straw dog, a publicity stunt, a brief storm before the iron calm.

For the governments of the developed West the problems of the East offered a welcome diversion. October had been a bad month for everyone but Italian politicians, who had finally managed to form a government. In the United States a Republican Presidency and a Democrat Congress were still deadlocked on all issues of substance. The riots of the summer had died away in blood and gas, but the root causes remained and no one had a coherent policy for extracting them. Only the Federal Reserve Board, acting in defiance of President and Congress alike, seemed to have a coherent policy of any kind. And, from all points of view but that of the transnational corporations, it was the wrong one.

Western Europe was still bumping along the economic floor. In Britain the politicians were still talking about freedom, the unions about free collective bargaining. The Employment Minister, Mrs Shirley Williams, had just resigned over new government plans for curbing the unions. Unemployment was approaching five million and hardly a week seemed to pass without some city centre erupting into flames.

In the former powerhouses of the Western economy, West Germany and Japan, the situation was little better; in both countries strong environmentalist and anti-nuclear groups had joined the opposition Social Democrat parties in campaigns which verged on civil disobedience. Neither country had seen such levels of unemployment since the thirties.

The governments of all these countries welcomed the news from Pushkin Square with unalloyed enthusiasm, but other highly-placed 'interest groups' were far from pleased. In international financial circles the talk was all of crisis and possible calamity. What if the Kremlin went down? Then the East European régimes would drop like cards, dragging their debts and the viability of many major Western banks with them.

Nor were the political implications purely favourable. It was Travkin's speech, of course, which received most of the attention, with its passionate denunciation of corruption and evil. The more low-key speeches, which stressed the commitment to the socialist system, were mostly ignored by Western commentators. But not all. As one expert noted on Radio 4's *World at One,* 'the system of public ownership in the Soviet Union is now more than half a century old and there are no indications that a majority, or even a large minority, of the population wants to see a return to a system based on private property. Whatever emerges from the present crisis — if that is

140

what it is — is unlikely to be a system sympathetic to our own. It is even possible that a new, democratic form of Soviet socialism could pose a greater threat to the *status quo* in the West . . . It must be borne in mind that the Soviet Union, over the last few decades, has acted largely as a force for stability, at least in so far as the developed West is concerned. If I may use a phrase that has become somewhat devalued over recent years, we may here be witnessing the breaking of the mould of international politics. The possibilities are enormous.'

TUESDAY 22 OCTOBER

Breaking the mould, breaking heads — something seemed bound to be broken. It was on the Monday and Tuesday of this anarchic week that the first 'personalities' of the upsurge shuffled onto the historical stage. The Politburo had, in effect, asked the workers to elect their leaders and in many cases this meant finding replacements for the spokesmen 'lost' during the spring crackdown. There seemed no shortage of candidates.

To have spoken in Pushkin Square was in itself a claim to 'leadership' of some sort. Those who had mounted the Rossiya rostrum had put themselves at risk and were, in the main, respected for doing so. Some were considered a little too young, a little too hotheaded for their own and everyone else's good; they tended to receive less support than members of the preceding generation, men and women in the late twenties to early forties bracket who had worked for a long period at the same plant or factory.

Some of these 'belonged' to one of the 'independent' networks and most of them, at least in Moscow and Ukraine, had absorbed the spirit of free trade unionism. But there was no 'independent' takeover of the upsurge. For one thing the situation was far too chaotic, for another the 'independents' had, in many areas, paid dearly for their temerity in the spring and the slow business of reestablishing links was still far from completion. The Moscow SMOT network had been hit particularly hard by the KGB in June and its members tended to act more as individuals than as a coherent unit during this week.

One of these members, Vladimir Nikitenko, was to emerge as one of the revolution's most prominent figures. Older than most of his fellow leaders, Nikitenko had been a fulltime member of the Party since 1956, working at the Moskabel factory in Kuncevo. Unlike most Party members he preferred life on the shop floor to life and privileges on the Party's promotion ladder; *his* growing cynicism had not been neutralised by regular visits to the special shops.

He had joined SMOT in 1984; both politically and personally the time seemed right. His long-waning faith in the system's workability had been finally destroyed by the authorities' actions during the autumn 1983 'norm war'. His wife had died in 1982, his children had now left home — there was only himself to think about. Still, Nikitenko was (and is) a cautious man by nature and he had no intention of martyring himself to no effective purpose. He kept his Party card, but began to recruit for SMOT among his long-term colleagues at the Moskabel. By the time of NEP 2's introduction he had a solid caucus of members within the giant factory and a growing network of activists and sympathisers in the Kuncevo district.

During the winter of 1984–85 he urged caution, believing that the reform programme should be given its chance to effect a fundamental shift in worker-management relations. When he realised, at some point early in the spring, that this shift was accelerating out of the authorities' control, he feared the worst. The events in the Dnieper bend towns and Nikolayev provided dismal confirmation.

Now matters were coming to a head once more and this time, Nikitenko thought, it might be different. 'Repression had obviously failed to provide an answer,' he said later. 'The economy was still sinking. It seemed to me that the authorities would have to take greater risks, in either the negative or the positive sense. And we were in a strong position to influence their choice.'

Nikolai Zakharov worked on the other side of Moscow, in Perovo's Vladimir Ilych Engineering Combine. Like Travkin in

142

Nikolayev, he had recently seen service in Afghanistan and been profoundly disenchanted by the experience. His parents were both members of the artistic intelligentsia, his mother a well-known children's writer, his father a film editor at Mosfilm, but Nikolai, on returning from active duty, decided to forego the privileges which beckoned one of such birth and to use instead the engineering skills he had acquired in the Kabul tank-repair shops.

This disdain for the good life was initially distrusted by his fellow-workers at the Vladimir Ilych, but Zakharov had a winning sense of humour, a lot of interesting things to say and, most important, an ability to use his head and feet which soon made him the star of the works football team. At this time he had no 'considered political opinions, only a sense that something, somewhere, was very wrong'.

The winter struggle and spring debacle hardened his attitude, honed his opinions and increased his sense of realism. Nikolayev was full of dead heroes. He eventually joined the much-weakened Perovo section of SMOT and soon developed into one of its most conscientious members. It had been his fiery certainty and persistence which, more than any other single factor, had got the Vladimir Ilych workers out of the combine and onto Enthusiasts' Highway. It had been his idea to call the rally in Pushkin Square.

Mariya Shestakova was an etcher at the new 75th Anniversary factory in the northwestern suburb of Chovrino. A long-standing Party member, she had been expelled in 1976 for talking to Western journalists about the psychiatric hospitalisation of her husband Pyotr. He had been one of the earliest members of Khlebanov's FTUA and had been categorised as schizophrenic for his pains. She had not joined the union, the couple agreeing that one of them should remain at liberty to care for their three children, but she did wholeheartedly share in its aims and beliefs. When the renewal programme was put into effect in the autumn of 1984 she became one of those most vociferously opposed to the new schedules.

In June she expected to be arrested, but the authorities, keenly aware of the West's interest in her still-interned husband, decided to gamble on leaving her free. They were already beginning to regret it. When the call went out for the rally in Pushkin Square, Shestakova was one of those most responsible for mobilising the workers of the Chovrino district.

Of her many attributes as a political organiser, not the least, in such a sex-conscious society as the Russian, was a striking beauty. Born in Alma Ata in 1949, the only child of a Russian father and Kirghiz mother, she seemed to combine the most graceful features of each race. Not surprisingly the Western TV coverage of the rally seemed equally divided between the rage of Travkin's words and the elfin intensity of 'la belle Mariya'.

Nikitenko, Zakharov and Shestakova were only three of a dozen or so leaders who sprang into prominence during these days. Since most of them had never met any of the others, much of their time was clearly going to be spent in coordinating action. All were highly conscious of the need for unity, of their vulnerability as individuals. But this was not the greatest fear. As Nikitenko said much later: 'What we feared, all through that first week, was that the authorities would somehow find an Aladdin's lamp, would conjure up an illusion so stunning as to be believable. We did not fear force, or arrest for ourselves; we knew that such actions would only increase the workers' determination. What we really feared, foolishly I suppose, was an answer to our questions which left the system intact.'

The need for unity was given expression by the creation of the Moscow Workers' Coordinating Committee. The idea was first discussed 'backstage' in Pushkin Square, but the conclusions reached on the Rossiya steps were given organisational form at a clandestine meeting in the Kutuzovskaya locomotive depot on Monday evening. Only one motion was passed — no plant or district would enter separate negotiations with the authorities. Those districts not represented at this meeting were to be asked to send delegates to the next, which would begin the coordination of the Moscow workers' programme for the forth-coming conference. In the meantime all available channels of communication with workers beyond Moscow should be utilised to the fullest — there was no telling how long the telephones and post would be allowed to operate should the situation deteriorate. A wall newspaper campaign was decided on, to be carried out as each district saw fit. The public transport delegates were asked not to take industrial action whatever the provocation — the workers' mobility depended on it.

Tuesday morning, Moscow woke up to a rare sight. Or a succession of rare sights. Graffiti, the art form of the decadent West, had finally reached the decadent East.

Across the plinth supporting Kutuzov's statue, on the Prospekt which bears his name, someone had scrawled LENIN WAS ONLY A MAN.

On the Stankevich Street side of the Moscow Soviet building another budding artist had written, rather more ominously, IF WE DON'T LOOK AFTER THE PARTY, THE PARTY WILL LOOK AFTER US.

On the path leading down to the Lenin Hills metro station, suitably in sight of the Lenin Stadium, the slogan SPORT IS THE OPIUM OF THE PEOPLE had appeared.

The Lenin theme was certainly the favourite; someone had painted LENIN MADE MISTAKES on nearly every metro platform from Marks Prospekt to Vernadskogo Prospekt. As if to emphasise the point, at the University stop someone had added EVERY FEW MINUTES.

Most blasphemously, however, the word NIKOLAYEV now lengthened the list of hero-cities by the side of the unknown soldier's flame.

The wave of industrial inaction sweeping through Moscow could not be accurately described as a wave of strikes. The workers were not sitting round at home or standing on picket lines waiting for their demands to be met; they were attending their work places with the object of formulating those demands. It was as if a thousand huge seminars had been arranged, and they took place in storerooms and yards and machineshops and paintshops across the city.

The notion of a 'wave' was also misleading, in that it implied simultaneity on a grand scale. In reality the seminar's progress was remarkably uneven; some factories were still working on Wednesday when others had already set up new organisations

145

and chosen their delegates to the new coordinating bodies. A few factories even continued 'storming' the monthly plan until their supply of inputs dried up.

The business of coordinating all this activity proceeded slowly. On the Monday the 'independents' and the most precocious factories were electing committees and councils (*soviets*), and these in turn helped to set in motion similar electoral processes at the factory, district and, finally, citywide levels.

Meantime there was talk. And talk, and more talk, as if all the years of not talking had to be made good in a week. In the first few days the purely economic issues were the main topics of discussion — complaints about the norm system, about bad and inefficient and corrupt management, 'Black Saturday' working, the lack of safety measures, the lack of housing, the lack of things to buy. But as these were discussed and as possible alternatives were suggested, the talk inevitably became more political. In the Soviet Union, as elsewhere, it was impossible to separate the two.

No one knew this better than those occupying positions of authority in the work places concerned. Here again, the reaction varied widely from plant to plant. The Party and official union members were accustomed to siding with the management, but as the week progressed many began to sense a fundamental shift in the wind and acted accordingly. There were also, of course, many such members who welcomed this shift wholeheartedly, who were just as ready to 'talk' as their erstwhile flocks. The managers fared less well overall, many being simply 'dismissed', thrown out or locked out, their offices given over to elected committees hammering out lists of demands.

The wide range of attitudes thrown into this industrial melting pot was well-illustrated by a piece written for the *Los Angeles Times* by their Soviet bureau chief, Bill Warner. On the Tuesday he had been invited to attend the Sverdlov Engineering Works 'in session':

'The reaction to our arrival was less than welcoming. When we showed our American press credentials to the workers manning the gate several of those present refused to believe that we had been invited. ''We don't want the capitalist press writing

146

lies about us,'' seemed to sum up the general feeling and it was only when our invitation was confirmed by those inside that we were allowed through the gate.

'It was not yet 9 am, but the ''session'' was already in full swing. It was taking place in a large, rather dark canteen, with the work force seated on chairs, tables, windowsills and the floor. One woman explained that the subject under discussion was the piecerate system, but as far as I could tell each speaker was treating the theme somewhat elastically. And usually disagreeing with his or her predecessor. I had, naively perhaps, expected a mirror-image of the authorities: workers united, a proletarian solidarity. I could not have been more wrong. The range of opinions being expressed would have made the staunchest democrat scream with frustration. I even found myself coming close to sympathising with the men in the Kremlin who had to forge some sort of order out of this unutterable chaos.

'One speaker started off talking about the piecerate system and then abruptly veered off into a heartfelt denunciation of the intelligentsia, the ''parasites who swim in our sweat''. I had always doubted the official tale of ''unpopular dissidents'', but here was a Soviet worker, apparently labouring under the delusion that Sakharov was Jewish, vigorously prepared to confirm at least one article of the Kremlin's faith. The dissidents were ''traitors'', pure and simple.

'This worker received a large round of applause from at least half his audience. So did another man who spoke at some length, and with nostalgic warmth, of the late lamented Comrade Stalin. I knew such feelings were widespread, but it was still discomforting to hear them expressed. Other speakers touched on the same general themes; they wanted strong government, someone to put the parasites in their place, to give the young hooligans a good kick up the backside, to stop the corruption, to get the country moving again.

' ''Corruption'' was definitely the prime target, though no one actually mentioned the Party élite in this context. It was the managers who received most of the abuse. ''Some of them,'' one speaker said, ''have cars and seven-room dachas, eat caviar and drink the best vodka, live off the fat of the land.'' But it wasn't only them. "You earn your bread honestly and you don't have a kopek to spare. And then you see another worker, at the same factory, doing much the same job, he suddenly arrives in a car. How did he afford it? You know the answer to that as well as I do. He sold someone or something to the bosses."

'A few approached the matter more analytically. "Corruption?" one woman said, "of course there's corruption. There always will be with the system we have. When there's not enough goods to go round then money means nothing — it all depends on who you know, on getting things *na levo.* * We have to produce more and that means running things more efficiently, which means running them ourselves. I'm not saying we should cut all the bosses' throats — someone has to sit up there and run the country. But this factory, that's different, no could run this factory better than us."

'On the same lines another speaker — who I later learned was Nikitenko — was more philosophical. "There's a lot of people out there, and quite a few in here as well, who carry Party cards. Most of them started off as I did, believing in socialism, believing that we were building communism here. And, like me, most of them found out it wasn't happening. Each year we were a little better off and each year they were a lot better off. The ones who live well out there, they're not communists, no matter what they say. They're only interested in themselves; so long as they're all right, the hell with you and me. They might as well be capitalists, for all the difference it makes.

' "But it's not everyone in the Party lives like that. I've never lived like that and I've been in the Party for twenty-five years. Yes, the bosses should get a little of their own medicine. Yes, we could run this factory a hundred times better than some Party creep from the management school. But it's not as simple as that. We've got to think about the whole system. At the moment we know what we don't want, but we don't seem to have a clear idea of what we do want. The bosses have been saying nothing but 'no' as long as we can remember; we've got to find a 'yes' somewhere."

* Literally 'on the left', colloquially 'through unofficial/illegal channels'.

148

'He got a huge ovation for this, not so much because every-one agreed with him — judging from the interruptions there was abundant scepticism attached to the Party and all its works — but because of his obvious enthusiasm and sincerity. There was a confidence in the way he spoke which brought out the uncer-tainty in the words of most others.

'The speeches went on. And on. No one seemed to tire of them, even though many simply regurgitated what had already been said. There was no stopping for lunch; people either disappeared or pulled hunks of bread out of their pockets. All afternoon it went on, until around five a list of specific proposals was voted on. These would be taken to the district level by the elected delegates, and after eight hours of political debate it was surprising to find that all the demands voted through were concerned with the day-to-day running of the factory. Its workers wanted their dismissal of the director ratified and the appointment of the new director subject to their approval after a three month probationary period. They wanted a move from piecerates to hourly rates for everyone, with bonuses for overfulfilment of realistic plan targets. If new machinery was introduced they wanted an automatic bonus for the transitional period. They wanted new trade union elections, an official five day week with double pay for voluntary Saturday working. There should be regular consultations between the director, the unions and the work force. And they wanted new toilets and a new canteen. The plan for the current month was officially declared abandoned and a holiday period proclaimed, during which discussions could take place for improving the running of the works.

'What most astonished me was the general feeling that these demands would be met. As one worker said: ''They've made a mess of things and they won't be sorry if we can sort it all out.'' At that stage, I must admit, I thought he was talking through his fur hat.'

Such scenes were repeated in factory after factory, from Kalinigrad to Magadan. Perhaps their greatest significance lay in a single fact. The young Hungarian dissident Miklos Haraszti had written, a decade earlier, that his co-workers were forever using the pronoun 'them' and knowing exactly what they meant by it, but never 'either by chance, or by slip of the tongue' did they use the 'us' which formed 'the counter-balance to it'. In the Soviet Union that 'us' was now being discovered.

WEDNESDAY 23 OCTOBER

The first, and arguably the most important, of the official meetings held that day, took place in Vitaly Fedorchuk's sumptuous third-floor office overlooking Dzerzhinsky Square. No minutes were taken, but Pavl Mazyakin, one of the few surviving participants, included an account of the meeting in his book *Divided Loyalties: The KGB in 1985*. Mazyakin's objectivity is somewhat suspect, but his account has been partly substantiated by others who were present.

'I arrived at the chief's office just before nine. Obviously I was aware of the reasons for this crisis gathering, but at the same time I had little idea of what to expect. The whole building was buzzing with rumours, most of which turned out to be untrue. Between the gate and the third floor I heard that the chief was resigning, that Warsaw was in flames, that the Army was taking over, that the Americans were poised to invade Cuba. It was incredible, the events of the past week seemed to have temporarily unhinged the whole organisation.

'Inside Fedorchuk's office the atmosphere was more restrained, if equally tense. There were nine persons present, including myself and the chief. They, and their positions of responsibility were as follows:

Yuri Andropov, who was still, to most intents and purposes, the real head of the Committee. Fedorchuk's office was still referred to as "Yuri Vladimirovich's office";

Vladimir Leonov was my nominal boss, the head of the First Chief Directorate;

150

Aleksandr Lobachev headed the Second Chief Directorate, dealing with most aspects of internal state security. Two of his Directorate heads, *Vlienin Panov* (Industrial Security) and *Stepan Malakhov* (Political Security), were also present;

Anatoly Shareyev was head of the 5th Chief Directorate, which dealt with certain specific aspects of internal security, most notably intelligentsia dissidence, students, religious fanatics and nationalists;

Sergei Darensky headed the Armed Services Directorate (sometimes called the Third Directorate), which was responsible for security within the Armed Forces.

'Fedorchuk opened the proceedings by summarising the events of the previous twenty-four hours. There had only been a few substantive breaches of public order, and none whatsoever in Moscow and Leningrad. This was the good news. On the industrial front the situation was, if anything, worsening. The response to Secretary Romanov's appeal for a return to work had been overwhelmingly negative; the strikes seemed to be spreading rather than stopping. And there were "unmistakable indications" that new organisational structures were being created in the most disaffected areas, beyond Party or trade union control.

'Fedorchuk delivered this report in his usual diffident tone — he might have been reading a railway timetable. He then asked Panov for the sector reports. Apparently the "first tier" production centres — those dealing with particularly sensitive materials and goods — were mostly unaffected. There was no sign of serious trouble on the railways.

'Malakhov delivered his report. The nationalist element in the present troubles was, with the exception of Central Asia, relatively insignificant. In Ukraine only a few extremist groups were trying to exploit the industrial situation for nationalist ends. The student population was mostly quiescent, again with the exception of Central Asia. The "dissidents" — he used the English word — were simply stunned by what was happening. "They talk and talk, but they represent no threat at present."

'Andropov asked him to judge the effect of releasing "the majority of our Article 70 detainees". Malakhov thought it would be "minimal in the short term". It would be "years" before "our dissidents" found "KOR-type roles". They didn't like "getting their hands dirty".

'Andropov nodded and wrote something down.

'I gave my report on the situation in the fraternal states, which basically consisted of thumbs-down for Romania, Poland and Czechoslovakia, thumbs-up for East Germany and Bulgaria, and thumbs at half-mast for Hungary. Leonov backed me up.

'Then the bombshell was dropped. Darensky had a list — "incomplete, and possibly not wholly accurate" — of high-ranking members of the Armed Forces who were actively considering a coup. They had "substantial support" on the Central Committee. However, planning was not advanced; most of those involved still believed that the Politburo could be pressured into a change of course. There was no immediate — meaning hours, not days — danger.

'Suddenly Andropov's presence at this meeting was explained. He neither looked nor sounded depressed by this information. "Comrades," he said, "this is the opportunity we have been waiting for. If we proceed carefully, Party opposition to the renewal programme can be reduced to insignificance."

'We went on to discuss the correct procedure.'

Many of the men on Darensky's list were at that moment gathered, for purely legitimate purposes, in one of the Defence Ministry's conference rooms. This meeting of the General Staff had been convened at very short notice — representatives from all sixteen internal military districts had been flown to Moscow overnight — to review contingency plans for dealing with large-scale civil disturbances. Tempers had not been sweetened by lack of sleep, and Ustinov's hectoring tone was no more appreciated than usual. Many high-ranking Army officers still considered him an upstart, foisted upon them by the Party bureaucrats.

That morning, however, more than Ustinov was needed to

close military ranks: the 'real' military had differences of its own. Many of the generals present contented themselves with a recitation of their difficulties, ranging from supply problems through obdurate local authorities to low morale, but some of their colleagues were unwilling to take such a narrowly professional view of current affairs.

The strongest emotion on show was not anxiety but distrust. Of the Party leadership, of the existing policies, of the 'unnecessary' conference. Where was it all leading? — that was the central question, never put directly, but alluded to in a number of ways. When was order to be restored? When would normal service be resumed? The Chief of Staff, General Olgarkov, poured scorn on 'the minor problems' most present seemed to be experiencing; the situation was now 'critical', and 'only the Armed Forces' could 'still be relied upon for the maintenance of order'.

This prompted General Mikhailov to ask whether Olgarkov was suggesting that 'the Armed Forces should usurp the function of the Party?' The Chief of Staff denied it; he was 'merely stating what appears to be a fact'. Mikhailov thought it 'a fact with rather dangerous implications'.

All of this seems to have passed right over Ustinov's head, but according to Mikhailov none of it was lost on the others present. 'Loyalties were going to be severely tested in the coming weeks. I had served as a military attaché in several African and Latin American countries and the atmosphere at this meeting was a familiar one. Ripening coups smell the same the world over.'

The Politburo session that afternoon was uneventful. The arguments continued, but in a distinctly desultory fashion; neither side had anything new to say and there were no reports of fresh trouble to stimulate the existing discord. Ustinov reported on his morning meeting with the generals, but despite persistent prodding by Chernenko, refused to admit that the General Staff had expressed serious anxiety about the current situation. Andropov said nothing.

After the East European developments had been considered

in some depth the session was adjourned. Solomentsev noted that his colleagues 'seemed both willing to wait on events, in effect to have decisions taken for them, and somewhat bewildered by this willingness. Tiredness had much to do with it. Holding one's breath for days on end tends to be debilitating.'

THURSDAY 24 OCTOBER

After a series of chill, cloudy autumn days, Thursday in Moscow offered bright sunshine and an abrupt rise in the temperature. An observer watching the white-collar workers pouring into the city centre that morning could have been forgiven for thinking that Soviet life went on as usual, that the events of the previous week had been no more than a disturbing dream.

The reports reaching the leadership were more substantive. Throughout the country further strikes and occupations were taking place, though instances of violence remained rare. One particularly serious incident had occurred in the Tadzhik capital Dushanbe, but news of this and the subsequent fighting would only emerge slowly in the days to come.

In Moscow it was a day for taking stock. The first stage, the fundamental shift of expectations engendered by the Pushkin Square rally, was now drawing to a close. The implications were sinking in, giving both workers and Politburo members pause for considerable thought. The latter's session that afternoon was the shortest and most relaxed of the week; most of it was given over to discussing a new report on the ecological implications of the Siberian river-reversal scheme. The new Moscow Workers' Coordinating Committee, which included the majority of Moscow's conference delegates, held its first full meeting at the Likhachev Auto Plant, but this proved a low key affair, overly concerned with its own credentials and the rules of formal debate. One Western correspondent who attended the meeting gloomily opined that 'the revolution is already digging its own bureaucracy'.

Outside the Soviet Union matters were proceeding at a greater pace, with fresh signs of serious discord in three of the Warsaw Pact countries. Prague was treated to a huge, silent demonstration, organised by the city's students in support of the Soviet workers. The authorities took no action and the evening passed off peacefully, but the number of people involved, few of whom were actually students, must have sent shivers down a few fraternal spines.

In Poland familiar scenes were being reenacted, with Silesian miners striking for higher pay and a near riot in Szczecin, but in Romania such activities were still dangerously novel. On this evening a full-scale riot took place in the oil city of Ploesti and in the ensuing armed confrontation some forty people were killed. This was to mark the beginning of a long week for the Ceaucescu family, whose tribulations and fall were to pass almost unnoticed in the shadow of Soviet events.

Thursday also bore witness to one of the revolution's more bizarre phenomena. At 11 am the previous morning *Pravda*'s editorial board had approved the Thursday edition and began work on Fridays's. On page four of the approved paper there was a full-page article on economic developments served by the newly opened Amur-Baikal railway, complete with map and photographs of the local Party fauna. So far, so predictable.

But when the paper appeared throughout the Soviet Union on the Thursday morning, this article had been replaced by another. Titled, innocently enough, 'Lenin and Working Class Democracy', the new article took a fresh and rather controversial look at some of Lenin's less publicised views. The following quotations were placed prominently in boxes:

> Is there any way other than practice by which the people can learn to govern themselves and to avoid mistakes? Is there any way other than by proceeding immediately to genuine self-government by the people?

All the revolutions which have occurred up to now perfected the state machine, whereas it must be broken, smashed . . .

We ourselves, the workers will organise large-scale production . . . relying on our own experience as workers . . . We will reduce the role of the state officials to simply that of carrying out our instructions as responsible, revocable, modestly paid 'foremen and bookkeepers' . . .

To develop democracy to the utmost, to seek out the forms for this development, to test them in practice and so forth — all this is one of the eonstituent tasks of the struggle for social revolution.

The author of this article was never discovered, leading many to believe that it originated high in official circles. The method and timing of the substitution also remained a mystery; only the ease with which the article had passed through the various checking procedures was instantly explicable — all concerned had assumed that Lenin equalled orthodox.

The effect of the article was easier to gauge. Most people, expecting the usual ideological porridge, ignored it at first, but the word soon spread. Since the idea that *Pravda* could be tampered with was unthinkable, many assumed that a major shift in Party policy was being, albeit circuitously, announced. The only real mysteries were the map and the Siberian photos.

Similar misconceptions were rife among the Central Committee's hardliners, who instantly recognised the article as a deliberate provocation by the reformists. The latter, meanwhile, had decided that the hardliners had manufactured a fictional 'reformist provocation' for their own ends. For a couple of hours Moscow resounded to the gnashing of Party teeth.

By mid-morning, however, such fears had been proved groundless and a major investigation was under way to trace the article's source. Simultaneously, a meeting was called to decide on corrective action. It was hardly practicable to recall eleven million copies, yet the article could neither be denounced as a forgery without admitting the enormity of the hoax, nor revoked without impugning of the purity of the Leninist gospel. It was eventually decided to run a second part on the following day, replete with 'corrective' quotes, to effect a dilution of the original message.

This second piece, reportedly penned by Ponomariev in twenty minutes, was reasonably successful in ideological sleight-of-hand terms, but in one sense the damage had already been done. Denying raised hopes could not restore the emotional *status quo ante* and in the days to come many of the 'new' Lenin quotes would stick in many a mind.

FRIDAY 25 OCTOBER

At 4.45 pm a train from Astrakhan pulled in to the Kazan Station on Moscow's Konsomol Square. Among the alighting passengers were the two conference delegates chosen by the Saratov city workers, Valentina Kosterina and Ivan Polyansky. They had reservations at the huge Rossiya Hotel, situated on the river a long stone's thrown from the Kremlin.

Neither of the pair had ever visited Moscow before and after registering at the hotel they took the obligatory stroll around Red Square. They watched the 7 pm changing of the guard outside Lenin's tomb and were suitably impressed. The huge red stars hung in the sky. The walls of the Kremlin might be intimidating, but the majesty of the square was reason for national pride.

They walked down to the river and along the Moscow Quay, searching for a way back up to the hotel. When they eventually found one the hotel was behind them and they found themselves approaching it from the southeast. From such apparently insignificant sparks are the flames of revolution kindled.

On that corner of the Rossiya stood one of the city's largest *beriozka* shops, intended only for those fortunate, foreign or criminal enough to possess hard currency. Polyansky had promised his family souvenirs. Why not buy them now — there might not be time later?

They walked in and were immediately amazed by the selection and quality of the goods available. The shop was soon to be closed for the day, the two had their best clothes on and no one took any notice of them. Since the prices were all marked in roubles they had no reason to think their custom might be unwelcome. Polyansky quickly decided on a set of matryoshka dolls for his daughter and a silk scarf for his wife. Kosterina settled for some perfume. They approached the till.

The saleslady finally deigned to look at Polyansky. 'You have foreign currency?' she enquired sarcastically. 'No, I pay in roubles,' he replied innocently. The saleslady smirked. 'Then you have no business here. You must put these things back.'

At this point the strain of the long journey from Saratov seems to have gotten the better of Polyansky. 'Whose country is this?' he shouted, his face red with anger. He held up a ten rouble note with its portrait of Lenin. 'Whose picture is this? Is this money or isn't it? It's what we work for, isn't it? I'm taking these goods and paying with this money.' He slammed the note down, grabbed the scarf and dolls and started for the exit.

The commissionaire was in his way, telling him to take the goods back. Polyansky tried to push him aside with an elbow and a few carefully chosen oaths.

Another voice appeared behind him. 'Citizen, you will accompany me please.' He flashed a card in front of Polyansky's face.

The latter lost his patience, lashing out at both the commissionaire and the plainclothes man. Other men came rushing towards them and Polyansky disappeared in a mass of flailing bodies. Kosterina tried to intervene and was thrown to the ground. By the time she had scrambled back to her feet the bloodied body of her colleague was being bundled into a Volga saloon. A crowd had appeared and once the Volga had roared away in the direction of Razina Street she was plied with questions. It turned out that most of the questioners were also conference delegates bivouacked at the Rossiya.

*   *   *

Within an hour the news of Polyansky's arrest had reached most of Moscow, or so it seemed at the time. The story had gained a little with each telling, but the basic theme — worker delegate arrested the moment he reaches Moscow — was disturbing enough, especially for those who wished to believe in the leopard's new spots. By 9 pm people had begun to gather in Pushkin Square once more, first in small groups, then in large impromptu meetings as these groups slowly coalesced. No one had called this 'rally', it simply happened.

More significantly, the composition of this crowd was very different from that of the previous Sunday. Then the square had been mostly packed with workers from the Moscow factories, all speaking with much the same voice, their demands clear and relatively limited. On this night there was no such sense of defined purpose. This was a mob, united only in anger, frustration and a desire for cathartic action. Many young people were present and not a few representatives of Moscow's criminal underworld. Mixed in with these were delegates from many parts of the country, both bemused and excited by their first taste of the big-time. Here they were defying the bosses only a mile up the road from the Kremlin.

The authorities were also having to cope, this time round, with the unexpected. Some of their representatives watched nervously from the windows of the 'Half Rouble' at the bottom of the square, while others desperately sought clear instructions from above. Had someone taken the responsibility and ordered the dispersal of the crowd while it was still relatively small, the night's events might well have been avoided. But no one did. Both the police inaction and the crowd's swift growth were signs of the times.

Word of the gathering had also reached the Hammer and Sickle, where it occasioned nothing but alarm. Most of the Coordinating Committee members present headed straight for the Metro.

Meanwhile, the mob in the square had become convinced that the unfortunate Polyanksy was being held in the 'Half Rouble'. (He was, in fact, in his room at the Rossiya — the KGB had released him on discovering that he was a conference delegate.) Stones were taken from the flowerbeds in the southern half of the square and several windows broken. Inside the building the lights went out, but no one else appeared.

This emboldened the mob, which crashed through the front door and began rampaging through the offices. The police had withdrawn through a back exit and, after releasing a bevy of drunks and whores from the basement cells, most of the crowd reerupted into the square. Many were carrying trophies of the conquest — typewriters, riot shields, furniture; one man was even observed with a pile of wastepaper baskets. Others carried out heaps of records and a bonfire was started on the paving stones. Inside, a group of students was hammering a computer terminal to pieces. There was still no sign of the militia.

The atmosphere grew a little less frenzied with the arrival of several well-known workers' leaders from the Hammer and Sickle, Nikitenko and Zakharov among them. They began pleading with members of the crowd, begging everyone to calm down, not to give the authorities the excuse for wholesale punitive action. At first they received short shrift for their pains — 'What authorities?' people replied — 'We'll string up the fucking authorities! — 'This is the only sort of conference they'll listen to!', etc — but gradually, as the excitement of ransacking the 'Half Rouble' wore off, they received a more reasoned response. Or so many assumed at the time.

But there was another reason for the crowd's increasing temperance. Largely unnoticed, some two hundred youths had left the square with a fresh target in mind.

Nor would the 'calm' descending on Pushkin Square prove very long-lived. An hour or so earlier people had begun to gather outside the Art Cinema on Kalinina Prospekt, a mile to the south. No one seems to know how or why this crowd formed; most likely it simply coagulated from the disparate streams of people available — those coming out of the cinema, and late evening shoppers, drinkers and diners emerging from the various establishments which huddle beneath the tower-blocks on either side of the Prospekt. The word quickly spread that a large and violent affray was taking place in Pushkin Square, but such happenings promised danger as well as excitement and this crowd was mostly composed of family groups, including a fair proportion of children happily slurping ice cream.

It was one of these who unwittingly, and tragically, was to precipitate another turn of the revolutionary screw. For reasons that remain obscure — there may not have been any — a fight broke out between two of the drunker men on the pavement between the Arbatskaya Metro entrance and the main thoroughfare. Seven-year-old Tatiana Dushkina, retreating out of range of the flailing limbs, retreated right into the Prospekt just as a taxi was speeding past. She was knocked into the air and killed.

The taxi didn't stop. And neither did the Zil limousine, also travelling at high speed, which travelled in its wake. It simply swerved to avoid the child's body and swept on towards the Kalinin Bridge and Kutuzovskaya Prospekt.

The Politburo's luck was certainly out that night. For some reason the taxi driver's escape seemed to pale into insignificance when compared with the Zil driver's callous indifference. Everyone knew that only Politburo members travelled in those cars, and no one stopped to consider that perhaps — as was indeed the case — only a chauffeur had been on board. To the crowd the whole incident seemed only too typical of the way these 'servants of the people' performed their service. Someone shouted the magic words 'Pushkin Square' and off most of them went.

The arrival of this angry throng rekindled the anger of those who had sacked the 'Half Rouble'. By this time the taxi had been forgotten; it was the Zil that had knocked down the child. Someone even claimed to have recognised Andropov's ascetic countenance through the smoked glass and others were ready to point out that he lived on Kutuzovskaya. It was an open and shut case.

In the meantime the breakaway group had taken a Metro ride to Nogina Square. Polyansky served as their inspiration, though most of them lacked roubles, let alone hard currency. It was as if an English football crowd had been let loose on Moscow. On reaching the Rossiya *beriozka* they simply stove in the windows and began to loot with gay abandon.

In Petrovka Street this news removed any doubts as to the advisability of action. Grishin, called out of a Politburo meeting, sanctioned the use of whatever force seemed necessary for the restoration of order.

Less dramatically, but more ominously for the régime, the larger crowd in Pushkin Square had set its sights on a new target. Only a few hundred metres to the south on Gorky Street stood the five storey cream and carmine mansion which housed the Moscow City Soviet. Lenin had spoken from its columned balcony on many occasions. A plaque on the wall announced that the building had been occupied by the Revolutionary Military Council which directed the October 1917 armed rising in Moscow.

At first the crowd, squeezing into the small Soviet Square which faces the mansion, confined itself to chants and slogans. Nikitenko was called on to speak and did so from the steps beneath the Prince Dolgoruki statue. His advice was the same as it had been in Pushkin Square, but the tone had changed; like everyone else he was becoming infected by the night's excitement.

The Soviet building had been in total darkness, but while Nikitenko was speaking it suddenly burst into light, first the ground floor, then the second, up to the fourth. Figures could be seen at the windows behind the balcony, and then one forced his way out through the door. For a moment there was total silence in the square; then the man called out: 'Come and speak from up here, comrade, let's do it right.'

At the Rossiya the looters were accumulating mounds of goods on the pavement, apparently oblivious to the arrival of lorry-loads of militia on the hotel's northern side. Others were drawing up below on the Moscow Quay. When the shadowy figures were at last observed, shouts went up and youths began running in all directions, as fast as their legs and overloaded arms could carry them. Some ran straight round the corner of the hotel into an advancing group of militiamen, who could do

162

nothing more than grab at flying sleeves. Their colleagues further back had more time and weapons were trained while megaphones shouted for surrender. The mob was moving too fast to hear or think. The troops opened fire.

On the other side of the hotel the sound of gunfire panicked both the youths and the militia. The former thought of nothing but escape, the latter assumed the worst had already occurred and opened fire themselves. Above the carnage hundreds of people, many of them delegates, leaned out of their windows to watch. The youths' unwitting mentor, Ivan Polyansky, was among them. This was life in Moscow?

Midnight arrived with bodies being carted away by ambulance from the Rossiya and Nikitenko addressing the Soviet Square crowd from the fourth floor balcony. 'You read your *Pravda*s yesterday morning? Just that once, eh? You can imagine the sort of things Lenin said to the crowds gathered here. He promised them a workers' state, not a *chinovnik* state. He promised them that even the workers' state would one day disappear. He promised them democracy, not rule by parasites. Self-government, not them-government. I tell you, if we're not given self-government, we'll take it. The people who 'work' in this building, they run this city, don't they? Well, the building doesn't matter but the function does. And when we go home tonight we'll take that function with us and we'll keep it at the Hammer and Sickle for a while, in trust for us all. From now on, when they tell you to get permission from the City Soviet, you'll know where it is, won't you — out on Enthusiasts' Highway.'

One of the others on the balcony was tugging at his arm, shouting against the noise of the crowd. After a moment Nikitenko resumed: 'My friends, we're told that the militia is on its way. There's some down Stankevich Street here, some at the bottom of Gorky Street. We don't want bloodshed — how could it help us? Now we've stolen their function there's nothing to keep us here. So let's go home. Nothing can stop the changes now, there's no reason to fight. We'll win without.'

As the week had worn on, the rest of the world's media had expressed growing astonishment at the forbearance of the Soviet authorities. After the events of Friday night, which had been witnessed by most of the Western press corps, there were few who doubted that the iron hand would now come crashing down. Rumours of mass arrests and troop movements flashed through the foreign compounds; one American tabloid, desperate to outscoop its competitors, actually brought out its Saturday edition with the headline TANKS ROLL INTO MOSCOW.

The rest of the world had misread the situation. Its knowledge was largely restricted to Moscow and Leningrad, and the relative quiescence of the latter was more typical of the country as a whole. The 'battle' outside the Rossiya, the emotional meeting in Soviet Square, were certainly extraordinary events by Soviet standards, but when all was said and done the only real violence had been provoked by the same sort of youngsters who, in recent years, had regularly run riot in the cities of the developed West. Such activity might be more unsettling for the paranoid authoritarians in the Kremlin than it was for governments in the West, but in neither case did it pose, on its own, a real threat to the socio-political system.

The widespread stoppages were of infinitely greater significance, but here too the situation was far from as clear-cut as most Westerners tended to believe. The 'strikers' were not staying at home, not marching through the streets, not seeking arms — they were holding apparently endless meetings. For the moment the authorities were prepared to accept the half-truth that such extensive consultations were a necessary part of the build-up to the much-heralded conference. Even this freedom to talk was less unusual than it seemed to many Westerners; the Soviet Union might not be a political democracy, but the level of formal participation, at all levels of society, had always been much higher than that existing in the West. The Soviet population was not used to deciding things, but it was used to discussing them and for a week or so the Politburo could afford, or so it thought, to blur the difference.

Most important of all, the rest of the world, still living with images of the spring crackdown, was unaware of the extent to which the Soviet leadership needed a positive *modus vivendi* with its industrial work force. Only this need made sense of the Politburo's restraint and only the workers' knowledge of — and, to some extent, their sharing of — this need made sense of their restraint. Both sides had invested a great deal in the conference and neither wanted a showdown while a show-up was still possible.

More than a thousand people had spent the night at the Hammer and Sickle, either talking the night away or sleeping on the hard office floors. 'It was like Gatwick Airport on a bad day,' according to one British journalist who shared the workers' hospitality, 'uncomfortable, overcrowded, but everyone was expecting to fly.'

The Saturday morning, according to an equally good-humoured Russian worker, saw 'less work than usual but a lot more activity'. The brief physical occupation of the Moscow Soviet, and Nikitenko's announcement of its metaphysical relocation, was known throughout the city by mid-morning and interested parties began flocking towards this new Mecca. Not all of them approved of Nikitenko's rhetoric and, as the morning wore on and the meeting grew larger, it became apparent that Nikitenko himself was one of them. His cold-light-of-day urgings were all for caution, for giving the conference a chance, for not pushing the authorities into an impossible position. 'We must not repeat the Polish workers' mistake.'

Such fears were shared by most of the Coordinating Committee, but Zakharov spoke for many of those present when he warned of making the opposite mistake. 'We must not over-estimate them. We must not become paralysed by their power. We have to provoke them, because any real demands are bound to be provocative; there is no way in which both sides can win this fight. Of course Comrade Nikitenko is right to talk of restraint — we must be as disciplined as they are, more so . . . what happened at the Rossiya played into their hands . . .'

At this point Nikitenko interrupted: 'Over the past few days there has been a definite pattern to their reactions. They're prepared to allow peaceful meetings, occupations, public discussion, but the moment violence breaks out they hit it very hard. I think it looks hopeful. If they'd wanted to break up the meeting in Pushkin Square they could have done so — most of us were expecting something of the kind. If they wanted to arrest me for what I said last night they could do so. The fact that they haven't — yet — I think they want this conference to achieve something. They must know the risk they're running, so there must be some reason for running it.'

'They're scared!' someone shouted.

'Perhaps. But not of people in the streets, not in the short term anyway. If they're scared of anything, it's of using their power, not because it won't work, but because it won't get them anywhere. They need us, that's our real strength. If they didn't there'd be no need for the conference.'

Four miles to the west a similar argument was under way in the Politburo chamber, with Andropov putting forward much the same line of reasoning. Chernenko was less impressed than the workers at the Hammer and Sickle. He found Andropov's remarks 'incredible'. The events of the previous night had been 'unacceptable,' 'disgraceful', 'intolerable' — words almost failed him. 'What level of disorder do we have to reach before this bureau finds the will to act?'

According to Andropov, action was being taken. 'All those responsible for the Rossiya affair are in the Lubyanka. We have to distinguish between talk and anti-state activity. Talk is cheap, people are letting off steam; if we react forcibly the chance of channeling all the discontent into constructive endeavour will be lost. The conference opens in forty-eight hours. Then Nikitenko and his friends will come up against the limits of practicality, will have to discipline themselves. A few days of wild talk is a small price to pay for a measure of real agreement, a way forward.'

Chernenko, according to Solomentsev, 'seemed beside himself with rage. 'Seizing control of the Soviet is "letting off steam''? This is absurd. I demand that those responsible be brought to justice. The conference must be postponed — better still abandoned. It certainly cannot take place in this atmosphere of total irresponsibility. The Party cannot negotiate with a mob — if that is ''a way forward'' then we are no longer socialists. Comrade Andropov has no understanding of the forces he is letting out of control and neither, apparently, have his friends at Dzerzhinsky Square. There must be action. A stop must be put to all this.'

Andropov replied as if he was addressing a well-meaning, but particularly stupid child. 'All right, Konstantin Ustinovich, let us examine alternatives to my proposals. We could arrest Nikitenko and the other prominent leaders, we know who they are. Others would fill their places but we could arrest them too. But what of the ones behind them. We cannot arrest everybody, though I suppose you might try. This is not the spring, when we could trade promises for obedience. The promises have all been made and most have not been kept. The situation continues to deteriorate. We have nothing to bargain with, only force. How would you force the thousands of strikers to work? How many Nikolayevs do you think we would need this time? I'll give you an idea. In many areas the militia is no longer completely dependable. Substantial parts of the Armed Forces have also become infected with the popular mood. When you talk so glibly of restoring order, you are really envisaging the use of chemical disabling agents against entire districts *as a first step*. You are talking about wholesale deportations to the North and East. You are talking about reintroducing coercion on a scale not seen since the Cult of Personality era.

'It could be done, I don't deny it. For a few months, a few years perhaps, we should sleep easy in our beds. The streets would be quiet and the workers would be working. But it would solve nothing, absolutely nothing. Our economic problems would grow steadily worse, with consequences for the Party which are easy to imagine. The distance between us and the people would widen alarmingly, at the very time when the need is for a narrowing, a drawing together. Let me speak personally for a moment. For all of my years in the Party I have believed that the Party acts as a parent — we protect, we guide, we educate, we provide the opportunities. And now our "children" have grown up and we must adapt the Party to take account of this. Your only answer, Konstantin Ustinovich, is to replace the parent-child relationship with a master-slave relationship. If we succumb to that answer we shall have been wasting our time. The one relationship has moral purpose, the other has not. With men we can build communism, with slaves only pyramids.'

Chernenko considered this 'ludicrous romanticism'. If the Party did not lead, then it was 'nothing'. 'If you, Comrade Andropov, are prepared to go cap in hand to those who hold the state to ransom, these "grown children" who loot shops, then you will deserve all that befalls you. The Russian people has a nose for weakness.'

After this exchange of views the rest of the session seemed anticlimactic. Ustinov shared both Andropov's 'faith in our future' and Chernenko's 'misgivings', but was unwilling to support the latter in his demand for a postponement of the conference. Romanov agreed: 'To put off the conference now would worsen the situation, not improve it.'

There was a majority for a general tightening of security and unanimity on the need for measures designed to improve the morale and reliability of the urban militia forces. Chernenko's demand for a curfew was defeated by eight votes to five.

There were other important matters to discuss. An hour was spent on the political crisis in Romania, with Ponomariev presenting a detailed rundown of the situation and a list of policy options prepared by the responsible section of the Secretariat. None was particularly appetising — the Romanian Chiefs of Staff were almost unamimously anti-Soviet, and the pro-Soviet security forces were counselling caution. This course carried a high risk factor, but it also put off the evil day of Soviet intervention, which might prove of some importance when the desperate need for grain imports was taken into account.

Solomentsev later wrote that 'the handling of the Romanian crisis showed the Politburo at its best, functioning as a team, concerned carefully to weigh all the possible courses of action and the implications therein. This approach was thrown into stark relief by the handling of the crisis within our own country.

In this matter we were continually talking at cross purposes, substituting ideology for reality, prejudices for facts, letting personal antagonism get the better of rational discussion.'

As the Politburo argued, the Soviet people was busy supplying supportive evidence for both Andropov's optimism and Chernenko's fears. In Moscow there was no significant mass activity — a fact not entirely unconnected with the visit of Dynamo Tbilisi for a match likely to decide the Soviet league championship — but elsewhere in the country demonstrations were a common occurrence.

In Leningrad several thousand workers marched down the Nevsky Prospekt and up Garden Street for a rally in the Field of Mars. Speeches were made, many of them highly critical, but generally speaking the atmosphere was friendly rather than angry and the authorities made no attempt to intervene.

In Kiev a large crowd gathered in Pushkin Park, but again the mood was good-natured. Groups of young workers shouted 'All Power to the Soviets' with broad smiles on their faces, while others carried portraits of Lenin and the current Politburo. There were no reports of friction between the crowd and the large police presence.

This was not the case, though, in several Siberian towns, where police fought running battles with groups of youths. In Novosibirsk there were more than twenty deaths when KGB troops from the local security school opened fire on demonstrators in Krasny Prospekt. Similar, if less serious, incidents took place in Irkutsk, Barnaul and Semipalatinsk.

Andropov, having left the Kremlin for Fedorchuk's office in Dzerzhinsky Square, must have read the incoming print-outs with mixed feelings. A further report from Darensky was also awaiting him; at that moment a cabal of senior officers was meeting on the fourth floor of the Defence Ministry to decide on possible unilateral action 'in defence of the motherland'.

The list of those present or involved made disturbing reading. It included two deputy ministers of Defence, senior officers — in some cases commanding officers — from fourteen of the Soviet Union's sixteen military districts, and more than half of the members of Glavpur, the Main Political Directorate of the Armed Forces. Even the Chief of the General Staff was involved, albeit tentatively.

The plotters did not lack support within the Party machine and Andropov must have been particularly satisfied with the proof supplied of Chernenko's involvement. On the previous Thursday Chernenko had conversed at length with the C-in-C of the Moscow military district and the KGB transcript contained enough ill-advised words to sink both men.

At 6 pm the meeting at Frunze Street broke up and within ten minutes Andropov had a full account of what had transpired. The plotters had still not mustered the resolution to take the final plunge, contenting themselves, naively, with the framing of a virtual ultimatum to the Politburo. The key sentence served notice that the loyalty of the Armed Forces rested 'on immediate action to halt the rising tide of civil disorder'. The plotters had, however, taken the precaution of ordering additional troops into Moscow, Leningrad, Kiev and Odessa. Which was enough for Andropov. The only question remaining was how wide to throw the net and what to do with the catch.

The purge would have severe implications; it would not be possible to decimate the senior echelons of the Armed Forces without weakening, temporarily, the confidence of those who remained. On the positive side, the links between the military plotters and Andropov's political opponents presented him with a priceless opportunity for consolidating the reformist majorities in the Central Committee and Politburo. Ustinov, for one, would be forever in his debt.

But still, a purge could work both ways. He would be throwing the ballast overboard, would, in effect, be cutting off the Party's line of retreat. At 8 pm, after spending two hours in conversation with Fedorchuk, he made several phone calls, gave instructions to his personal staff and left for his dacha in the Moscow river village of Zhukovka.

Two hours later, Solomentsev arrived to find him watching a video recording of Wadja's *Ashes and Diamonds*. According to the Control Commission chief's later account, Andropov turned off the machine, stared at his visitor for several seconds and then matter-of-factly recounted the discovery of the projected military coup. He showed Solomentsev Darensky's reports and invited him to study a list of people to be arrested that night. To Solomentsev's amazement, it contained half the members of Glavpur and three of his Politburo colleagues — Chernenko, Grishin and Rashidov. Andropov told him that Romanov, Ustinov and Shcherbitsky were expected shortly.

Solomentsev's first reaction 'was purely practical'. I asked whether Ustinov had sufficient support in the Armed Forces High Command to guarantee acquiescence in these dismissals. Andropov said there was, but he sounded less than certain. I next asked whether Viktor Vasilyevich [Grishin] was a party to the plot — the evidence shown me only implicated the other two — and he admitted that there was no solid proof. He simply added, almost as an afterthought, that "the Moscow Party needs a new leader".

'He seemed tenser than I had ever known him and it wasn't hard to see why. This was a gamble for the highest stakes. If Romanov, Ustinov, Shcherbitsky and myself supported him, then most of the others would swing into line, giving us an automatic majority in the chamber for the foreseeable future. We would also have some juicy bones to throw to the workers' conference.

'But if the rest of us decided to fix up an eleventh hour compromise with the plotters, then Andropov was finished. The Party seemed to have a clear choice — subservience to either the Armed Forces and the hardliners or the KGB and the reformists. For myself, the decision was easy to make. I knew I would not survive a plotters' victory.

'Shcherbitsky, Romanov and Ustinov arrived in quick succession, each of them brandishing the letters delivered by the KGB dispatch riders. The General Secretary looked exhausted, as if he were carrying the weight of the whole Socialist World around on his back. Ustinov looked ill; he would look more so as the evening progressed. Shcherbitsky, by contrast, seemed as ebullient as ever. He boisterously complained that he'd been dragged away from his TV football and that only a successful harvest could justify such impertinence.

They were given large brandies and copies of the evidence to peruse. Shcherbitsky read his with an ironic smile, Romanov his with a deepening frown. Ustinov seemed devastated.

' "Yuri Vladimirovich," Shcherbitsky eventually asked, "do you have any information regarding their plans for us?"

'Andropov smiled for the first time that evening. "You, Dmitri Fyedorovich and Grigori Vasilyevich will be retired. Mikhail Sergeyevich and I will be arrested, pending an investigation into the accident on Kalinina Prospekt."

' "Retired? I don't believe it."

'Romanov was more interested in the arrests envisaged by Andropov. "From the names on this list I see that you intend using this plot to good effect. Almost everyone who has opposed the renewal programme is here. Is it wise to go this far? We might be misinterpreted."

'I could see Andropov relax the moment Romanov used the word "we". Shcherbitsky supplied the answer: "Misinterpretation is the least of our problems. There can be no half-measures . . ."

' "And we cannot miss such an opportunity," I added. "Chernenko has cleared the path for us and we should take it. Even those in the Party who oppose our policies will support us against a plot of this kind."

"All the more reason not to risk alienating them by arresting all their friends," Romanov suggested.

"That is a valid point," Shcherbitsky said. "I think we could prune this list a little without putting ourselves at risk."

'The conversation turned into a bargaining session. Viktor Grishin and a few Central Committee members were reprieved. Eventually Andropov had an agreed list.

'He had one last point. "I propose General Mikhailov for Chief of Staff, if Dmitri Fyedorovich has no objections. I have spoken to him and he is willing."

'Ustinov said nothing. He seemed to have aged ten years in an hour and a half. Riding home I felt both relief and an intense foreboding. We had thrown off the past, but the future still seemed just as inpenetrable.'

* * *

While Solomentsev was pondering the vagaries of history, the reborn 'Moscow Soviet' was trying to push through them. To outside observers it was clear that the mood of the Moscow workers, or at least that of its representatives gathered in the Hammer and Sickle machine hall, had radically changed in the past forty-eight hours. As late as Thursday the talk had mostly been of piecerates, managerial incompetence and corruption, Saturday working and flooded toilets. Now it was all of workers' control, of industrial democracy, Party corruption, the state of the nation. A vision of the future was taking shape.

At around 10 pm a delegate from Kalinin was reporting on his local situation when one of the Moscow Committee members interrupted him to make an announcement. Someone had just phoned in from the railway offices in Konsomol Square — all lines to the east were being cleared for incoming troop trains.

There was bedlam in the hall, with people shaking their fists at the vaulted ceiling, screaming defiance into the smoke-filled air. One delegate, blessed with a particularly stentorian voice, could be heard shouting for an immediate arming of the workers. Another cried out that many weapons were stored at the militia barracks on Nizhegorodskaya Street.

Nikitenko took the microphone and patiently waited for the uproar to subside. 'Yes,' he said, 'we could nip over to Nizhegorodskaya Street and relieve the militia of a few rifles. But that's not the answer. I could tell you that we're not — or at least most of us haven't had any military training for a long time. I could tell you that the rifles we'd get would be next to useless against what they'd bring up against us. I could give you a hundred reasons why we'd lose and lose badly. But it's all beside the point. Our weapons' — he held up his hands — 'are these. We are workers, not soldiers and we must fight with *our* weapons, our most powerful weapon, our ability, our willingness to work.' He stood there, looking at his audience, which for some mysterious reason had gone completely quiet. And then, equally unexpectedly, there was a huge swell of applause. Nikitenko later said that this moment had meant more to him than any other — it had 'lain flesh across all the theories'.

The Kalinin delegate retook the microphone and Nikitenko,

along with several other members of the Coordinating Committee, moved upstairs to one of the managerial offices. One Polish reporter went with them, his tape recorder on. What follows is a partial transcript of the ensuing conversation. No names are mentioned; the different voices are identified by letters:

A: Fine words will not defend us, Vladimir Nikolayevich
Nikitenko: We cannot risk violence.
B: Why now? A week ago it would have made sense to bring troops in.
C: Their patience has run out, that's all.
A: Perhaps it's just insurance.
D: Martial law, more likely. Poland again.
C: Look, what does it matter. We shall continue the strike, that's all.
D: For how long? Winter is coming, Fyodor Ivanovich. Food is short enough as it is. We can't go on forever.
C: We have no choice.
D: We do, you know we do. Direct action. Storm the Kremlin [*general laughter*].

As this conversation was taking place General Aleksandr Dmitrevich Mikhailov, Chief of the General Staff designate, was walking into the brightly-lit conference room on the third floor of the Ministry of Defence building. The four generals around the table began to welcome him and then noticed the squad of armed soldiers at his shoulder. Mikhailov pulled a service revolver out from inside his coat. 'Comrade Generals, I regret to inform you that you are under arrest.'

'On whose authority?' muttered one, as if indifferent to the answer.

'Comrade General, the warrant is signed by the General Secretary of the Central Committee, the President of the Supreme Soviet and the Chairman of the Committee for State Security. The charge is conspiracy to overthrow the state.'

At roughly the same time KGB squads were knocking at the doors of Chernenko, Rashidov and thirty-seven other high-ranking Party officials. Only one proved hard to find and he was traced the following morning to the apartment of an internationally famous gymnast. By mid-morning they had all been taken out of Moscow and out of Soviet history.

At the Hammer and Sickle the session of the 'Soviet' was still in full swing as midnight approached. At five to twelve another message arrived from Konsomol Square — all the troop trains had been halted and shunted into sidings pending further orders. Normal traffic was being resumed. No one knew why.

SUNDAY 27 OCTOBER

The view of Soviet events presented by the Western media was almost universally distorted in one crucial aspect. All talked as if the unfolding struggle was an all-embracing phenomenon. The *Guardian,* when it editorialised on 'the Soviet people taking the first, tentative steps into a dangerous and uncertain future', offered one such example.

The truth of the matter was very different. These 'steps' were being taken by the Party leadership and the increasingly organised industrial working class. Sections of Soviet youth, fuelled with vodka or best Afghani hash, were the only other active element in the situation. The vast majority of the Soviet 'people' were, like the Western media, mere spectators to the drama.

Spectators, moreover, who were uncertain whether to cheer or boo. The workers might have justice on their side, but they were causing a lot of trouble and surely there was no chance of them winning? The authorities might be a corrupt bunch of no-goods, interested only in feathering nests, but at least a clear-cut victory for them would bring some much needed stability.

Of course, it all depended on who you were. In the higher reaches of the Party, Government and KGB machines there were many people whose careers, even lives, were riding on the decisions being taken by their immediate superiors. Central Committee members, for example, felt as impotent during these weeks as the average kolkhoz worker and a lot more vulnerable. The Committee had not been convened by the Politburo, because neither of the factions in the upper body felt confident enough of the lower body's support. And with good reason — the Committee was full of frightened, uncertain people. Anna Ostrevnaya's account of a dacha weekend argument between three of its members amply conveys the prevailing mood:

> Masalov was arguing as logically as ever, his eyes twinkling with perverse pleasure. 'The social reality does not actually contradict the Party's position. We have built the foundations of socialism and now we can push ahead, into the "radiant future", towards communism. The administrative methods we have used up to now couldn't be expected to work for ever and they haven't. But that's no reason for panic; it's just a new phase, I'm sure we'll find a name for it eventually.'
>
> Garagan agreed. With a laugh he added, 'There's not many other ways of looking at it, is there? We always said that the working class was the leading element in our society.'
>
> At this point Bobryshev, who was more than a little drunk, finally lost his temper. Masalov's logic had been bad enough; Garagan's cynicism was simply too much. 'You morons,' he shouted, 'when the blood starts spouting do you think anyone's going to notice how progressive you are?'

The same argument was also to be heard in the corridors of the KGB building. No one much fancied adorning a lamppost, but few, as yet, could actually imagine the noose around their necks. Change was inevitable so let's supervise it — that was the general reaction. Who else in the Soviet Union had more experience of supervision?

Lower down the hierarchical ladder, the vast army of Party functionaries had much to think about. One trade union official from Minsk later described a typical incident. 'I came out of the director's office and walked towards my car. As I did so a couple of workers walking in front of me deliberately spat on my windscreen as they went past. My first reaction was to beat the hell out of them, my second to report the matter. But I quickly reached the third — to take it as a lesson. Here I was, a union man earning only a few kopeks more than the others on my shift, who'd worked like a madman to save up for that car, and this was the sort of thanks I got. The Party kept giving me new instructions, telling me not to interfere with the elections, to accept a temporary reduction in wages, to keep clear of the black market, everything above board, to let the workers do what they wanted. And what did they want? They wanted to spit on my car. That day I mentally resigned from the Party. I kept the card just in case, but no one was going to get me out on a limb from then on.'

The industrial functionaries were at least close to events. For the rest of the Soviet intelligentsia the world of the shop floor remained as remote as Sausalito. Each section saw the issues through its own prism of interests. The planners had been fighting a rearguard action against the Leninist renewal since its introduction; they were now banking on an agreement between workers and government which gave them a pivotal role. The economists, or at least the perceptive ones, had backed renewal to the hilt, but their in-built assumption had always been that the working population would have to pay for it. If the intelligentsia was given the bill, there might be a few second thoughts.

Most of the vast bureaucracy had hardly considered politics. In the Soviet Union such philosophising was unlikely to advance one's career. And at least that had been simple. Now that career advancement was beginning to rest on so many imponderables, it was hard to avoid the political realm. The prevailing feeling seems to have been an ardent desire for a swift compromise; the régime should devolve some of its powers and the workers should work harder.

The 'dissidents', though a special case, were no more united in their response. Now that all the negative statements they had been circulating were being shouted to the cupola-tops, the lack of any coherent direction forward was more marked than ever. Proponents of military-religious dictatorship argued with lovers of Western democracy. Only the Marxist dissidents, many of whom had close links with the reformists inside the Party, seemed comfortable with the way things were going.

The student population was just as divided. In Moscow and Leningrad the universities were generally quiet, with only a small minority of youngsters from the rural areas insistent on making themselves heard. Outside these two cities it was a different matter; in Siberia and Central Asia the students had quickly made contacts with striking workers and were often at the forefront of the local struggles for political change.

In the rural areas there was hardly any sign of the turbulence afflicting the cities. The Party functionaries might be keeping their heads a little closer to the ground, but in general the work went on as usual.

This diversity of response was much in evidence on the Sunday. For those living in Dushanbe it must have seemed as if a violent revolution was already well under way. The city had been sealed off for several days, with the airport closed, the railway south and the road north blocked by the Army at Denau and the Anzob Pass respectively.

Since the first night of rioting in Rudaki Square, which had claimed fifteen lives and the modern Dushanbe Hotel, there had been something close to guerrilla warfare in the city, with the apparent daytime calm succumbing at dusk to sporadic armed clashes between security forces and self-styled 'fedayeen'. More troops had been brought in, many of them straight from duty in neighbouring Afghanistan, but the derelict alleys of the old city were ideal for hit-and-run warfare and little progress had been made. The city's Russian population was staying indoors.

On this particular day the troops had a rather unusual task, that of hunting down four tigers deliberately released from the city zoo during the night. All were recaptured before noon, but the other escapees, the zoo's bountiful collection of vultures, proved harder to reach with the tranquilliser guns. They seemed to be enjoying themselves, for rather than fly north to their home in the Gissarskiy Mountains, the huge birds had taken up residence on the tall buildings lining Lenin Prospekt. From these new perches they watched and waited for the revolution to deliver its dead.

The 27th was the day for the provinces to ape the big cities. While the latter remained quiet, serious disturbances broke out as far afield as Magadan on the Okhotsk seacoast and Yerevan in Armenia. In Magadan the spark was supplied by one more non-arrival of the supply ship from Sovetskaya Gavan; the workers wanted bread to go with the salmon they caught and the lack of it cost the city its Party offices that day. In Yerevan the trouble was more traditional in origin — in the previous weeks there had been serious communal clashes between Azeris and Armenians in the Karabagh oblast of Azerbaijan and on this day a huge demonstration was held in the city to protest the injustices and reassert the old demand for the region's return to Armenian control. The local militia overreacted and what had started out as a demonstration of nationalist fervour swiftly turned into a display of anger against the city authorities. Several people were injured before the tear gas and water-cannon were brought in to clear Marx Street and Shaumyan Square.

There were also outbreaks of active dissent, against a wide range of targets, in Tashkent, Alma Ata, Chelyabinsk, Saratov, Lvov and Mogilev. But, as if to emphasise the unevenness of developments, such large centres as Sverdlovsk, Frunze, Odessa, Kuybyshev and Kharkov remained free of trouble; for their citizens Soviet life proceeded much as before, with Sunday devoted to the outdoor pleasures of the vanishing autumn.

In Moscow the Politburo gathered in an atmosphere of high tension. Its members, according to Solomentsev, spent much of the morning 'searching for fingernails which had not yet been bitten to the quick'. The unmasking of the military conspiracy, the arrests of Chernenko and Rashidov, 'had evoked images of years long past', when knocks on the door in the middle of the night had been almost an occupational hazard. Several of the people arriving at the chamber that afternoon must have wondered whether they too were headed for political oblivion; Grishin, for one, must have known how close he had come to sharing Chernenko's ride south.

The session began with a long and detailed account of the conspiracy and its uncovering, delivered by Romanov in a voice 'devoid of all possible inflection'. Andropov supplied a list of those arrested, Solomentsev a list of their replacements hurriedly cobbled together by the Secretariat. There was no further discussion of the matter.

One reason for this lack of debate was an understandable desire to let sleeping Stalinists lie, another was the existence of more urgent claims on the Politburo's attention. During the night a letter had been received from President Reagan; it threatened unspecified but dire consequences should the Soviet Union intervene in Romania. It could of course be another White House publicity stunt and the public release of the letter encouraged such a view. But the Kremlin's American experts had almost despaired of ever understanding the present administration's foreign policy; it seemed to one of them 'like a new game — call it "American roulette" — in which only one chamber of the gun is left empty'. The Soviet leadership could no longer afford to assume anything but the worst.

This new burst of White House 'roll-backing' in Eastern Europe was bound to aggravate the already deteriorating situation in Poland. The previous day an Army attempt to disperse a large Solidarity demonstration in Katowice had ended ignominiously in massive troop defections. More troops had been hurriedly brought in and the city was now under a dusk to dawn curfew, but the long-term prospects of the four-year-old Polish junta were looking anything but promising.

And, of course, there was the conference opening on the following day. This would have to be orchestrated with great skill if the desired outcome — a more realistic approach to the country's economic problems — was to be achieved. The Politburo had a mountain on its plate.

Across the city the reborn 'Moscow Soviet' was also experiencing serious difficulties. Every attempt had been made to convene the conference, unofficially and a day early, at the Hammer and Sickle, but more than half the 'foreign' delegates had declined the invitation. Some were Party members who considered 'Nikitenko and Co' crypto-subversives, but most were workers who viewed both the Moscow 'independents' and the régime with equal distrust. They were here to attend the conference, not to risk life and limb by attending revolutionary meetings.

Those that did attend found the 'Soviet' torn by internal dissension. Half the speeches delivered that day amounted to calls for unity and the other half showed why — it was like a British Labour Party conference. Many still believed that they were there to represent their fellow workers' interests as workers, to put forward demands concerning pay and conditions. They found the more 'political' approach of others disturbing, dangerous and, quite possibly, counterproductive. 'We're here to do deals, not indulge in day-dreams,' as one worker from Mozhaisk pithily put it.

But there was a growing minority, led by delegates from Moscow's assembly line plants, which was quite prepared to deal in dreams, to cross the artificial border which separated the economic from the political. This group vehemently opposed the call for a general return to work whilst the conference was in session and it was only at the urgings of Nikitenko and Shestakova — 'The threat will be infinitely more useful than the fact,' the latter said — that the motion for an indefinite general strike was defeated. As the session broke up early that evening it was far from clear how many workers would be reporting for work on the following day.

The graffiti explosion continued. The word SOLIDARITY began to appear on walls all over the city; ALL POWER TO THE SOVIETS adorned the pedestrian underpasses in Pushkin Square and Marks Prospekt. Commuters coming into the city by rail on Monday morning received further enlightenment from a wall outside Ostankino Station — TO INHERIT THE FUTURE WE MUST RECOVER THE PAST.

More succinctly, but equally to the point, one tram on the Kutuzovsky route had the single word YES emblazoned on its side in bright yellow paint. It made two round trips before a conscientious official decided the motor needed servicing.

And at least one Muscovite had read the third issue of *Waterfront* — THEY WOULD HAVE PROSPERED UNDER THE TSARS had been painted along the northern face of the Central Exhibition Hall. One passer-by with a paintbrush must have been dissatisfied with the tense; he or she had added THEY STILL DO in bright red.

By 8.30 on the following morning the Troitsky Bridge into the Kremlin was jammed with conference delegates, queueing to pass through the security checkpoint beneath the Troitsky Tower. In twos and threes they were passed through to the Palace of Congresses, where the more detailed accreditation procedures were taking place in the fourth floor hall usually reserved for intermission buffets.

Of the five and a half thousand delegates some 40 per cent were Party members, but this fact counted for considerably less than it would have done a month earlier. The events of the last few weeks had polarised the Party at all levels and, while a substantial minority of those present had experienced a hardening of attitudes, the rest had been radicalised in the 'liberal' direction. The non-Party delegates were no more united. Most were unused to the public eye, unaccustomed to the Victorian-style formality of official gatherings, unpractised in the politics of power. Some, initially at least, were cowed by the event, others responded with nervous defiance. No one knew what to expect.

The leadership's crystal ball was also fogbound. As the delegates' credentials were being checked inside the hall, the Party Secretariat was still wrestling with the Conference agenda. The problem here lay not so much in the matters to be discussed, as in the manner in which the discussion was to be conducted. Was the conference to consist of a series of lectures, a no-holds-barred exchange of views, or something in between? The hardliners obviously inclined towards the former view — they would rather there was no conference at all — while the reformists found it hard to decide the number of holds they wanted barred. The process had not been helped by the arrest, only the day before, of several of the agenda drafters.

Of course the success of an agenda rests on a willingness to follow its script and it soon became apparent that one Party leader had no intention of doing so. The opening address delivered that afternoon by Vladimir Shcherbitsky was nothing short of sensational, eliciting obvious parallels with

Khrushchev's famous 'Secret Speech' twenty-nine years before.

Perhaps Shcherbitsky, mounting the rostrum with his prepared speech in hand, was struck by the difference between this audience and the hundreds of others he had addressed in his long career. The audience looked much the same — the long lines of grey suits, the apparent sea of conformity poised for the applause cues — but the atmosphere was very different. There was an air of expectation, partly as a result of what had already occurred on the streets, partly because so many of the people present lacked experience in collective docility. But the key factor was the calling of the conference itself. The Party had called it, true, but few doubted that the Party had been forced to do so. The power balance had shifted, no matter how slightly, and Shcherbitsky must have seen that shift reflected in the faces of his audience.

'Comrade delegates,' he begun, 'this extraordinary conference, convened for the discussion of industrial policy, is now beginning.' He paused, leaning against the lectern. 'I have a speech here, written by speech-writers. It is exactly what you all expect it to be, full of self-congratulation, optimistic forecasts, solemn entreaties. It is not what I want to say.'

Shcherbitsky, amidst complete silence, tore his speech in half. At this point, several hundred yards to the east in the Politburo chamber, his colleagues' eyes were riveted to their closed-circuit screen. Solomentsev later wrote that 'the sound of twelve men drawing in breath was metaphorically deafening. Viktor Grishin dropped his glass of Coca-Cola.'

'A year ago,' Shcherbitsky was saying, 'the Party put into effect the NEP 2, the policy of economic renewal. Since then, as you and I know all too well, there have been serious problems in the life of our country. Serious mistakes have been made in the implementation of the policy, in explaining it, and the results have been less than we hoped for. But we have no intention of abandoning the policy. I hope that by the end of this week there will be a greater all-round understanding of the problems involved and of the steps we must all take to overcome them.'

Shcherbitsky then went on to talk of Soviet successes: 'Before we explore our failures, let us be sure that we do not forget what has already been achieved.' He talked of increases in production, of the opening up of new areas in the East, of the improvements in services. 'You have all heard this before, this rosy picture of life in our country. You know it is not the whole picture; we have all experienced the other side of things, the cock-ups, the waste, the goods that arrive late or not at all, and even then of poor quality. But I urge you, do not go to the other extreme, do not imagine that everything is that way. There are strides we have taken and strides we have yet to take. If any here doubt the truth of this, let them ask anyone who was alive during the Great Patriotic War what life is like now. They will tell you that we live in paradise!

'But, as the proverb says: "the belly is ungrateful — it always forgets that it has already been fed". I am not going to talk of specific measures or problems. I want to speak to you of the wider picture, to pose questions for your consideration during the coming days. How can it be that the planners who have guided the enormous growth of our country have also been responsible for the problems we see today? Are they not the same people, pursuing the same aims in much the same way? Let me give you an example of the problems they face. Much of our natural wealth lies in the East, yet there is no rush of comrades leaving for Siberia. People don't like the weather out there, or the conditions. Tyndinsky is not Moscow! But we must develop this area. How can we get people to go there? Pay them more money? Lay stress on socialist duty? Appeal to people's spirit of adventure? We do all these things, but it is not enough. This is a real problem, comrades. We all want to be richer, but not enough of us are willing to bring those riches out of the East. No one is to blame for this; we cannot turn around and say it's his fault or her fault or their fault.

'There are many such problems without easy solutions and it is for this reason that I urge you to approach this conference in a constructive frame of mind. In recent days many wild things have been suggested, many irresponsible statements made, and we must keep things in perspective. The Party cannot wave a magic wand and make everything work perfectly.

'Another thing, we are not alone on this planet. For almost seventy years now we have needed to defend ourselves against the onslaughts and the threatened onslaughts of the imperialist powers. This we have done, of course we have, but it has cost us dear in money and talent, in lives lost. I know no Soviet citizen resents the resources devoted to our armed forces, to our role in the preservation of world peace, but there are many citizens who do resent, unknowingly, the consequences of our devotion. Each missile built is a factory unbuilt, each new fighter plane equals a thousand kindergartens. We cannot have it both ways, comrades, we have to live in the world as it is.

'We try to import grain and sometimes we cannot buy enough. Do you know why? It is not because we cannot pay for it. Let me read you one sentence from an American official. He said, "We have the food and the hell with the rest of the world." That is the kind of world we have to survive in.

'Let me give you another example of trying to have it both ways. In the last few days there has been much talk of "the right to strike", as if any group of workers had the "right" to harm the life of his fellow citizens. Ah, they say, but even under capitalism they have this right and, it is true, in some capitalist countries they do. But comrades, they need it, and for one very good reason. The capitalist has the "right to dismiss", to throw his workers into the street, and this is a "right" which our society would rather not have. Again comrades, we cannot have it both ways. Strikes point to problems — sometimes they are the only way in which the problems can be pointed to — but they solve nothing. Not working is no answer to the problems of work.

'Some argue that the capitalist economies are more "efficient" and, it cannot be denied, in some cases this is so. But there is a price to pay; the current rate in the capitalist countries of Europe is tens of millions without work. We are socialists and though we desire an efficient economy — who would not? — we must put the right to work as our first priority. This need not mean that socialism is inefficient, that our stores are doomed to bare shelves, but it does mean that we must strive harder, that our workers must be better-educated, more mobile, more inculcated with a socialist spirit, more ready to respond to challenges in a flexible manner.'

And so Shcherbitsky went on, aggressively outlining the country's problems, challenging his audience to respond positively, talking what sounded eerily like common sense. When he sat down, after speaking for almost two hours, the audience reaction was equally unprecedented. Though the applause was long and formalistic, the moment it faded a thousand furious arguments seemed to break out all over the hall. In the Politburo chamber, according to Solomentsev, everyone was slumped back in their chairs, 'as if we had all just completed an Olympic marathon'.

The rest of the afternoon session, barely an hour of it, was inevitably anticlimactic. It was given over to statements by various worker-delegates, ostensibly picked out at random, but in fact carefully selected by the KGB Industrial Security Directorate, which had devoted the morning to weeding out the required number of moderate reformists, men and women who would say neither too much nor too little. With one exception they proved suitably dutiful in their approach, welcoming the Party's decision to promote discussion of the contemporary industrial situation.

The exception, a female delegate from Tula, had apparently been inspired by Shcherbitsky's frankness to offer some of her own. She raised two unsettling points — the continued detention of workers arrested the previous weekend, most notably Vladimir Travkin, and the media coverage of the conference. She wondered why the television network was not carrying live coverage of the proceedings, giving 'the tremendous importance attached to this conference by the whole Soviet people'. This issue, in coming days, would prove one of increasing importance.

At the end of the first day, however, Andropov and Shcherbitsky had good reason to be satisfied with the course of events. The mood of the delegates, as interpreted by the countless KGB plants in the hall and hotels, was neither angry nor distrustful. Shcherbitsky's speech had been well received and had not, as some on the Politburo had feared, been interpreted as evidence of weakness. On the contrary, one delegate summed up the opinion of many when he called it ' a man's speech'. There was no evidence that the more militant delegates were gaining the upper hand. Indeed, the partial return to work that day in the major cities pointed to the opposite conclusion. There seemed, on Monday evening, every chance the reformists' strategy was working.

Historians have debated the extent to which this strategy was clearly formulated, but Solomentsev's evidence suggests that there was no lack of clarity in Andropov's thinking. He describes the strategy thus: 'Andropov's basic aim was to reach agreement with the industrial workers by reasoning with their delegates and to hold the Party together (including the enforcement agencies) by asserting the Party's right to lead the process of radical change. The workers would be constrained by realism, the Party by its own commitment to reform. Of course, appeals to national unity and ideological solidarity (in that order) would be used to strengthen the Party's boat as it entered these stormy waters, and judicious pay rises (particularly for the enforcement agencies) would also play a part. Through all this the Party would retain the strictest control over all forms of communication.'

The reform envisaged did not seem particularly radical, since in most aspects they seemed no more than a restatement of those announced the previous year. But Andropov and Shcherbitsky were now more than sufficiently aware of the workers' opposition to their first version of renewal and, unlike most of their colleagues on the Politburo, were prepared to contemplate a greater degree of workers' management. In this respect, as Solomentsev notes, 'both men realised that their real enemies lay within the Party, not beyond it'.

It is perhaps easy now to condemn such arrogance, to see that Andropov and Shcherbitsky, in setting out to convince both the workers and the Party that a particular and hitherto untried course of action was the only correct one to follow, were attempting the impossible. But on that Monday evening, as the bars of Moscow hummed to discussions of Shcherbitsky's address, the impossible seemed less than a miracle away.

The industrial workers, as events were to show, did share a vision of the Soviet future not too different from that propounded by the more adventurous reformists, but their basic lack of trust in the authorities as a whole prevented any immediate meeting of minds. The bulk of the Party, long inured to methods of administration which ran directly counter to the thrust of the envisaged reforms, did not even share the vision. Naturally there were important exceptions, particularly among the Party member conference delegates, but this was one of those few times when the exceptions really did prove the rule. The reformist leaders, thinking themselves in the vanguard of necessary and potentially popular change, were in fact climbing out onto a fragile limb. They were losing the Party without gaining a comparable power base elsewhere.

Tuesday was the day of transition, the day when the more percipient of the reformist leaders became dimly aware of the gaping chasm beneath their feet. It began badly, with what many saw as a particularly insensitive piece of reporting in *Pravda*. The newspaper had not been the same since the 'Lenin edition' and on this occasion an overzealous identification with orthodoxy was shown to be just as damaging as the most subversive hoax. Shcherbitsky's speech was not printed in full and from the excerpts quoted no one could have guessed its revolutionary tone. 'Vigorous' and 'forthright' were the two most dangerous adjectives on view; the speech itself had been gutted of all but the most mundane of statements of 'the difficulties confronting the Party'. The workers' delegates' speeches, with the single, glaring exception of that delivered by the Tula critic, were reported verbatim.

Such coverage undid most of the good work Shcherbitsky had done. It seemed to emphasise that nothing had really changed in the authorities' attitude and it brought home to many delegates, in a very direct way, just how selective the Soviet media was. The reservoir of trust was low enough already.

The Tuesday session of the conference did nothing to

rekindle the emotions of the previous afternoon. The main event of the morning was an address by Gorbachev on the problems facing Soviet agriculture, complete with visual aids. The content was radical enough and depressing enough to engender the 'positive realism' which the reformists desired, but Gorbachev had none of Shcherbitsky's style. He lectured and the Party clichés kept popping out of his mouth like escaping puffs of wind. As one delegate put it, indicating the droning speaker: 'As you hear the solution, you see the problem.'

The afternoon was supposed to be spent in discussing the agricultural problems and in a way it was. The delegates were interested in food, if not its production, and the session turned into a litany of complaints about shortages and the inefficiency which gave rise to them. The mood was totally different from that of the previous day; now the dutiful ones were the exceptions and most of them were howled down. The applause rang out for those full of angry, vague demands for change.

The Politburo, though, had other matters to discuss as evening approached. Across the length and breadth of the region under its ultimate control, signs of approaching catastrophe were making their appearance.

In Eastern Europe the situation had continued to deteriorate. For two days now, the Sunday events in Katowice had been evoking echoes throughout Poland, with strikes fostering strikes and marches fostering riots. The authorities in Warsaw seemed paralysed; without the certain support of the Kremlin they resembled rabbits frozen by the approaching headlights of the recharged Solidarity bandwagon. In Romania the situation was even worse, with bloody clashes reported in many of the Danube plain cities and widespread refusals to fire on the part of the troops. Yet the Ceaucescu family still clung to power in Bucharest, complicating the task of those still hoping for a peaceful transfer of the reins.

The Politburo was in crisis session all afternoon, discussing these events. The acuteness of the problem was concentrating minds wonderfully, with the reformists giving voice, for the first time in forty years, to doubts concerning the wisdom of the Soviet position in Eastern Europe. It was as if the scales had been lifted, albeit slightly, from their eyes — complaints about the cost of shoring up the fraternal régimes were nothing new, complaints about the difficulty of enforcing ideological uniformity were merely commonplace, but the thought that perhaps, just perhaps, the game was worth less than the candle presaged a formidable break with the past. It was more than a matter of bowing to the inevitable; it was a reappraisal, under pressure, of what purpose that extra five hundred miles served in the missile era.

This discussion — it was no more than that — was abruptly cut short around 7 pm by incoming reports of a new crisis point within the Soviet Union. The Donetsk-Makeyevka city authorities, whose handling of the original miners' strike had left much to be desired, had failed to learn from their experiences. A housewives' march protesting food shortages had been brought to a halt by the militia on Artyoma Street and ordered to disperse. The housewives, not to be so easily dissuaded from carrying their grievances to the City Soviet, had begun pelting the troops with bricks from a convenient building site and the militia commander had panicked. Shots were fired, several women were knocked down and the remainder had charged the small detachment of frightened young men responsible. Several were kicked to death.

As usual, word had spread with astonishing speed and by early evening a huge crowd had gathered in Lenin Square. Opinions subsequently differed as to the mood of this crowd: official reports described it as 'hysterical', while several of those who had been present claimed the atmosphere, initially at least, was 'carnival-like'. Either way, the least sensible option available to the local authorities was the sending in of more troops, yet this is precisely what was decided upon.

Several armoured cars nudged their way into the square and were quickly surrounded by chanting, taunting citizens. The Army commander, unable to communicate any orders, found himself conducting a debate with the crowd from his armoured turret. Perhaps out of sympathy with the aspirations expressed, perhaps through an understandable desire for self-preservation, he agreed to withdraw the troops. The centre of Donetsk was left to the mob, most of which continued its 'carnival' in the corridors of the City Soviet. An angrier (or hungrier) section went on a looting spree down Artyoma Street.

The 'ordinary citizens' were not the only ones reconsidering their loyalty to the leadership in Moscow. That same afternoon the Republican Party leadership in Tbilisi, alarmed and dismayed by the 'reformist mania' on show in the Kremlin and highly conscious of the threat such an ideological shift posed to their own position, were meeting in emergency session. Political and quite possibly physical survival was at stake for the Georgian leadership and no cows were sacred; according to one unsympathetic Politburo member 'the word "secession" was being tossed to and fro like a live grenade.' It seemed incredible and yet strangely logical. The Georgian bosses, if the worst came to the worst, saw more chance of salvation in an independent Stalinist Georgia than in a reformist régime imposed from Moscow.

Three thousand miles to the northeast the Soviet intelligentsia was making its presence felt for the first time. Akademgorodok was a town built, as its name suggests, for academics. Situated a few miles outside the giant industrial centre of Novosibirsk, on the shores of the artificial Ob Sea, it was the intellectual capital of Siberia. Though apparently untouched by the current crisis, its inhabitants had, by the previous weekend, almost abandoned academic work in favour of newspaper-reading, TV-watching and intense debate.

Their concern with the crisis 'surfaced' at a council meeting on the Monday morning, with several of the students and younger researchers suggesting a meeting with representatives of the workers in Novosibirsk. The idea had been enthusiastically endorsed by the majority, the Novosibirsk Coordinating Committee had responded positively and, on the Tuesday evening, the town's largest building, an applied engineering lecture theatre, was packed to its stainless steel rafters with students, staff and workers.

The meeting was 'chaotic', providing evidence of both the Soviet 'class divide' and the ties which bound all Soviet classes together. Nothing was decided, but that hardly mattered. It was the fact of the meeting which was significant, the feeling that such meetings were both necessary and desirable. As one ageing professor said: 'I felt ashamed of the joy I experienced. For twenty years I had been a Party member in our "workers' state", yet it was not until that evening, at a meeting frowned upon by many of my Party friends, that I communicated, man to man, with industrial workers.'

Such emotions were obviously dangerous. The keepers of the holy Leninist writ in Moscow needed no reminding of the part played by worker-intelligentsia cooperation in the toppling of the Tsar. It was vital that such links be kept to a minimum.

Unfortunately for them, no advance publicity was given to a particularly crucial piece of link-forging which took place that evening in Moscow. Several members of the Moscow Coordinating Committee had prevailed upon Roy Medvedev to address an audience at the Hammer and Sickle, and it is difficult to imagine how they could have made a better choice.

Roy Medvedev was a dissident with a long pedigree, having devoted some two decades to the study of Stalinism past and present and to the publicising, by whatever means available, of his conclusions. These, though profoundly unflattering to the régime, were at least couched in a language the Kremlin could understand, for Medvedev, almost alone of the prominent Soviet dissidents, was a committed Marxist. Indeed, one cynical dissident dubbed him 'the last believer'.

The cynic may have been right, but clearly the current situation was tailor-made for someone of Medvedev's convictions. The basics of Soviet socialism were not being questioned by the vast majority of the workers he addressed that evening; they were too busy denouncing the gaping gap between state rhetoric and reality. By offering, or at least appearing to offer, a way to close that gap, Medvedev helped to provide a focus for what were essentially negative feelings. He gave the workers something to argue *for*.

The theme of his address was democracy, and he made it plain from the start that the country, and not just the intelligentsia, needed it badly. 'It is the total restriction of freedom of speech and press which stops our country from overcoming all its other shortcomings. For the first condition of solving any social problem is the right to study and judge it freely.' All Soviet life, he argued, was stifled by this lack of democracy; it meant that instead of 250 million people offering ideas, the whole country had to rely on the brains of the mere hundreds of people who took the key decisions. 'Of course, 250 million people cannot run the state, but they can expect that those they choose to perform such functions are accountable for the decisions taken.'

Moving on to the conference, Medvedev thought it 'absolutely essential that it is conducted in the open, with the whole country taking part, in so far as that is possible'. He believed that 'while there are many in the Party, even at the highest levels, who earnestly wish for fundamental reform, there are many others who will fight it tooth and claw. These people will seek to plot in the shadows. They must be dragged into the light of day.'

The lack of openness served neither the Party nor the people; it was simply 'a habit of the Stalinist era'. 'Take foreign travel. It is restricted because the régime fears that the terrible truth will come out — that capitalism works better than socialism. And of course that is exactly what the restrictions encourage people to think. Since the régime says that nothing in the West works, our people tend to assume that everything must work, that it's nothing short of perfect over there. Neither is the case — the West has problems as we have, it has advantages as we have. This is not to say that the two systems add up to the same thing. It is a complex business and one that we desperately need to understand. But we can only begin to understand it if we have access to the facts.'

There was also a need for new elections, to the Soviets at all levels, to the Trade Unions, to the Party itself. 'For the reforms to work, they must be run by people who want them to work, who believe that they can work. Anything else is a waste of time.'

In the ensuing discussion Medvedev's arguments were vociferously endorsed and applied with some force to the media coverage of the conference. The television report that evening offered one obvious target; it had featured large chunks of Gorbachev's indigestible speech and as many expressions of delegate goodwill as could be found. It was decided, by a unanimous show of hands, that future sessions would be covered less selectively. Or else.

All these events, in their different ways, offered hard evidence of the erosion of central authority. The Party now seemed to be facing in two contradictory directions: it stood for both change and the *status quo*, it was the undermining the order for which it was responsible. In simple terms, it was pulling the rug out from under its own feet.

This was not of course the intention and it is conceivable that the leadership's stance might in more favourable circumstances have gained it the active support of those who favoured the middle way of substantive but limited reform. Indeed, all the signs were that the vast majority of the Soviet population was in favour of such a course.

But the circumstances were not favourable. The leadership bore, with some justice, the burden of the Party's history. Economic hardship was widespread. Most important of all, the events of the preceding fortnight had traumatised the body politic and Soviet society, wrenched from its normal rut, was drunk on debate. As the proponents of both change and the *status quo* found reason for disaffection, so the reformist leadership found that it was its enemies, and not its friends, which were proliferating.

The different agencies of Party rule reflected the lack of unity within the political hierarchy. The KGB, with very few exceptions, remained loyal to the centre and the centre remained loyal to Fedorchuk and Andropov; the arrest of the entire Georgian Politburo on the following morning was carried out with exemplary efficiency. The city militias remained loyal, again with few exceptions, to the local Party machines, but these demonstrated a wide diversity of political stances. Some, like those in Kuybyshev and Sverdlovsk, had made up their collective minds to wait on developments and in the meantime were turning a blind eye to everything but flagrant criminality. Others, sensing a fundamental threat to their own survival, went out looking for excuses to take punitive action, to 'reestablish respect for socialist legality'. The argument that such tactics, so long successful, now produced the opposite effect from that intended, had been proved that day on the streets of Donetsk. But unfortunately for the Kremlin leadership a similar display of short-sightedness was soon to be witnessed in Leningrad.

The armed forces were far from immune, and one of the more worried men in Moscow that evening was the new Chief of Staff, Marshal of the Soviet Union, Yevgeny Mikhailov. Both the internal and external situations were giving cause for grave concern and Mikhailov could expect little help from his immediate superior — Defence Minister Ustinov had been confined to the Kremlin Clinic since Monday morning, a victim of age, illness and the shock of the weekend's attempted betrayals.

Mikhailov's most pressing problem was Eastern Europe, where a combination of domestic grievances and perceived Soviet weakness was threatening to topple more than one régime. The Marshal had himself served in Budapest in 1956 — he had been part of the military staff at the Soviet embassy during Andropov's term as Ambassador — and had never forgotten the experience. The night of 4 December, with every window in Budapest candlelit in solidarity with the broken revolution, was engraved on his memory.

But, like many high-ranking Soviet officials who had visited the West in the 1980s, Mikhailov remained staunchly loyal to the Soviet way and, if ordered to crush a satellite rebellion, would do so. What worried him most was the lack of any orders at all.

The loyalty of his crack troops in East Germany and on the Chinese border was not yet in question, which was more than could be said for the vast mass of the conscript army. 'Soldiers' Soviets' seemed to be spreading like Rubik cubes, particularly among the large bodies of troops immobilised inside the Soviet Union. Using such troops to quell civil disturbances was likely to prove a risky business.

Nor could Mikhailov rely with much confidence on his immediate subordinates, many of whom had sympathised with his predecessor's plan for the country. In the upper levels of the hierarchy, mirroring the 'Soldiers' Soviets', the so-called 'Rodina' (or 'Motherland') clubs were gaining recruits by the hour, preaching views which even Tsar Nicholas I would have found autocratic and reactionary. As the Soviet system began to crumble at the edges, its armed forces seemed ill-equipped to hold the centre fast.

WEDNESDAY 30 OCTOBER

The conference continued. Despite everything the majority on both (or all) sides of the 'dispute' preferred arguing matters out in the Palace of Congresses to fighting them out in the street. The authorities still had too much physical power, the workers too much economic power.

It was Solomentsev's turn to experience the strange atmosphere in the conference hall, facing an audience finely balanced between awe and contempt. His subject was the industrial economy and his address, when seen in cold print two years later, seemed a model of depressing clarity.

He talked of 'the second Industrial Revolution', of the strains it imposed on the existing structure of the economy. He outlined the various attempts at reform — from Khrushchev's through to NEP 2 — with a frankness which, ten days earlier, would have amazed all those present. He stressed the difficulties of the transition period which the economy was now entering — 'even if the agricultural situation was favourable, even if the international situation was such that we could immediately cut defence expenditure in half, there would be no escape from the need to dramatically improve industrial productivity.' The purpose of the conference was not to lament this state of affairs, but to seek agreement on how such improvements could be brought about. There was a need to 'abandon methods which no longer serve to realise the potential of the socialist system'. No one was blameless here; the planning organs, enterprise management, the workers, the Party itself, all had clung for too long to methods of administration and production which had outlived their usefulness. There had to be 'widespread experimentation with new methods, undertaken in a constructive and responsible spirit'. Dogmatism was 'the greatest obstacle to progress'.

Solomentsev gave a vivid and somewhat rose-tinted account of several enterprises where such experimentation had proved successful, before turning gloomily to those unfortunate enterprises where obstructionism had been the order of the day. 'But,' he added, 'I do not wish to suggest that our problems can be solved overnight. They have been growing for decades, growing even while we have been gaining remarkable successes. And we can see that the two are closely related, for as the economy grew and our lives became richer, the difficulties of running the increasingly complex system grew too. It may be said that corrective action should have been taken earlier, and I say to you — of course it should.'

There was a gasp from the audience at this remark, a collective inflow of breath which sounded like 'a vast balloon deflating'. 'But what is done is done,' Solomentsev continued. 'If you don't crack the shell you can't eat the nut, and this shell remains to be cracked. I offer you two stark choices in this matter. We can make the necessary sacrifices, all of us, in a spirit of unity and resolve, for one, two, three years, and so create the potential for renewed growth. Or we can refuse to make sacrifices, argue bitterly with each other, consume what there is to consume and find ourselves, in a year or two, having to make even greater sacrifices for less reward. There is no escaping this choice, no easy third way. And in reality there is no choice at all; the nut must be cracked.'

All of which made sense but little impact, as the first speakers from the floor soon made clear. It was not the economic logic they objected to, but the existing balance of power within which that logic was to be followed. The first speaker welcomed 'Comrade Solomentsev's emphasis on unity and resolve'. He came from Karaganda, 'where the butchers' shelves have been bare since spring. Yet here in Moscow I see window displays bulging with meat.' He demanded immediate rationing on a national scale, so as to 'ensure fair distribution of all goods'.

Other speakers demanded a forty-hour week, an end to 'Red Saturdays'. When, one wondered out loud, had the bureaucrats ever worked on Saturdays? But the most popular demands centred around the power relationship within the work place. Speaker after speaker insisted that enterprise directors should be appointed by, and accountable to, their work forces, and that elected councils of the latter should negotiate production policy with the planning authorities.

The implications behind these proposals were most clearly expressed by Zakharov, the first of the well-known Moscow leaders to address the conference. 'What is required is real consultation, continuous consultation, between the workers and the authorities. This conference does not constitute such consultation — you say what you want, we say what we want and then you take the decisions. It will not suffice, either for our purpose or, I suspect, for yours. The workers must have a *continuing* say in the renewal, through freely elected trade unions. These can negotiate with the planning organs and can help to foster that sense of unity and resolve of which Comrade Solomentsev has spoken.'

Zakharov's ideas were echoed by many speakers in the course of the afternoon, but it was also noticeable, as the session progressed, that the mood of the delegates was slowly shifting. There was no withdrawal of the political challenge to the reformists' economic programme, but a greater sense of 'realism' was definitely creeping in. Perhaps the cumulative effect of three gloom-ridden addresses from the Party podium was making itself felt, perhaps the delegates were beginning to feel the weight of the responsibility which 'cooperation' entailed, but anyone prepared to read between the lines of the delegate speeches could detect a growing willingness to think in terms of compromise. It was in this mood that the conference broke up around 4 pm, prompting more than one delegate to express a sober but decided satisfaction with the day's work. At this stage the news from Leningrad had not yet broken.

When, in any society, the natural linkage between incumbent authority and the enforcement of order shows signs of breaking down, the temptation to settle old scores becomes harder to resist. In Soviet society, with its interlocking networks of informers, there was ample scope for such 'settlements', and one of them was to play a crucial role in the unfolding of the revolutionary process.

Late on the Tuesday evening a group of extremely drunken workers from the Leningrad docks had called upon one of their colleagues, a known KGB informer. They swapped unpleasant-ries, dragged him out of his flat, used him as a football and then flung him half unconscious into a convenient piece of the Gulf of Finland. The ripples were still spreading when a militia squad, summoned by the victim's wife, arrived to arrest them.

This seemed like an eminently reasonable piece of law enforce-ment. However, by the following morning it had been turned by rumour, prejudice and wishful thinking into a flagrant violation of human rights. A protest meeting was called for that after-noon.

Kazan Square was the designated point of assembly and by 2 pm several thousand people had gathered beneath the golden-domed cathedral. It was here that Russia's first major workers' demonstration had taken place in the previous century, and one of those to address it had been Plekhanov, one-time mentor of Lenin. Here too several people had been shot on 1905's Bloody Sunday, whilst *en route* for the Winter Palace and an audience with the Tsar's cannon. The place was full of ominous portents.

The Soviet era had left its mark on both cathedral and square. The former now housed the Museum of Religion and Atheism, the latter, sliced into gardens as if to preempt such gatherings, no longer sufficed to hold all those wishing to condemn their rulers. The gathering crowd was soon overflow-ing up and down Nevsky Prospekt and along the banks of the Griboyedov Canal. Most of those present had only a dim notion of why the meeting had been called, but there was anger to express and rumours to spare.

Unfortunately, nothing much seemed to be happening. According to one participant, 'the meeting had obviously not been properly organised. There was no sound system and apparently no speakers, just a large crowd, waiting for something to take place, ever more tightly packed and increas-ingly restive. When people started shouting "To Palace Square!" it was as if a vast weight had been removed from the collective mind. Like a huge herd of angry sheep, we started off down Nevsky Prospekt.'

During all this time the city authorities had been doing more than wringing their hands. The Leningrad Party had a reputation for toughness to maintain — many of its leading members considered their erstwhile leader Romanov a 'traitor' — and it was determined that there should be no Muscovite-style street anarchy in 'the Venice of the North'. By the time the crowd began surging down Nevsky in the direction of the Admirality, lines of visored, gas masked troops were blocking off the Prospekt's northern egress and all the side streets leading east and west.

The leading echelons of the crowd, confronting this space age army, hesitated, but those at the rear, unaware of the obstacle ahead, continued to push forward. The troops fired their canisters and soon the tear gas was rolling down the road.

A large body of people sought shelter by turning left down either side of the Moika Canal, where only a few militia were stationed. One of these men attempted to fire on the crowd; he was swiftly disarmed by his colleagues and thrown into the water. The rest embraced the demonstrators and joined them, throwing their weapons after their spluttering colleague. The retreat along the canal now turned into a new line of attack, as more and more people pushed along each bank in the direction of St Isaac's Square, demonstrating their political flexibility by exchanging cries of 'To the Palace!' for the geographically relevant 'To the Soviet!'

It proved, in military parlance, a classic flanking manoeuvre, for in St Isaac's Square the mob found only a group of officers, busy directing their troops on Nevsky Prospekt. Seeing this crowd debouching into their rear, these officers revved up their vehicles and disappeared in the direction of the Neva. The crowd, wrongly as it turned out, began celebrating victory.

A large group poured through the arched entrance to the Soviet building, intent on remonstrating with the city's government, but the building was empty, having been hastily evacuated by a back entrance only minutes before. Revenge was taken on the files, which were flung from the windows to cheers from the crowd.

By 3 pm there were some 15,000 people in the square, drawn by political magnetism to the centre of events. From the front steps of the Soviet building to the colonnade of St Isaac's Cathedral was a sea of faces, with people hanging at all angles from the statue of Tsar Nicholas I, and one man even sharing the saddle with the late ruler of all the Russias.

But still there was no sound system, no speakers who could make themselves heard. This crowd had no focus, no lightning rod for its anger, no reason to stay or go.

The authorities did have a sound system. As the digital clock on the Soviet building registered 16.16 a voice crackled out the order to disperse. Almost simultaneously two helicopters arrived to hover above the square and moments later tear gas canisters were dropped into the middle of the densely packed throng.

The crowd disappeared as fast as it could, pouring through the dozen or so exits from the square. For most this escape meant safety, but for those unfortunate enough to choose the Nevsky exit it meant disaster. The troops who had originally beaten them back were still there, deprived of officers and waiting for orders. Seeing hundreds of people running towards them, some men panicked and ran. Others panicked and opened fire, cutting down the leading ranks of the fleeing demonstrators.

Still the people kept coming, driven forward by those desperately intent on escaping the gas-filled square. The troops fired again, killing or wounding another twenty, but there would be no third volley. By this time the crowd was within wrestling distance and the unfortunate troops disappeared beneath the feet and fists of the enraged populace. Barely ten minutes after the dispersal order had been given, more than fifty bodies were littered across the last hundred metres of Nevsky Prospekt. The authorities in Leningrad had, albeit clumsily, lived up to their reputation.

In his offices on the tenth floor of the Moscow Television Centre, Director-General Sergei Medvedev (no relation) had spent the afternoon trying to make sense of the directives issued by his political superiors. On Sunday night he had been issued with copious instructions for coverage of the conference, but these had apparently proved insufficient, for that afternoon another fifty pages of studied vagueness had arrived. He was now to offer 'a balanced view of conflicting viewpoints', firmly set 'within politically constructive limits'. Since the definition of what was 'politically constructive' seemed to be changing from day to day, this hardly amounted to definitive guidance and Medvedev had no desire to follow last week's editor of *Pravda* into media oblivion.

That afternoon the reports from Leningrad were also flooding in, but his instructions in this regard were commendably precise. Peaceful demonstrations which did not explicitly attack the Party's leading role were acceptable for screening, violent confrontations between the public and the forces of order were not. So no Leningrad.

His news editors were busy 'balancing' coverage of the conference, and at 5 pm Medvedev viewed the ten minute report for inclusion in the 6 pm news. He ordered one reference to 'free trade unions' to be cut, more for its tone than content, but left Zakharov's short speech alone. If they wanted balance, then balance they would have.

It was a particularly Soviet piece of political short-sightedness. The telephone lines between Moscow and Leningrad had been humming with news and the men gathered round the communal TVs at the Hammer and Sickle were waiting for a report on the events in the northern city, not a faithfully 'balanced' report of the day's conference session. In a way, the presence of the latter made the absence of the former all the more enraging. It seemed to suggest that things could change, but only when the authorities were subjected to intense pressure. 'You tell them to tell the truth or the conference is a waste of time, so they tell you the truth about the conference and carry on lying about everything else.'

It was decided to send a delegation to the Television Centre and a dozen or so members of the Coordinating Committee set off in a lorry. On arrival, they were granted an audience with

Medvedev's deputy Masalov — Medvedev had gone home — and were told in no uncertain terms that the state television service was responsible to the Soviet people, not a few trouble-makers. They were then escorted from the building by security officers.

Back at the Hammer and Sickle, it was decided that Masalov's strictures could not be taken lying down and, despite the pleas of several moderates, the decision was taken to call an immediate demonstration outside the Television Centre. Communications between the various industrial areas had been greatly improved during previous days and by 8 pm people were flooding towards Ostankino from all directions.

By this time Medvedev had been called back to the Centre, perhaps by Masalov but more likely by the KGB officer in command. He arrived to find the square in front of the building and the adjoining Academician Korolyova Street fast filling with demonstrators. One placard which particularly stuck in his mind proclaimed WE ARE YOUR NINE O'CLOCK NEWS.

Medvedev thought that the crowd seemed good-natured and at this stage of the evening it probably was; large gatherings of people were still special enough for the fact itself to be enter-taining. But beneath this affable exterior there lurked a hard resolve, particularly where the industrial workers were concerned. In the previous week they had suffered the mis-reporting of the conference and, now, the non-reporting of important events in Leningrad. Roy Medvedev's speech the night before — the cyclostyled copies of which had been circulating throughout Moscow that day — had put a lot of doubts in their political context. The media had become a matter of crucial import, and Masalov's crude dismissal of their protest had only served to increase their determination to put things right. Further evidence of the issue's significance could be found in the simultaneous, and apparently spontaneous, gathering of another, smaller crowd outside the *Pravda* offices two miles to the southwest.

If these two demonstrations had been the only signs of active dissent in Moscow that evening, things might have ended up very differently. As it was the whole city seemed to be out of doors, with crowds, large and small, gathering at hundreds of street intersections and in the major squares. Perhaps the weather had something to do with it, dry and warm for the time of year. More likely, as one Western journalist put it: 'Everything seemed to be coming to a head. There was no obvious reason why it should have been that day rather than the day before or the day after — it just happened to be that day. The rumours flying around about what was happening in Leningrad had an effect, but no one I spoke to really believed that workers were being massacred or factories bombed. People didn't seem to know whether they wanted a revolution or a street party. But they did want action.'

Back at the Television Centre Medvedev had been on the phone to the Kremlin, where the Politburo had been in session since early afternoon. At 2 pm the Romanian Government had officially requested fraternal assistance in the maintenance of order and an hour later the American Ambassador had delivered a message from President Reagan which seemed to withdraw American opposition to the provision of such 'assistance'. Half an hour after that, however, another message had restated the original position. The Soviet Embassy in Washington reported that the State Department and the US Treasury had locked horns over the issue, the one demanding a firm stand against Soviet intervention, the other stressing the financial calamity which might flow from a simultaneous debt default by both Romania and Poland.

Not surprisingly, the Politburo had little time to spare for Medvedev's problems which, from their turreted perspective, they assumed to be less serious than was actually the case. The television boss was told to use his common sense, the KGB commander on the spot to resist any violent attempt on the Centre with as little force as seemed prudent.

Medvedev agreed to see the delegation that Masalov had snubbed, reasoning that this would at least keep the rest of the crowd quiet. One of its members described the audience: 'We were herded, rather like prisoners, into the Director-General's office. He sat behind an enormous desk in front of us, the armed guards stood by the door. He asked us what our grievances were, and Shestakova began to criticise the coverage of the conference. Why were the delegates interviewed always the ones who agreed with the Party spokesmen? Why were the more critical comments of the Party spokesmen themselves omitted? Why was such an important matter not being given continuous live coverage? Did the Director-General think Tadzhik folk dancing and the breeding habits of the Siberian weasel more important?

Medvedev defended himself vigorously, appealing less to ideology than to our sense of 'reality'. Where did we think we were living? How long would he last in his position if he indulged in 'irresponsible sensationalism'. Television had to present a 'balanced view' of events, and it was inevitable that some people would consider themselves hard done by. In any case, when people got home from a hard day's work they wanted to be entertained, not to be subjected to endless discussion of problems which they already knew about.

As this debate was proceeding on the tenth floor, the crowd below grew increasingly impatient. There was no news from inside and more troops were said to be arriving in Ostankinskaya Street, on the other side of the Centre. A long line of army lorries with lights extinguished was observed at the southern end of Novomoskovskaya Street. At around 9.30 the distant but unmistakable sound of gunfire was heard.

In Pravda Street the crowd was composed mostly of young people: workers, students and *bona fide* hooligans. Half an hour earlier a group of these youths had 'held up' a newspaper delivery van near Belorusskaya Station and 'liberated' a bale of the following day's *Pravda*. These had been distributed among the crowd outside the dark grey newspaper building and predictably enough were found to contain no news from Leningrad.

Predictable or not, the youths were given further fuel for their anger and a hail of missiles, mostly pebbles and flakes of stonework, was aimed at the building. Chants went up for an audience with their editor, but those inside the offices made no response.

At this point two ostensibly empty newspaper vans arrived back from one of the railway stations. They were seized by the crowd, apparently for use as battering rams, but on closer inspection were found to contain arms — rifles, small arms, gas grenades and protective gear. These were quickly shared out among the demonstrators, despite protests from some of the students. Minutes, or even seconds later a shot was fired, probably by accident. A student dropped to the ground.

It seems likely that the KGB guards on the door reacted by assuming that the shot was meant for them and quickly retreated into the building. The crowd interpreted this move as guilt and surged after them, only to be thrown back by a hail of bullets and glass as the panicking guards opened fire through the doors. Those that could still move rushed for the cover afforded by parked cars and vans. Some began directing shots through the ground floor windows. The lights went out.

This distant volley of gunfire electrified the crowd outside the Television Centre. No one had any doubts as to who was pulling the trigger, but whom were they aiming at? What was going on?

At this moment the delegation reappeared from inside the Centre, still escorted by the armed KGB guards. One of the women then tried to address the crowd, but only those nearest the front could make any sense of what she was saying. The delegation had nothing good to report, but they advised people to go home — the matter could be taken up at the conference on the following day, under threat of a mass walkout if necessary.

Even if audible, this advice would probably have been ignored. The sound of gunfire had introduced a new dimension and, while the delegate had been speaking, a column of army vehicles, comprising an armoured car and several armoured personnel carriers, had been slowly forcing its way through the crowd in Academician Korolyova Street.

The commanding officer consulted with the delegation and a KGB officer in front of the Centre while the crowd exchanged words with the nervous-looking troops in the carriers. Someone was sent in search of a loud hailer. The troops were ordered out of their vehicles to form a line in front of the building, a move which subsequent accounts suggest was misinterpreted by many in the crowd.

There was a renewed volley of shots in the distance and then, with dramatic suddenness, the crack of a shot in the immediate vicinity. Opinions differ as to who fired it and why: some claimed that a young KGB officer clubbed a worker who spat at him and then used his gun in self-defence against the man's friends, others that one of the troops accidentally discharged his gun when alighting from a carrier. Perhaps neither, perhaps both. Either way the impact was sensational. Several of the troops still struggling through the crowd had their guns wrenched from their hands; some of the KGB troops in front of the Centre opened fire for no apparent reason, dropping two demonstrators and at least one Army man. There was pandemonium, with people running in all directions. The Army commander reportedly tried to stop the KGB fire, but was himself badly wounded by a bullet fired by no one knows who. By this time most of the demonstrators were running at full pelt in the general direction of Mira Prospekt.

The second exchange of fire on Pravda Street had occurred when another military convoy had tried to intervene in the battle raging between armed youths and the KGB guardians of the newspaper building. The youths had fired on the column and the latter had returned the compliment with a machine gun, causing several casualties. The youths had retreated, first into Leningrad Prospekt and then south into the square facing the Belorusskaya Station. When it became apparent that there was no pursuit, an orgy of destruction began, with cars dragged across the northern entrance to the square and set ablaze.

The reason for the lack of pursuit was simple enough: the troops in Pravda Street, shocked by the sight of riddled fifteen- and sixteen-year-old bodies, had refused to proceed further without explicit instructions from higher authority.

In Mira Prospekt things were calmer. The fleeing demonstrators had discovered the highway already full of troop carriers, but delegates managed to speak with their commander and he had the good sense to realise that this crowd was trying to escape a fight, not find one. Gunfire could still be heard from the direction of the Television Centre and some reports later claimed that a full-scale shoot out took place between Army and KGB troops. This has never been confirmed.

Back in Belorusskaya Square events were moving towards a long drawn out climax. More troops moving into the city down Leningrad Prospekt had come up against the barricade of burning cars and been fired upon. In the square itself the scene was extraordinary. One Western reporter who arrived earlier than most noted that 'there were about a thousand youths, not many of whom were armed. To remedy this state of affairs a thriving Molotov cocktail production line had commenced operation in the station forecourt. Other people kept blundering into the situation, including a whole trainload of night workers from the suburbs. Some helped the youths, some tried to remonstrate with them, but most vanished as fast as their legs would carry them. The one truly bizarre aspect of the scene was a Japanese cassette recorder, perched against a tree, pouring out Western rock music from the sixties era. Petrol tanks exploded to the sound of John Denver extolling country roads in West Virginia, gunfire vied with whipcracks on Neil Young's "Southern Man". I waited in vain for the Beatles' "Back in the USSR".'

The troops were ill-equipped for this sort of fighting (let alone this sort of music), being armed with killing rather than disabling weaponry. Their commander wisely forbore from using the former and little progress was made in shifting the barrier of burning cars until water cannon arrived from the militia HQ on Petrovka Street. Surprisingly, no attempt was made to outflank the rioters; Gorky Street had already been cordoned off just above Mayakovsky Square, but these troops were not ordered forward.

When the barrier was breached around midnight, the siege turned into a running battle down Gorky Street, with windows smashed and more cars overturned and set afire. The rioters were eventually halted by a warning volley from the troops ahead and, finding themselves blocked in both directions,

208

many sought escape through the back streets. A last major confrontation took place among the flats between Gorky and Krasina Streets, with thousands of silent watchers leaning from their windows providing an eerie counterpoint to the sound and fury below. By 1 am the riot was over, with most of the youths loaded into black marias for the trip to Petrovka Street.

Meanwhile a new focus of conflict had appeared in the eastern part of the city. A large number of troops had been brought in along Enthusiasts' Highway, only to find their progress blocked by lorries parked across their route. A member of this convoy later recounted the events and the troops' state of mind:

'The boys in my unit were no different to those in any Russian unit (the Asian units were another story). Most of us had fathers or brothers who were ordinary workers and we didn't fancy the idea of looking at them down the barrels of our AKSs. We understood why they were angry; we'd lived with it as well. But we were told — and at first we believed it — that the serious trouble was being stirred up by a few individuals, that the mass of the workers wanted peaceful change. The preservation of order, as they kept reminding us, was in everybody's interest, and if a few hooligans had to get their heads busted open then that was too bad.

'Some of us began to have doubts after we'd cleared out the Krivoi Rog complex in May. There seemed to be a good number of "individuals" stirring up trouble, practically the whole work force by the look of it. But there were good reasons for keeping these doubts quiet — one officer had refused to give the order to fire that day and he'd been taken behind some rail wagons and shot. When it comes down to you or them, it's not often you. There's never enough heroes in the same place at the same time.

'For the next four months we were on standby in Serpukhov, and then, when things were starting to go badly wrong, we were moved to barracks at Kupavna, about thirty kilometres from the Moscow city line. Some of the men had families in Moscow and we were getting a lot more news. The number of "hooligans" seemed to be rising dramatically.

'What we weren't seeing much of was decent food. Nor were any passes being issued and the officers generally seemed more inclined to dish out punishments. They were probably feeling the tension more than we were, but at the time we weren't interested in their problems. We tried sending a delegation to complain about the conditions, but they came back refusing to say anything. The next day we were told that they'd volunteered for service in Afghanistan.

'After that the rest of us kept quiet and the conditions just got worse. On the day before the Enthusiasts' Highway business we were informed that our pay was being upped 20 per cent, but the borsht seemed thinner than ever. There were also rumours flying around that one battalion, which had been parked in a railway siding outside Moscow for over a week, had gone beserk, shooting its officers and sending out parties to look for food. Apparently they'd come across this dacha in the woods belonging to some Party boss and found about four refrigerators stacked to bursting point with Western packet foods. I don't know if this really happened, but for some reason we all wanted to believe it had.

'So, when we were ordered into the BTRs on Wednesday night, our sense of duty was hardly overpowering. And as we drove through the outskirts of the city mine dropped still further. As a driver I had a pretty good view of things, and many of the people watching us go by were making gestures which could hardly be described as welcoming. This was a shock, despite everything. The ordinary soldier might be treated like shit by his superiors, but in our country he expected and usually got respect from civilians. And here they were sticking fingers at us.

'I could see the lorries stuck across the highway when we were still a mile away. Trouble, I thought. But our commander that night, Major Stenkin, was one of the better officers, a bit regulation-happy at times, but a reasonable enough man and I didn't think he'd try and plough straight through.

'He didn't. We were ordered to halt about a hundred metres from the wall of lorries and the Major went forward to talk with the men behind it.'

*   *   *

The blockade had been arranged only an hour or so earlier. As news and rumours of events elsewhere in the city had spread, a sizable crowd had gathered at the Hammer and Sickle as the most likely source of accurate information. The only solid fact that transpired, flashed by telephone down the five mile stretch of factories, was the passage of Stenkin's convoy. A spontaneous decision was taken to impede its progress, more it seems from a desire to do something than from any rational appreciation of what such a blockade might achieve. More than a few workers were armed, mostly with rifles seized from the militia in the previous week's affray in Iljica Square.

When the convoy halted and the Major commanding walked forward to talk, several members of the Coordinating Committee, Nikitenko and Zakharov among them, advanced to meet him. They tried to pump the Major for information, but at first he refused to answer any questions, simply insisted that the lorries be moved at once. After some argument, in which Nikitenko stressed the risk of bloodshed and broadly hinted that the workers behind him were in no mood to surrender, Stenkin revealed that his orders were simply to take up position on the Solanka Bridge over the Jouza Canal. He had no information concerning events in the city centre. Yes, he would check his orders with his superiors, but that was all he could do.

'The Major walked back with a grim face and called up Command on the radio. He reported the situation, adding that in his view there was no point in making an issue of the barricade; the battalion would reach its deployment area sooner if an alternate route was taken. Command was apparently not impressed by this advice and, after winding up the conversation with a series of increasingly resigned grunts, Stenkin gave the order for the men to deploy on the highway.

'We dismounted, trying hard not to catch each other's eyes. The men behind the lorries were taking cover, the Major was standing in his turret with a loud-hailer.

'He didn't say anything though, for at that moment a single shot knocked him backwards out of the armoured car.

'There was a total silence for what seemed like minutes, but was probably just a few seconds. It was broken by the clatter of an AKS hitting the road, and then more followed. I found myself dropping mine and joining the others, walking forwards, towards the barricade with a nervous smile on my face. The workers didn't seem to know what to do for a moment and then they rushed out to greet us and the night was full of shouting and hugging and back-slapping.'

This account of the night's main 'actions' — those in Ostankino and Belorusskaya Square, on Enthusiasts' Highway — gives something of a false impression, for though in retrospect they seem the key events, there were many, many others. In Moscow itself both the Chovrino and Reutov districts witnessed the erection of barricades and, in the smart Lenin Hills area, another large mob of youths went on the rampage. There were at least three other recorded instances of troops refusing to use force against demonstrators.

But listing 'events' cannot do justice to what happened in the capital that night, for the talking was as important as the fighting, and on nearly every street, in nearly every towerblock square, there was enough talk to fill a five year plan. It was the night itself which was the event, and describing a few of its myriad facets cannot conjure up the atmosphere of an entire city convulsed by the tremors of uncertainty.

Nor was Moscow alone. In the Leningrad district of Ligovo, in the Black Sea cities of Nikolayev and Kherson, in the Ural cities of Pervoural'sk and Chelyabinsk, similar scenes were being enacted, apparently each in isolation, but in reality all linked by the invisible threads of a people's impatience. It was not an insurrection. There was no attempt to seize the levers of power or vital installations. It was an expression of raw political emotion; the people were serving notice on the régime, on all its supporters both active and passive, that such an insurrection was no longer unthinkable. It was a way of saying that things could never be the same again.

And if, as the darkness lifted over Moscow, the authorities were still in control, in one sense the revolution had already occurred, for that control was now dependent on popular forbearance. It could no longer be enforced against the people's will. All that remained was the striking of a new bargain between rulers and ruled, if that were still possible.

THURSDAY 31 OCTOBER

The next morning a British correspondent in Belorusskaya Square watched the commuting office workers 'picking their way through the flotsam of battle with a look of stunned disbelief on their faces'. As they walked down Gorky Street 'silence gave way to fierce whispering'. Another journalist tried to check out the situation on Enthusiasts' Highway, but was turned back by troops at the metro station. 'One soldier, a very young-looking sergeant, admitted with a grin that the barricades were still up.'

In some ways the general situation paralleled that existing ten days before. The bureaucrats were working more or less normally, the industrial workers were merely attending their places of work and the régime seemed to be running out of ideas. At the Palace of Congresses only a handful of delegates turned up for Day Four of the conference; the decisions were being taken, or not taken, elsewhere.

The centres of power were still the same: the KGB Internal HQ on Dzerzhinsky Square, the Defence Ministry on Frunze Street, the Politburo chamber overlooking Alexandrov Gardens, the new upstart focus of disaffection at the Hammer and Sickle. At each of these centres the morning was spent evaluating, debating, deploring, celebrating the events of the past twenty-four hours. Where, each group was asking, do we go from here?

The Politburo had gathered at 9 am, looking, according to Solomentsev, 'as if we had not slept for days, which was perilously close to the truth'. For most of the previous evening

213

they had been agonising over the Romanian crisis, pausing only to sanction the Moscow Party's decision to call in the Army. No decisions had been reached. The Ceaucescu régime was clearly bound for oblivion, but there was no obvious successor. If a more liberal, Titoist alternative could be found, then there would be no need for Soviet intervention — indeed, such interference might well prejudice the chances of such an amenable outcome. But if extra-Party forces did seem to be gaining the upper hand, then the Soviet Union could hardly stand aside. It was hard to believe that the Reagan Administration would go to war over Romania, but the Soviet Ambassador in Washington had not yet sent any encouraging news. Meanwhile, Bucharest was becoming a battleground.

The early hours brought more bad news from the international front. The Far Eastern Military District reported a notable concentration of Chinese forces on the Amur and Ussuri rivers, in the region of the disputed Damanskiy and Goldinskiy Islands.

But the main topic, inevitably, was the deteriorating situation within the Soviet Union, and in this context a bout of Chinese bellicosity was almost welcome — there was nothing like the 'yellow peril' when it came to appeals for national unity.

This ray of light apart, gloom presided. It was not a disciplined discussion, with each member more inclined to dwell on the mistakes and lost opportunities of the past than to consider the options still open. 'The only person who seemed sure of himself that morning, astonishingly enough, was Viktor Grishin. Perhaps this was because Moscow, which he had run for fifteen years, was now at the centre of events. Perhaps he was simply less tired than the rest of us. Assuming Chernenko's fallen mantle, he made a strong appeal for the taking of drastic measures and no one, not even Shcherbitsky, seemed to have the energy to argue the case against. The practicality of such a move was by no means certain, but for once this seemed almost unimportant. If Mikhailov had not arrived at that moment I think Grishin's motion might have been passed and then events would have taken a far more violent course.'

*   *   *

Mikhailov had been attending a meeting of the Main Military Council at the Defence Ministry and had been appalled by the deterioration in the Armed Forces' ability to perform the tasks set by their political masters. On the one hand were the reports flooding in of troop disaffection, ranging from simple surliness to outright mutiny, on the other was the steady expansion of the tasks themselves. The Soviet Army was now facing the prospect of fighting a war on two fronts against NATO and China, of occupying and subduing Romania and of maintaining internal order. At the best of times such a menu would have been cause for chronic indigestion and these were far from such times. Something, somewhere, would have to give.

This was the message he brought to the Politburo. 'Mikhailov stood just inside the doors, as if uncertain of the correct procedure. Andropov gestured him to the chair which Chernenko had always occupied, which turned out to be rather ironic. He delivered his report as if speaking from memory, but the gist was clear enough. The Soviet Armed Forces could guarantee the defence of the Motherland, could effectively assume the administration of Romania within 72 hours. The Chinese could not launch a major land offensive for three weeks, which, given the time of year, ruled out any major incursion until the spring. Local successes could not be prevented without the use of nuclear weapons. Troop morale in both the Eastern and Western operational sectors was high.

'But, and it was the biggest but any Defence Minister had come across since 1921, morale among the domestically-stationed conscript units was "uncertain". The Chiefs of Staff could not "categorically guarantee the maintenance of internal order with the forces presently at its disposal". Much would depend on the "possibilities of cooperation with the other organs of internal security".

'Everyone looked at Andropov, who had not said a word all morning.'

Andropov had met briefly with Fedorchuk before the Politburo session and received the latest KGB assessments. The Committee itself was holding together remarkably well. Though a few provincial offices had erred on the side of overzealousness, only a handful had exhibited mutinous intent.

That was the good news. The reports reaching Dzerzhinsky Square from all around the country made more ominous reading. They confirmed Mikhailov's assessment of the mood among Soviet conscripts and suggested that the resolve of the industrial workers was hardening. The will of the Party, at provincial and town levels, was being rapidly eroded by the leadership's apparent reluctance to take decisive action. Not that such action would solve anything. The Dzerzhinsky Square experts predicted that any decisive move by the leadership would, initially at least, split the Party down the middle.

Andropov recounted the substance of the KGB's views to his Politburo colleagues, adding that there were some grounds for considering them 'optimistic'. But far from sobering the meeting, his account served to enliven the proceedings. 'Grishin's motion was now vigorously debated, and defeated. But there was no clear alternative presented; the importance of the decisions which most of us realised had to be taken seemed too overwhelming. Grishin counterattacked by demanding the convening of the Central Committee, but this too was defeated, the majority holding to the view that bringing more people into the discussion would confuse rather than clarify the issues.'

At the Hammer and Sickle the same issues were being debated, the same lack of unity being displayed. The machine hall was overflowing with people — most of the conference delegates were there — and the proceedings were no less chaotic than usual. The principle topic of debate was the future of the conference, and in this matter the *de facto* leadership was split. Nikitenko was all for perseverance, Zakharov now considered it a 'charade'. The Leningrad delegates were refusing to consider attendance until their city authorities had been brought to book for the 'St Isaac's Square Massacre'.

This division of opinion among the leaders reflected a general polarisation of views. A clear majority of those present that morning could be described as moderates, workers who, despite or because of recent events, favoured reform of the Soviet

216

system. A minority — just as clear but less apparent because it included many of the influential Moscow and south Ukrainian spokesmen — were now openly talking of overturning the old system and creating a new one. In terms of the desired end the two sides were not far apart; both condemned the same elements of the existing system and shared a similarly nebulous vision of a brighter future. But in terms of means there was a growing divergence. The moderates were still willing to make use of those Party-made structures, like the conference, in which the extremists had lost faith.

Eventually a motion was passed which sidestepped the main issue. The 'conference as constituted in the machine hall' would formulate a list of demands. These might, at some future date, be presented to the 'conference as constituted in the Palace of Congresses'.

The moderate majorities emerging in the Kremlin and at the 'conference' also reflected public opinion, in so far as it could be gauged that day in Moscow. Western journalists, busy seeking instant reactions to the night before, found that most 'ordinary Russians' expressed a strong desire for a 'return to normality'. Two main reasons were quoted: the fear of anarchy, much heightened by the destructive violence of the previous night, and the fear of endangering national security. 'The Americans will be the only winners in all this,' was a recurrent refrain.

The debate in the Kremlin went on. 'We have to face the central fact,' said Solomentsev. 'The Party has lost its position as the single source of political and ideological authority. This is not an irretrievable disaster. In time we can emerge stronger than before. But we must act swiftly to broaden the basis of our support, we must push ahead with the broadening of democratic procedures. This is not a betrayal of Party policy, it is, and has always been since the beginning, inherent in the commitment to renewal.'

Shcherbitsky, of course, agreed. Furthermore, he had 'an

interesting historical parallel' to offer. 'In the 1920s it became apparent to the Party that someone was going to have to make enormous sacrifices, to pay, in effect, for the industrialisation programme. It could only be the peasants — there was no one else. Comrades, someone has to pay for the renewal. There is no way round this. The rural sector is in enough trouble already. The workers are making it painfully clear that they have no intention of paying the price we asked and, according to Comrades Mikhailov and Andropov, our ability to force the issue is, to say the least, questionable. The conclusion is obvious. Only the intelligentsia remains.

'But we all know that renewal cannot succeed without the active support of our intelligentsia. So we must buy their sacrifices and there is only one means of payment to hand — that suggested by Mikhail Sergeyevich — a broadening of socialist democracy. This need not mean throwing all restraints aside, that would be utterly foolish. But properly presented, I believe it offers a broad direction for policy which would gain widespread support.'

Solomentsev claims that a lengthy silence followed this peroration, 'interrupted only by the click of cigarette lighters and the fizz of drinks being poured'. Eventually Ponomariev, 'straining for self-control', asked whether Shcherbitsky had forgotten that 65 per cent of Party members were from the intelligentsia stratum.

'No, I had not forgotten. According to the Committee 50 per cent will oppose us whichever way we turn. I would rather dispense with the careerists.'

This was more than Demichev could bear. 'Have we all gone mad, listening to this old fool carelessly cutting the Party in half? Listening to insane ''historical parallels'' . . .'

'Pyotr Nilovich,' Andropov broke in, 'there is nothing insane about Vladimir Vasilyevich's suggestions. We have an extraordinary situation to deal with. Administrative measures are not appropriate, so what would you have us do — abdicate?'

Andropov's voice had steadily risen; Solomentsev had 'never seen him so angry'. 'Can you imagine what would happen,' he continued 'if we abandoned our responsibility? Russia will become nothing, just an orderless mob grabbing what it can. No one can replace us. Make it impossible for us, yes. Cast us aside, yes. But not replace us. The peasants would go back to tilling their little plots, the workers would sit around all day drinking, the dissidents would try and ape their Western friends, create a bourgeois democracy which would talk forever and never decide a thing. We would be set back a generation, two generations. I refuse to countenance such a defeat.'

Another silence, this one broken by Romanov. 'But what are we to do?' he asked pathetically. Solomentsev thought that 'at this moment he looked like a little boy who'd lost his ball'.

Gorbachev, however, had a suggestion. 'Deal direct with the workers' leaders. With ten rather than ten million. Convene a meeting ostensibly to discuss the reconvening of the conference.'

This was discussed at length and eventually agreed, despite a notable lack of enthusiasm. It was better than doing nothing and, as Andropov noted, 'at present we are better able to threaten a showdown than to precipitate one'.

Working on the old principle that when Moscow leads the rest of the country follows, the invitation 'to discuss, in a fraternal atmosphere, the resolution of present difficulties' was addressed to the Moscow Coordinating Committee. It was not delivered, as some myths have it, by tank; the letter bearing the General Secretary's signature was personally conveyed by the conference chairman, Zavrek Ivanov, in a common Chaika.

The Committee considered it with some trepidation. Nikitenko later admitted 'how strange it felt to be holding a slip of paper with Andropov's signature on it'. But he never 'considered refusing such an invitation'. As he told the packed machine hall, it offered both 'proof of our strength' and 'an opportunity for putting our case at the highest level'. He dismissed suggestions that it was a trap: 'what could they hope to gain from such a manoeuvre?'

The majority, in the hall and on the committee, agreed. The rest of the afternoon was spent in selecting the five delegates who would attend this Soviet 'summit'.

* * *

At some point in all revolutionary processes, attention becomes focussed on the state machine and those who run it. Are it and they to be destroyed and a completely new machine created? Or is the machine to be seized and its previous controllers ejected from power? Or will those who control it, under pressure from their opponents, 'voluntarily' relinquish their positions and powers?

In the Soviet Union of 1985 none of these three options appeared feasible. The 'destruction' of a state machine is usually bound up with the dismantling of an entire socio-economic structure, and there were few Soviet citizens, in October 1985, who envisaged such a far-reaching transform-ation. The basics of the 'socialist' system were not widely questioned; it was the manner of its operation, both economic and political, which was under challenge.

Nor, at this stage, was there any possibility of the state machine being seized. As Andropov had pointed out, the workers' power was essentially negative; it lay in their ability to obstruct the machine, not to assume its running.

For the same reason there was little possibility of the Party relinquishing power. To whom could they hand it? Who else could run the machine which existed, which only made sense in terms of the command economy that the Party itself had created? An Army takeover would mean nothing more, in the medium term, than a shuffling of Party faces. The KGB could not run the country, a high political profile would destroy its *raison d'être*. No, the only possible inheritors of power were the citizens of the Soviet Union and the only way they could inherit it was through an agreement between the various interests groups to share the state machine.

The industrial workers, on the whole, wanted no more than this. They wanted to influence decisions, not take them. The reformist Party leaders also had strong reasons for pursuing such a course. If they set about democratising the existing machine, there was a good chance that renewed public support (or, at worse, a lessening of violent opposition) would follow. In such a situation the Party would not find it difficult to retain considerable powers.

It would not be easy. The implications were staggering — the loss of the Party's monopoly of power, a difficult period of transition wherein the formal Soviet political system was made real, a new role for the security forces, not to mention the impact on an economy already groaning under the strain of failure. But it was, in the end, these implications which added up to a revolution. In the Soviet Union, until October 1985, the defining characteristic of the system was the Party monopoly of power. To share power, to break that monopoly, was to redefine the parameters of Soviet existence.

There have been many accounts of the meeting held that evening, on 'neutral ground' at the House of Trade Unions on Pushkin Street. Most of them have been substantially inaccurate and none more so than the two American films which sought to dramatise the event. The workers' delegation did not arrive on foot, the Politburo members did not draw up in a fleet of Zils and there was no crowd gathered outside to cheer the one and hiss the other. Nikitenko never mentioned Nikolayev, much less launched a five minute harangue against KGB genocide. Nor were Soviet workers inclined to spice their arguments with quotes from Solzhenitsyn.

Most accounts stressed the nervousness of the five committee members — Nikitenko, Shestakova, Zakharov, Grigori Cheverov and Leonid Poznyakov — and the beaming assurance of the five Party leaders — Shcherbitsky, Romanov, Gorbachev, Solomentsev and Andropov. Solomentsev, however, claims that the opposite was the case: 'they were more used to dealing with higher authority than we were to dealing with equals'.

Nikitenko was most struck by the unreality of the occasion, as the ten men spent the first few minutes of their historic encounter deciding on refreshments and ordering the replacement of a light bulb.

Eventually they were all seated along either side of a table meant for thrice their number. The Committee delegates waited for Andropov to set the meeting in motion, but it was Shcherbitsky who spoke first. 'This has gone on long enough,' he said, in a voice which Nikitenko later described as 'a mixture of sad and matter-of-fact'. Scherbitsky's following words echoed this impression: 'I do not say this as a threat, merely as a statement of the obvious. Throughout our country the difficulties are increasing — economic difficulties, violent disturbances on the streets, many of which bear no relation to the real problems facing us. The threat from the imperialists is increasing, almost by the hour — I have here the latest cables from our Ambassador in Washington, the latest military intelligence reports from the Far East. And these are not the only threats.'

Andropov entered the fray, outlining the military coup attempt of the weekend before, detailing the links between the generals involved and certain figures 'high in the ranks of the Party'. He explained the plotters' intended strategy for the reimposition of 'discipline', including for good measure a technical description of the incapacitating gas Diphenylchloroarsine. Nikitenko was struck by Andropov's manner. 'I had rarely come into contact with such an undemonstrative man. Of course, at that time I saw him simply as the Party's *éminence grise,* fifteen years in charge of the KGB, Enemy No 1. I had no idea that he had been as responsible as anyone for pushing through the reform programme.'

Shcherbitsky continued. 'I will be totally frank with you. The plotters are all behind bars, but there are others on this side of the table — though not in this room — who would still not hesitate to use such measures, regardless of the consequences for our country, our people, our socialist system. And we know that there are those on your side of the table who, either from ignorance or misplaced determination, will try to push matters to the point where the use of such measures may become unavoidable. Time is short. We must reach agreement, get the conference in motion again, make it succeed. There is no one else who can do it for us.'

After this dramatic opening, anything that followed should have been anticlimactic. It was not what Nikitenko had been expecting. 'I had anticipated threats, bluffs, endless lectures on socialist responsibility, all delivered by a row of dead faces. I suppose the disclosure of the coup attempt could have been construed as a threat, but it was done in a totally unthreatening manner. And instead of dead faces, those opposite us wore worried faces, almost appealing faces. But the clincher was Shcherbitsky's use of the word "us". It sounded so odd, yet he was clearly sincere. I barely resisted the temptation to say "thank you". That was the way it was then.'

Nevertheless, the workers' delegates' negotiating skills had been honed over the last year and they did not 'thank' the Politburo. On the contrary, they insisted that they lacked a mandate from the 'conference' for 'reaching agreements'.

'We aren't here to sign pieces of paper,' Solomentsev said. 'This is a purely informal meeting; we are here to discuss opinions, yours and ours. If we in this room can find a measure of agreement then that will be an important step forward. And let us be honest: you may have no formal mandate, but you are influential people. I do not say that all the industrial workers of Moscow will follow your lead in these matters, but many will.'

The talks lasted fourteen hours, surviving several near-breakdowns and consuming nearly seven hundred cigarettes. Additional electric fans were introduced at the halfway stage.

In those fourteen hours the outlines of a different Soviet Union were sketched out. Matters were discussed which Nikitenko had thought 'indiscussable', most notable among them a programme for the gradual — and, in Western eyes, partial — democratisation of Soviet institutions. The first candidate for such treatment was to be the official Trade Union organisation, with fresh elections, on a new basis, scheduled for the near future. Multiple candidature was to be the rule and was not to be restricted to Party members, only to those ascribing 'to the basics of the socialist system of property relations'.

New elections would also be held, more gradually, to all State and Party institutions. In the spring of 1986 the Party, Supreme Soviet and Trade Unions would join with the State planning authorities in formulating a new five year plan embodying the principles and aims of renewal.

When the discussion turned to industrial work practices the delegates found themselves on more familiar ground. They presented a 'provisional list of demands', based on the half-decisions taken at the Hammer and Sickle that morning, which included a guaranteed forty-hour week, no 'Red Saturdays', an accelerated transition from piecework to hourly-paid work, greater worker control over the distribution of investment, planning assessments, directorial appointments and marketing decisions. It was in the middle of this discussion, somewhere between three and four in the morning, that Andropov 'flabbergasted' Nikitenko and his colleagues by waxing coldly lyrical about the productive record of the Nikolayev workers the previous spring. Zakharov interrupted this panegyric to ask why 'three hundred of those workers had been murdered?' Nikitenko expected an explosion at this point, 'but only Romanov and Gorbachev reacted with even a semblance of anger. Andropov simply remarked, in that offhand manner of his, that "the decision to use such methods had been taken by people no longer holding positions of responsibility within the Party." It was not a satisfactory answer, but it was a hopeful one.'

PART SIX

AFTERMATH

*Workers' management is not a
panacea. It is a starting-point.*
> (N Zakharov 6 March 1986)

*The right to speak freely and the
right to work cannot be separated,
as the governments of both East and
West have now found to their cost.*
> (from a *Le Monde* editorial, 7 July 1986)

The ten men who walked, bleary-eyed, through the portals of the House of Trade Unions that Friday morning had shifted Soviet history into a new course. There was nothing much else they could have done. By meeting at all they had set the seal on the events of the past fortnight, had implicitly recognised the new political balance of power. All realised, with varying degrees of enthusiasm, that there could be no going back. The door to the past was closed.

The Party had been split, first by its attempts to solve the chronic problems of the Soviet economy, second by the need to reduce the level of opposition which those attempts had provoked both within its own ranks and in the country at large. The scale of the reformists' victory over the hardliners had been made necessary by the growing resistance of the industrial workers and it had of necessity cost the victors dear. By removing the Chernenkos, the reformists had placed themselves in their victims' position — now they were the defenders of Party rule, of the crumbling *status quo*. For the moment the industrial workers still needed them as a bulwark against, on the one hand anarchy, on the other the still smouldering embers of Stalinism in the Party, State and military structures. But, as the reformists knew only too well, the more successfully they doused these embers the more redundant they themselves become.

All this, in retrospect, seems clear, but at the time the issues seemed far more confused, the outcome far less predictable. In the first week of November any generalisations seemed out of place, as the rest of the country sought to follow the course already run in the capital. In Leningrad the Party authorities refused to accept the writ of the reformist Politburo and tried instead to demonstrate an alternative solution. A chaotic week of purges, arrests and some executions followed. But the local KGB proved more loyal to the centre and, by mid-November, the Leningrad authorities had been brought back to Moscow's heel.

In several south Ukrainian cities the position was reversed, with significant sections of both the authorities and the population beginning to act as if the Party had ceased to exist. Red stars were torn down, streets renamed, Party offices commandeered for conversion into workers' flats. It would be some weeks before economic circumstances forced these areas back into the new mainstream of Soviet politics.

The nine men and one woman who had met that night at the House of Trade Unions became, in a highly informal manner, the *de facto* ruling body of the Soviet Union. They met at frequent intervals, always in the same room, bringing suggestions from, and taking back compromises to, their own organisations. These meetings were anything but easy, anything but calm, but slowly a new consensus was being prised from the wreckage of the old system.

Within both the Party and the new workers' organisations there was intense political manoeuvring, as people sought to direct or jump aboard the bandwagon of change. The conference continued on a more democratic footing; it had become a seminar on the Soviet future, screened live on TV each day, throwing up more ideas than the country could cope with. This, in a way, made it easier for the leaders, for by the middle of November the Soviet public was crying out for clarity, for decisions.

Many had to be taken. The weeks of disturbances had all but destroyed the remaining viability of the economy and the reestablishment of some form of central control was clearly in the general interest. In consequence the initial measures announced were decidedly draconian, giving rise in the West to the misleading impression that nothing much had really changed. Certainly the new penalties for food hoarding could hardly have been stiffened by Stalin and the imposition of comprehensive food rationing brought back memories of wartime.

But in other respects the 'democratic-liberal' aspect of the transition was more apparent. There had been no Soviet intervention in Romania or Poland, where Party rule had to all intents and purposes been overturned. In Poland Solidarity was finally at the helm and wondering what to do with the bankrupt economy; in Romania a coalition similar to that now existing in the Soviet Union had taken over. Late in November the Kremlin signed agreements with the two new governments, agreements which amounted to a virtual granting of political independence. Membership of the Warsaw Pact was to be renegotiated, a process likely to be made much easier by the parallel disintegration of NATO. In future, the more realpolitik-inclined members of the Soviet leadership decided, the friendliness of Eastern Europe would be better guaranteed by the facts of economic life than by a costly military presence.

The new liberality was also noticeable in several of the political measures announced, or at least promised for the near future. The internal passport system was to be overhauled, perhaps to the point of extinction. A near-total amnesty was granted to political prisoners — the only exceptions were the October coup plotters. All jamming of Western broadcasts was stopped and simultaneously rendered almost irrelevant by the new honesty of the Soviet media. Most significantly of all, the elections for the new trade unions and the Supreme Soviet were being pushed through with all possible speed.

Of all the old institutions of neo-Stalinist rule the Party was being transformed the most rapidly. A large outflow — and, surprisingly to many, a large inflow — of members was transforming its social and ideological composition. The KGB was maintaining a low profile in security matters, but was playing a more open role in the fight against black marketeering. Like the Okhrana before it, the Committee was proving extremely adaptable.

In the Party's highest reaches there was less paranoia than expected. Things were just moving too fast. Politburo meetings were, astonishingly, 'more relaxed'. The reason, Solomentsev thought, was that 'many thought they had got off lightly. They still had their privileges — the less visible ones, at least — and they retained a great deal of their former power. If we'd been younger men this "demotion" might have rankled more. But none of us was facing many years in exile or the wilderness and to spend our last few years in this fairly pampered situation, sharing the burden of political responsibility, was hardly unacceptable. Many people in the West,' he added rather pathetically, 'failed to understand the intensity of the pressures exerted on high-ranking Soviet officials in the pre-October situation.'

But for one of his colleagues there would be neither relaxation nor responsibility. On 3 December, at the opening ceremony for the BAM railway in Ust Kut, Yuri Andropov was assassinated by the wife of a KGB victim. He was to be the last of Lenin's heirs to be buried in the Kremlin wall.

Ironic though it now seems, the governments of the developed West had welcomed the Soviet leadership's surrender of monopoly power. They had barely a month to enjoy their old enemy's discomfort, before it became apparent that the Soviet workers had, unwittingly and circuitously, pulled the rug out from under more régimes than their own.

It was not the revolutionary spirit, but the tendrils of economic collapse, which spread. The first intimations of the Western catastrophe came from Kinshasa, not Moscow, with the 23 November announcement of Zaire's incapacity to repay its debts. This, and the almost simultaneous 'request' by the Mexican government for yet another rescheduling, brought the overexposed Western banking system to the brink. When, two weeks later, and as a direct consequence of Soviet events, it became obvious that both Romania and Poland had defaulted in all but name, the dominoes began to fall, first the trickle of minor West Germany, British and Japanese banks, then the flood of major finance houses.

The ensuing traumas of the West are another story — one told with exemplary skill by Stephen Perryman in his *The Greater Crash* — but their impact on the new Soviet Union cannot be ignored. There is absolutely no doubt that the economic collapse of Western Europe saved the ex-satellite countries from a descent into political chaos. The régime in East

Berlin, for example, would not have lasted a week alongside a strong West Germany. For the people of East Germany, of Hungary, Czechoslovakia and the others, there was no longer a potential Western saviour; self-reliance was now the name of the political game and caution one of its cardinal rules. The old order was subject to change, but not at the cost of order itself. The old economic ties with the Soviet Union were subject to re-negotiation, to a new spirit of equality, but they were not to be thrown blithely asunder. In early 1986 a lifeline was a lifeline, no matter how ragged, no matter who held the other end.

The West's problems, and the new era of autarchy they had brought into being, had also dealt the death-blow to the long-crumbling transatlantic alliance. The strategic map was being withdrawn, allowing the Soviet leadership to rethink its military posture along more economic lines. And, at last, it was able to do so creatively: for the first time the direction of Soviet military policy was in the hands of men not scarred by memories of World War II.

The military were naturally loth to accept cut-backs, but the will to oppose them was not overwhelming; even the Generals had become infected with the mood of change. Over the next year the decisions were taken. Since the withdrawal of American forces from Europe, the chances of a conventional war in the West had been much reduced and the chances of fighting one in the East were lessened by the February 1986 border treaty with China, which cost Vladimir Shcherbitsky a round-trip to Peking and the Soviet Union thirty-seven square miles of empty territory.

Which left the United States, hobbled by depression and racial discord, stunned by the Oyster Creek nuclear disaster, led by a President apparently half way into senility. The Soviet leadership decided on a minimal counter-city strategy, three hundred well-protected missiles, mostly seaborne. Attempts were made to interest the Americans in nuclear disarmament talks, but without success. Negotiations were already under way with the Callaghan and Mitterand governments in Britain and France for the creation of a nuclear-free Europe.

Within the Soviet Union the economic rethink took longer, was, for some time, subsumed in the general atmosphere of austerity which gripped the whole northern hemisphere. But slowly, as 1986 wore on, the new government came to some sort of grips with the situation. There were no easy ways forward, but there was, at long last, a general willingness to examine critically all the shibboleths of the Bolshevik inheritance. New people, younger people, were gaining positions of influence. New ideas were springing forth.

The planning organs were finally adapting themselves to the requirements of a more decentralised system and were much helped in their tasks by the freeing of capital occasioned by cutbacks in military, space, police and propaganda expenditure. The democratisation of institutions was proceeding, with many operational powers being shifted from the Party to the State organisations, the new trades unions and the Supreme Soviet. The Party itself was mutating into a *de facto* civil service; its rapidly changing ideology now underpinned, rather than guided, the socio-economic system.

For many people the rate of change was still too slow, but the country's new leaders, drawn in increasingly equal proportions from the industrial workers, the liberal intelligentsia and the reformist wing of the Party, were determined to take no unnecessary risks. The economic situation remained difficult, the fear of political anarchy was still uppermost in many minds.

Those who had expected a re-run of 1918 were disappointed. There was neither civil war nor, with a few artistic exceptions, a libertarian explosion. The impression brought back by the few Westerners to visit the country in 1986 was of a highly moralistic, even puritanical atmosphere. This, in retrospect, was not particularly strange. For once the people of this vast Eurasian area were creating their own system, not merely adapting Western ideas brought home to them by the likes of Peter the Great or the cosmopolitan Bolsheviki. Dostoyevsky and Tolstoy, each in their own way, would have recognised the *tone* of the new Soviet Union, no matter how much the one would have detested its continuing commitment to collectivism, the other its obsession with historical progress.

One of those who did visit Moscow was Marion Lennox. She

found that 'at first sight nothing seems to have changed. The officials at Sheremetyevo still seem to believe that at least one passenger on every plane poses a mortal threat to the fabric of Soviet society. Red Square looks the same as ever; the queues outside the Mausoleum, the queues outside the shops, still stretch interminably. *Izvestia* remains as interesting as a fashion show in Omaha.

'But walk into a bookshop, pick through the pages of *Pravda,* read the graffiti which seems to adorn one wall in two, above all, feel the atmosphere. Moscow has become a city where things happen, where minds are active.

'There is no dancing on the streets, no kaleidoscope of extrovert happenings, but the change in mood since my last visit is quite extraordinary. The apathy and the cynicism have been washed away. People are actually optimistic, not wildly so, but quietly, determinedly, thoughtfully so.

'Partly it is the changes, partly also the feeling that the changes are under control. ''We have a government again,'' one woman told me, ''people who are prepared to do what needs doing.'' A taxi-driver admitted that ''there is hardship, much hardship. We have not overcome a tenth of our problems. But we have begun to do so. *We* have begun.'' '

While in Moscow, Lennox managed to secure an interview with Nikitenko, now a deputy premier in the Council of Ministers. She asked him what he considered the most important task now facing the Soviet Government:

'The immediate tasks facing us are, first, the reinvigoration of the economy and, second, the thorough democratisation of our institutions. But looking beyond these, I would say that the major problem confronting us — and you in the West — is the real harnessing of technology. For many years now, longer in the West than here, technology has been directing itself and the results have been nearly fatal for us all. The linkage between work and the payment for work has been broken down to the point where only a tenuous connection remains. We have reached a situation where what is considered economically efficient is social nonsense. People want to work. Of course the nature of that work will change, away from purely physical labour towards, in the long run perhaps, purely mental labour.

The rewards are potentially enormous, but only if there are still human beings around to enjoy them. If we permit this transition to occur faster than our ability to control it — as we have been doing — then humanity, in a real sense, will be lost.

'We have confused the economic with the real. I don't mean just in terms of the world situation — absurdities like there being no economic demand for food while half the world goes hungry. Take your own home, your own life: there is always something to be done, something that will make life a little more rewarding. Societies are the same, but we have refused to see it. Economics has become a calculated avoidance of human reality, a new religion almost. The opium of governments, perhaps.

'A society can only be judged in the terms of those who comprise it, in human terms. The standard of living is a matter of human satisfaction, not of statistics. Both we in the Soviet Union and you in the West have tried to measure it mathematically, in things, assuming that more and more means better and better. Sometimes it does. But look at us. After a century and more of unbelievable economic growth, do you detect a parallel growth in human satisfaction?

'We believe that work, creative, useful work, is at the root of human satisfaction. The primary duty of governments is to ensure that no one is denied the opportunity to work. This means planning. We have seen in the West where the free-for-all leads; it not only debases human beings, but it has even failed on its own economic terms. But we have also seen at first hand where the lack of democracy, of real participation, takes a society. So I think that these two things, planning and democracy, are the building blocks of a human society. They fight against each other, of course they do, but that is the human condition, the dialectic. Our task as a government, is to find the optimal balance between them.'

Lennox asked him whether the new Soviet Government would call itself 'Marxist'?

Nikitenko laughed. 'Does it matter? Marx was a great thinker, one whose predictions have borne the test of time better than most. But we here have relied on those thoughts rather too much; we are doing some thinking of our own now.

But, then again, a society which could take according to ability and give according to need — that would not be such a bad society to live in. But we are a long way from that.'

But nearer perhaps than we were. Will the new Soviet experiment 'work'? — only time can tell. Certainly there is no going back, for either East or West, to the societies of the pre-revolution, pre-Crash era. The future is fluid and that can only be welcome, when compared to memories of the deadening apprehension which gripped both blocs in the early 1980s. Now there is at least a chance of nuclear disarmament, a chance of a new deal for the Third World, a chance that the mad, random rush of technology can be channelled into human directions. Who could have said that in, say, 1983?

FALSE FLAGS
by Noel Hynd

'. . . *some sort of false flag job. It means someone is
made to look like he's working for one country when
actually he's in the employ of another.*'

Bill Mason, ex-CIA, survivor of a Chinese prison,
contemplating an empty future . . .

Robert Lassiter, the man who taught Mason everything
he knows, the man who now urgently needs his help . . .

Six silicon chips, tiny micro-circuits that could mean
everything or nothing, found in a London flat. They are
the triggers in a devil's game of life and death and
betrayal . . .

NEW ENGLISH LIBRARY

THE SANDLER INQUIRY
by Noel Hynd

Thomas Daniels sits in the charred ruins of his law
office, pondering the riddle of the late Arthur Sandler.
The answer could unlock an inheritance conservatively
valued at fifty million dollars. To find it, Daniels must
probe the labyrinths of the Intelligence community on
behalf of his client, who purports to be Sandler's
daughter.

Her father, she alleges, murdered her mother and twice
tried to eliminate her. *Why* is not at all clear, except that
it had something to do with the key espionage network
Sandler operated.

But who did financier Arthur Sandler work for during
the war? The Americans? The Nazis? The Russians?
Or all three? The trail has had thirty years to grow cold.
Now, suddenly, it is a blazing hot fuse, as past
treacheries come alive and the shards of Sandler's
unfinished business fall horrifyingly into place.

NEW ENGLISH LIBRARY

NEL BESTSELLERS

All The Rivers Run	*Nancy Cato*	£1.95
Brown Sugar	*Nancy Cato*	£1.50
Forefathers	*Nancy Cato*	£2.50
North-West By South	*Nancy Cato*	£1.75
Adventures in Two Worlds	*A.J. Cronin*	£1.75
The Citadel	*A.J. Cronin*	£1.95
Grand Canary	*A.J. Cronin*	£1.75
Hatter's Castle	*A.J. Cronin*	£2.25
Keys of the Kingdom	*A.J. Cronin*	£1.95
Shannon's Way	*A.J. Cronin*	£1.75
The Stars Look Down	*A.J. Cronin*	£2.25
Women's Work	*Anne Tolstoi Wallach*	£1.95
Acts of Kindness	*Charlotte Vale Allen*	£1.50
Believing In Giants	*Charlotte Vale Allen*	£1.75
Daddy's Girl	*Charlotte Vale Allen*	£1.75
Hidden Meanings	*Charlotte Vale Allen*	£1.75
Love Life	*Charlotte Vale Allen*	£1.50
Meet Me In Time	*Charlotte Vale Allen*	£1.25
Moments of Meaning	*Charlotte Vale Allen*	£1.50
Perfect Fools	*Charlotte Vale Allen*	£1.50
Times of Triumph	*Charlotte Vale Allen*	£1.25
Almonds and Raisins	*Maisie Mosco*	£1.95
Children's Children	*Maisie Mosco*	£1.95
Scattered Seed	*Maisie Mosco*	£1.95

NEL P.O. BOX 11, FALMOUTH TR10 9EN, CORNWALL

Postage Charge:

U.K. Customers 45p for the first book plus 20p for the second book and 14p for each additional book ordered to a maximum charge of £1.63.

B.F.P.O. & EIRE Customers 45p for the first book plus 20p for the second book and 14p for the next 7 books; thereafter 8p per book.

Overseas Customers 75p for the first book and 21p per copy for each additional book.

Please send cheque or postal order (no currency).

Name ....

Address ....

....

Title ....

While every effort is made to keep prices steady, it is sometimes necessary to increase prices at short notice. New English Library reserve the right to show on covers and charge new retail prices which may differ from those advertised in the text or elsewhere. (8)